Prospective
MEMORY

Cognitive Psychology Program

Senior Consulting Editor
James S. Nairne (Purdue University, USA)
Consulting Editors
Martin Conway (University of Leeds, UK)
Stephan Lewandowsky (University of Western Australia, AUS)
Elizabeth F. Loftus (University of California at Irvine, USA)
Mark A. McDaniel (Washington University in St. Louis, USA)
Hal Pashler (University of California at San Diego, USA)

SAGE Publications is pleased to announce a new, international program of titles in cognitive psychology—both textbook and reference—brought together by a team of consultant editors led by James S. Nairne: the *SAGE Cognitive Psychology Program*. Featuring books written or edited by world-leading scholars (or younger academics "on the rise") and infused with the latest research in the field, the program is intended to be a self-contained, comprehensive resource that meets all the educational needs of a cognitive psychology program including and beyond the introductory level.

The aim of the *SAGE Cognitive Psychology Program* is to offer both breadth and depth. Student textbooks are written by leading and experienced scholars in a style that is carefully crafted to be stimulating, engaging, and accessible. They are scholarly, comprehensive, and up-to-date, and boast the appropriate pedagogical devices and supplements—thus making them appropriate for building courses around a variety of levels. Reference works, including handbooks and encyclopedias, survey the landscape with an even broader sweep and should become benchmark volumes for years to come.

Existing and forthcoming titles:

- **Handbook of Cognition** (Koen Lamberts, *Warwick*; Rob Goldstone, *Indiana University*)
- **Cognitive Psychology, Second Edition** (Ronald Kellogg, *St. Louis University*)
- **Fundamentals of Cognitive Psychology** (Ronald Kellogg, *St. Louis University*)
- **Cognitive Psychology & Metacognition** [forthcoming] (John Dunlosky, *Kent State University*; Janet Metcalfe, *Columbia University*)
- **Attention: Theory & Practice** (Addie Johnson, *University of Groningen*; Robert Proctor, *Purdue University*)
- **Culture & Cognition: Implications for Theory & Method** (Norbert Ross, *Vanderbilt University*)
- **Rational Choice in an Uncertain World: The Psychology of Judgment & Decision Making** (Reid Hastie, *University of Chicago*; Robyn Dawes, *Carnegie Mellon*)
- **Handbook of Understanding & Measuring Intelligence** (Oliver Wilhelm, *Humboldt-University, Berlin*; Randall Engle, *Georgia Tech*)
- **Cognitive Science: An Introduction to the Study of Mind** (Jay Friedenberg; Gordon Silverman, both of *Manhattan College*)
- **Handbook of Implicit Cognition & Addiction** (Reinout Wiers, *Universiteit Maastricht*; Alan W. Stacy, *University of Southern California*)
- **Human Memory: Structures & Images** (Mary Howes, *SUNY-Oneonta*)
- **Prospective Memory** (Mark A. McDaniel, *Washington University*; Gilles O. Einstein, *Furman University*)
- **Cognitive Modeling** [forthcoming] (Jerome R. Busemeyer, *Indiana University*; Adele Diederich, *International University, Bremen*)
- **Handbook of Cognitive Aging: Interdisciplinary Perspectives** [forthcoming] (Scott M. Hofer, *Pennsylvania State University*; Duane F. Alwin, *University of Michigan*)

Prospective MEMORY

An Overview and Synthesis of an Emerging Field

Mark A. McDaniel
Washington University in St. Louis

Gilles O. Einstein
Furman University

SAGE Publications
Los Angeles • London • New Delhi • Singapore

For information:

Sage Publications, Inc.
2455 Teller Road
Thousand Oaks, California 91320
E-mail: order@sagepub.com

Sage Publications Ltd.
1 Oliver's Yard
55 City Road
London EC1Y 1SP
United Kingdom

Sage Publications India Pvt. Ltd.
B-42, Panchsheel Enclave
Post Box 4109
New Delhi 110 017 India

Printed in the United States of America

Library of Congress Cataloging-in-Publication Data

McDaniel, Mark A.
Prospective memory: An overview and synthesis of an emerging field / Mark A. McDaniel, Gilles O. Einstein.
     p. cm.
Includes bibliographical references and index.
ISBN 978-1-4129-2469-6 (pbk.)
   1. Prospective memory. I. Einstein, Gilles O., 1950- II. Title.

BF378.P76M35 2007
153.1'3—dc22

                                              2006035647

This book is printed on acid-free paper.

07   08   09   10   11   10 9 8 7 6 5 4 3 2 1

Acquisitions Editor:	Cheri Dellelo
Editorial Assistant:	Anna Marie Mesick
Production Editor:	Libby Larson
Copy Editor:	Rachel Keith
Typesetter:	C&M Digitals (P) Ltd.
Proofreader:	Word Wise Webb
Indexer:	Julie Grayson
Cover Designer:	Glenn Vogel

Contents

Acknowledgments

Nearly 20 years ago when we first started thinking about prospective memory, we could not have imagined the present worldwide involvement of researchers in the area. At that time, there were just a handful of investigators conducting research on prospective memory—most memory scientists either did not appreciate the theoretical and practical issues related to prospective memory per se or were busily involved in mining the paradigms and theoretical developments in retrospective and implicit memory. We owe a debt to those early pioneers, almost entirely in Europe, who initiated prospective memory paradigms and importantly helped to define the topic as one worthy of study. We want to thank Ron Kellogg, who alerted us to the potential richness of this nascent field, and Gus Craik for not only developing theoretical perspectives that stimulated our initial experimental ideas but also encouraging our work.

We also are indebted to our many students through the years at Furman University, Purdue University, the University of New Mexico, and Washington University, whose creativity and enthusiasm have sustained and enriched our efforts in this area. As well, we have been graced with intellectually curious graduate students in several prospective memory seminars at Washington University, whose thoughtful discussions helped refine our thinking as we developed the themes and issues for the book. Over the years, we have had the good fortune to benefit from a remarkably close-knit cadre of international prospective memory researchers who continue to stimulate our thinking, encourage our efforts in prospective memory, and generously share their time and thoughts.

One hallmark of the enthusiasm among these researchers is that we have already had two hugely successful international conferences devoted entirely to prospective memory. These conferences have helped us include the most up-to-date theoretical and empirical work in this book. We are grateful to the organizers and participants of these international prospective memory conferences.

Further, our research and our writing have been sustained through generous funding from a number of organizations, including the National Aeronautics and Space Administration and the National Institute on Aging. We are also grateful to our academic institutions and administrators at Furman University and Washington University in St. Louis, who have encouraged and supported our work by providing a superb intellectual environment and resources.

The book has greatly benefited from the careful and insightful work of the reviewers of the initial manuscript, all of whom are listed below. They were tough when appropriate, yet encouraging, and they were attentive to important detail. From the book's conception to its final copyediting and production, the staff at Sage has been pleasant and professional. We especially thank Jim Brace Thompson for his enthusiasm about the project early on, and Cheri Dellelo for keeping us on a strict time schedule. They gave us "sage" advice at every opportunity. We are extremely grateful to Mary Derbish at Washington University for taking care of the enormous number of important details associated with generation of tables, figures, manuscript drafts, and so on.

Finally, this book could not have been written without the encouragement, support, and love of our families.

—MAM and GOE

Sage Publications thanks the following reviewers for their contributions to this book:

Ute J. Bayen
The University of North Carolina
   at Chapel Hill

Martin Bink
Western Kentucky University

James Erskine
University of Hertfordshire

Melissa J. Guynn
New Mexico State University

Dr. Tom Heffernan,
   Senior Lecturer in Psychology
Division of Psychology
Northumbria University

Joshua D. Landau
York College of Pennsylvania

P. Andrew Leynes
The College of New Jersey

Richard L. Marsh
University of Georgia

Robert West
Iowa State University

We thank Lynn, Austin, Jesse, Leda,
Grant, and Tyler,
and Patty, Julie, and Alex,
who understand and enthusiastically support
our interest in uncovering the processes
underlying prospective memory.
Their ability to appreciate humor helps
them tolerate and even laugh at
our own prospective memory failures.

1

Prospective Memory

A New Research Enterprise

The failure of memory that caused me the most pain was the time I forgot to pick up my 3-year-old son and his friends after nursery school and take them to their play group.

—Eugene Winograd, *Practical Aspects of Memory*

This poignant example refers to an aspect of memory commonly termed prospective memory.* Prospective memory is remembering to carry out intended actions at an appropriate point in the future. Even minimal reflection prompts the realization that the texture of our daily existence is inextricably bound with prospective memory tasks. These tasks include mundane

---

*The term prospective memory is not favored by some researchers because it implies that the task is purely a memory task. As is apparent throughout this book, prospective memory involves a complex array of cognitive processes in addition to memory. Accordingly, the more neutral term realization of delayed intentions is sometimes used. In contrast, other researchers want to limit the focus of study to a memory process that is relatively unique to prospective memory tasks; these researchers favor the term prospective memory proper (Graf & Uttl, 2001). We have adopted prospective memory because it is widely used in the literature, is a crisp label, and perhaps reflects a good middle ground in the debate on terminology.

demands such as remembering to pick up bread on your way home, remembering to mail the letter in your briefcase, remembering to give your housemate the message that a friend called, and remembering to load your bicycle into the car for a ride after work. Prospective memory tasks are integrated into our work lives: The waiter must remember to pick up extra cream for a table on his way back to the kitchen, and an instructor has to remember to make sure the reserve readings for her class are available before meeting her seminar. Prospective memory is also involved in activities that are critical to maintaining life. Remembering to take medication is a common example. Failure to remember to check the backseat of the car after an appropriate period of time has elapsed has produced tragic deaths for young children left in the car (see Chapter 9 for discussion of real-world prospective memory challenges).

Given the ubiquity and central importance of prospective memory, surprisingly little experimental and theoretical investigation on the topic has been conducted. By comparison, retrospective memory (memory for events that have occurred in the past, such as the plot of a movie seen the previous week, or a list of words studied in an experiment) has been examined and considered thoroughly by experimental psychologists for over a hundred years. What we today call prospective memory was touched upon in early work, but very rarely. A survey of memory published in 1899 by Colegrove included a question on how people remembered to keep appointments, and Lewin's essay "Intention, Will, and Need" (1926/1961) considered aspects of prospective memory. But by 1985, in sharp contrast to the large amount of available material on retrospective memory, there were only 10 published experimental studies on prospective memory. Most of these studies were reported primarily in edited volumes (Harris, 1984) and had relatively little impact on the mainstream memory literature. It is probably safe to say that many memory researchers were unaware of research concerning prospective memory. It was not a topic mentioned in our graduate training during that era. By 1996, still only 45 published papers had appeared in the entire literature, and of these just about half included experimental work (Kvavilashvili & Ellis, 1996).

But the landscape is changing. The past decade has seen an explosion of experimental research on prospective memory (Kvavilashvili & Ellis, 1996). From 1996 to 2000, approximately 135 published papers appeared, and in the subsequent 5-year span (from 2001 to 2005) over 150 additional studies on prospective memory were published (Kvavilashvili, Kyle, & Messer, in press). As demonstrated in Figure 1.1, citation counts of prospective memory research have shown a parallel upswing. Laboratory paradigms for careful investigation of prospective memory have been developed, papers

on prospective memory are appearing regularly in the journals, and important theoretical perspectives are being developed. Researchers from around
the world are involved in prospective memory research. Since 2000, there
have been two international conferences focused on prospective memory as
well as many more-general cognition conferences that have included sessions on prospective memory. Students in many areas of psychology are
expressing interest in prospective memory and conducting theses on the
topic. Courses on prospective memory are being included in the curricu-
lum in graduate programs. Prospective memory considerations are now
included in government-sponsored efforts concerned with such things as
aviation safety and space exploration. Although once appropriately characterized as a "forgotten" topic (Harris, 1984), prospective memory is clearly
a vibrant topic at the beginning of the 21st century. The primary literature
is now sufficient to allow an informed and broad examination of prospective memory, and this book is intended to provide interested researchers
and students with an accessible and integrated foundation for the scientific
study of prospective memory.

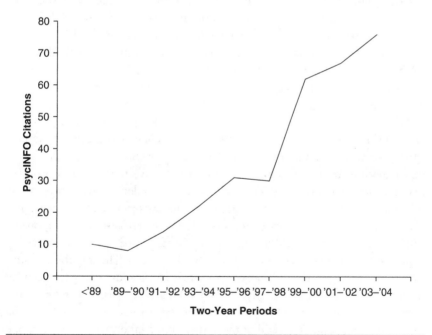

Figure 1.1   The Growth of Prospective Memory Research

SOURCE: From Marsh, R. L., Cook, G. I., & Hicks, J. L., An Analysis of Prospective Memory.
In D. L. Medin (Ed.), *The Psychology of Learning and Motivation, 43,* copyright © 2006.
Reprinted with permission from Elsevier.

What Is a Prospective Memory Task?

Our first order of business is to consider what constitutes a prospective memory task. In writing this chapter, we had animated discussions as we struggled with this issue. Here we distill the key features of our thinking with the thinking of others who have grappled with the issue. We started this chapter with a brief definition of prospective memory: remembering to *do something* at a particular *moment (or time period) in the future*. For the most part, researchers assume that this brief description activates a fuzzy set (Harris, 1984) that captures a common set of intuitions about what is and what is not a prospective memory task. In a strict sense, this definition can include almost any experimental task.

To illustrate, consider the following experimental task: Subjects are instructed that they will be shown a short word list, after which they will be asked to write down the words in the list. In addition, when some of the word lists are presented, a series of digits will be read concurrently, and subjects are to press a handheld counter every time they hear two consecutive odd digits. Subjects are further told that if they ever encounter the word *rake* in a word list, they should press the F1 key on the keyboard. In this kind of experiment, researchers have considered pressing the F1 key to be the prospective memory task. Yet a careful reader might justifiably ask, "Why aren't the other tasks also considered prospective memory tasks?" In all cases, the instructions convey an intended action, and the subject has to perform that action at some time after the instructions are given.

We need to sharpen our characterization of prospective memory to help guide our exploration of the topic and to help delineate our area of inquiry. Most generally, one might think of almost all everyday tasks and all laboratory experimental tasks as having both retrospective memory and prospective memory components. To perform an intended activity, one must remember to recall there was an intention (the prospective component) and also remember the contents of the intention (the retrospective component) (Einstein & McDaniel, 1996; Ellis, 1996; Graf & Uttl, 2001). In everyday contexts, both memory components can be challenged. The intention to stop by the store on your way home from work to pick up five items can be unsuccessful because prospective memory fails (you forget to stop at the store or because retrospective memory fails (you remember to stop at the store, but forget one or several of the items). In the laboratory, however, one component can be minimized so as to isolate the other component for study. The study of memory has historically emphasized tasks in which the prospective memory component is not challenging and the retrospective component is. The subject in a typical experiment does not have to remember to recall an intention to remember the studied items because the experimenter explicitly tells the subject to remember. In Tulving's (1983) terms, the memory experiment places the subject in a "retrieval mode." The study of prospective memory changes this emphasis by focusing on the prospective component and minimizing focus on the retrospective component.

In a retrospective memory experiment, the challenge for the subject is to remember the contents (recall the list of words studied). The parameters of laboratory retrospective memory tasks ensure that remembering the contents is challenging, so as to reveal the properties, processes, and dynamics of memory. If we decide to present one word for study and a short time later ask someone to recall that word, all of us would agree that this is a retrospective memory task. But this task likely would not tell us much about retrospective memory. In a similar vein, prospective memory tasks are designed to challenge remembering to recall (whereas the contents to recall are simplified). Paralleling retrospective memory tasks, prospective memory tasks can have a continuum of difficulty, such that remembering to recall can range from easy to challenging. If the demands of the tasks are too easy, we may not have incisive and revealing experiments for scientific study of prospective memory. In the next section, we synthesize the thinking of prospective memory researchers to offer some guidelines for creating interesting and informative prospective memory tasks.

Parameters of Prospective Memory Tasks

Execution of the intended action is not immediate. First, we will agree that, in normal populations, actions that people begin to carry out immediately after the intention has been formed are trivial in terms of prospective remembering (Harris, 1984; Kvavilashvili & Ellis, 1996). When subjects are given the instruction to recall or recognize a list of items and begin doing so, this is immediate execution of the intention. Because remembering to recall is certain, there is no sense of prospective memory here. Of course, these kinds of tasks, including the recall task in the illustrative experiment above, characterize a tremendous amount of the literature on memory.

The prospective memory task is embedded in ongoing activity. Second, a delayed intention—one that must be realized only at some point in the future—is not itself sufficient to produce an interesting or challenging prospective memory task. In the experimental setting, many tasks introduced at some delay after the instructions are given require that initial intentions be postponed. In our example, the intention to monitor for odd digits is postponed until later in the experiment when the digits are presented. These kinds of tasks would not be the focus of prospective memory research because the presentations of the stimuli supporting the intention are implicit, unambiguous signals to perform the instructed activity (see Einstein, Smith, McDaniel, & Shaw, 1997, and Harris, 1984). The presentation of the stimulus essentially serves as a proxy for the instruction. In the experimental setting, the stimulus (the auditorily presented digits) demands a response, thereby requiring that the person recall the instructions, but there is no sense in which the person is challenged to remember at a given moment to recall the instructions.

In contrast, in a typical prospective memory task, the stimulus that signals the appropriate moment for execution of the prospective memory activity does not directly or unambiguously demand performance of the previously intended action. The prospective memory cues (or stimuli) appear as a natural part of another task or situation (see Graf & Uttl, 2001). To achieve this, in laboratory paradigms the prospective memory task is embedded in an ongoing activity. Here the stimuli support performance of the ongoing activity, thereby satisfying the experimental demand to "do something." In our above example, the presentation of the word *rake* is part of the ongoing demand to maintain words for a short-term memory test. The prospective memory intention need not be retrieved for the subject to respond in the experiment. Consequently, nontrivial demands are placed on the subject to remember to recall that there is another "something" that must be done. This critical aspect of the prospective memory task occurs regardless of the nature of the retrieval occasion. The occasion can be event based, such as a particular stimulus item (see examples in Cherry & LeCompte, 1999, and Einstein & McDaniel, 1990). The occasion can be time based, such as a particular time or a period of elapsed time during the ongoing activity (d'Ydewalle, Luwel, & Brunfaut, 1999; Harris & Wilkins, 1982; Park, Hertzog, Kidder, Morrell, & Mayhorn, 1997). The occasion can be activity based, such as when a particular experimental activity has been completed (Kliegel, McDaniel, & Einstein, 2000; Loftus, 1971).

As just mentioned, in typical laboratory paradigms the prospective task is embedded in an ongoing activity, and performance of the ongoing activity must be interrupted or suspended to allow execution of the prospective memory task. This aspect captures another feature of prospective memory that some theorists consider to be central: Prospective remembering involves interrupting a daily routine or activity (see examples in Morris, 1992, and Shallice & Burgess, 1991). Other theorists, however, distinguish types of prospective memory tasks on this very dimension. Kvavilashvili and Ellis (1996) acknowledge that event- and time-based prospective memory tasks involve interrupting an ongoing activity, and that such interruptions represent an important component of these types of prospective memory tasks. For example, in remembering to buy bread on the way home from work, one must interrupt the drive home when encountering the grocery store. When remembering to attend a meeting at 11:00 A.M., one must interrupt the ongoing work activity at hand.

In contrast, Kvavilashvili and Ellis (1996) contend that activity-based prospective memory tasks do not require interruption of the ongoing activity, precisely because these tasks are signaled prior to initiation of an activity or upon completion of an activity. For example, remembering to take medication after finishing breakfast involves doing something during the gap between finishing breakfast and initiating the next activity in one's routine. One might argue, however, that this assertion depends on the extent to which normal, routinized activities are interconnected. For instance, taking medication after breakfast requires interruption of the normal routine of driving to work after breakfast (instead of walking to the car, one must fetch the medication). Similarly, an activity-based task in the laboratory might interrupt the normal flow of experimental tasks. For example, when subjects are asked to remember to request their watches at the conclusion of the experiment (an activity-based prospective memory task) (Kliegel et al., 2000), there is a sense in which the normal routine of departing the laboratory when the last task is completed is interrupted. Thus, it remains unclear whether interruptions to ongoing activity should be considered an important feature of all types of prospective memory tasks or whether interruptions are not present in some prospective memory tasks.

The window for response initiation is constrained. A third consideration is that prospective memory is characterized by a window of opportunity in which an intended action can be appropriately performed. My intention to clean the attic is appropriately fulfilled if I do it today, tomorrow, next month, or next year. Typically, such intentions are not classified as prospective memory tasks. Instead, definitions of prospective memory have included a constrained window of opportunity, and this window is how we define prospective memory forgetting and remembering. Remembering is manifest only if we remember the intention within the window of opportunity. The length of the window may vary (see Ellis, 1988a, 1988b) from several seconds to several days. The prospective memory task of remembering to pick up your child from nursery school involves a window of opportunity that is framed in minutes. The window for remembering to give your colleague the message about purchasing play-off tickets is framed in terms of several days. Not remembering the tasks within these windows of opportunity reflects prospective memory failures.

The time frame for response execution is limited. A fourth guideline often included in characterizations of prospective memory concerns the time frame needed to execute the intended activity. It seems strained to classify reading a book as a successful completion of a prospective memory task or the failure to read the book as a prospective memory failure (Roediger, 1996; Winograd, 1988). A similar observation can be made for writing a grant proposal, writing a book, taking a trip, or getting a job. Yet these are behaviors that arise from intentions that cannot be realized immediately and are not signaled by explicit requests to remember or unambiguous cues. The key distinction between these tasks and those that most of us are comfortable calling prospective memory tasks is that their execution requires a quite extended time frame. They cannot be executed in a matter of minutes, and they "cast a long shadow forward in time" (Winograd, p. 352). Taking a trip, writing or reading a book, or training for a job requires significant and concrete alterations in day-to-day activities. Be clear that here we are not referring to the time frame between the formation of the intention and the opportunity to execute the intended response, but rather the time needed to execute the intended action itself.

Thus, to capture the common assumption that prospective memory involves those intentions that do not require overly extended time frames for execution of the intended response, at this point laboratory paradigms reflect this limit. More precisely, Kvavilashvili and Ellis (1996) regard prospective memory tasks as those that can be accomplished in no more than several hours: for example, going shopping. Even within this constraint, the demands and processes associated with tasks requiring on the order of a couple of hours for completion are likely different from those of tasks needing seconds or minutes for completion (Kvavilashvili & Ellis). Because prospective memory research has dealt with only those intentions accomplished in the shorter time frames of seconds or minutes, this book must necessarily be limited to discussion of prospective memory involving intended actions that require relatively short time frames for execution. However, as theory and understanding of prospective memory progress, it may be of some value for future prospective memory investigations to consider tasks that require extended time frames for execution.

There must be an intention. Finally, an aspect of prospective memory that is more subtle but perhaps critically important in distinguishing prospective memory from other kinds of behavior is the extent to which a conscious intention is formed, at least initially (in habitual prospective memory tasks, the intention may not be formed prior to each occasion on which the task is executed, but the intention has been consciously formed at least once). Readiness to act in a certain way in the future can be considered to capture an intention (see Kvavilashvili & Ellis, 1996). But this idea of intention seems too broad. Consider classical conditioning: By virtue of pairings of an unconditioned stimulus with a neutral stimulus, the organism has a readiness to act in a certain way when the conditioned stimulus is encountered in the future. As in prospective memory tasks, the stimulus may well be encountered in the context of another ongoing activity (for example, divided-attentions studies). We would not want to suggest, however, that classical conditioning be studied under the umbrella of prospective memory. Thus, we believe it is useful to restrict definitions of prospective memory to instances that include consciously formed intentions or plans (Morris, 1992; see also Graf & Uttl, 2001).

Another consideration. Graf and Uttl (2001) further suggest that prospective memory proper takes place in only those situations where the formed intention is one "of which meanwhile we have not been thinking" (p. 444). The suggestion is that when an intention remains active in working memory, the task is more properly termed a vigilance task. Figure 1.2 provides a schematic of Graf and Uttl's distinction between vigilance and prospective memory tasks. According to their distinction, the more completely the intention is maintained in working memory, the more it resembles a vigilance task. Conversely, the less the intention is maintained in working memory, the more it resembles a prospective memory task. We are sympathetic to this approach, as it clearly circumscribes prospective remembering as the process by which the memory system ensures recall of the intention during the specified window of opportunity (rather than maintenance of the intention in working memory). Describing and characterizing this process is clearly a key issue (Morris, 1992), and one which we take up in some depth in following chapters.

Researchers have generally not endorsed this additional restriction in identifying a prospective memory proper task. They have preferred instead to designate the specification of underlying processes in a prospective memory task as the object of study, rather than strictly limit their study to situations in which subjects "meanwhile have not been thinking" (in much the same way as the study of recognition is not restricted to examination of processes that underlie recollection and not familiarity, but instead involves tasks in which subjects must determine whether test items have been previously encountered).

Conclusions

We believe that the above parameters are important considerations for characterizing a prospective memory task. However, we caution students and researchers not to take them too literally. There may be worthy prospective memory issues outside the general bounds outlined above. For instance, in keeping with the characterization that intentions that can be carried out immediately are rather trivial in terms of their prospective

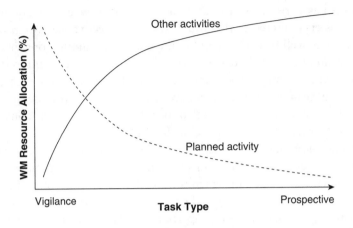

Figure 1.2   Resource Allocation for Vigilance and Prospective Memory Tasks: A Conceptual Model

SOURCE: From Graf, P. & Uttl, B. Prospective memory: A new focus for research, in *Consciousness and Cognition: An International Journal, 10,* copyright © 2001. Reprinted with permission from Elsevier.

memory demands, researchers might be tempted to introduce rather long delays between intention formation and the opportunity to execute the action. We believe this temptation may overly limit potentially fruitful avenues of research. We have found, for example, interesting losses of intentions within 5 to 10 seconds of activation of the intention (Einstein, McDaniel, Manzi, Cochran, & Baker, 2000; McDaniel, Einstein, Stout, & Morgan, 2003) (see Chapter 7).

Scientific Study of Prospective Memory

The next several chapters investigate the cognitive processes that underlie prospective remembering. Before turning to this research, we describe the standard experimental paradigm that has been developed to investigate prospective memory.

One reason that research on prospective memory has only recently emerged is that the standard paradigms on which the science of memory rest do not capture prospective memory. Further, figuring out how to implement a prospective memory task in the laboratory that reflects the key characteristics described above and that also allows the kind of control and sophisticated manipulations that are a hallmark of retrospective memory work is not straightforward.

Early work relied on semi-naturalistic prospective memory tasks. Typically, subjects were already at the laboratory for an experiment. Before leaving, they would be instructed to remember to call the laboratory at a certain time several days hence (Moscovitch, 1982), or they would be given a packet of postcards to mail on certain days (Meacham & Leiman, 1982). The appeal of these paradigms is that they allow subjects to become engaged in ordinary day-to-day activities, as they would with any prospective memory task. Clearly, however, these paradigms have limitations in manipulating and controlling various factors that potentially influence prospective memory; in monitoring subjects' compliance with instructions and their possible use of external aids; and in precisely measuring prospective memory behavior and processes.

These limitations likely discouraged the memory research community from giving serious attention to prospective memory work. Accordingly, development of rigorous laboratory paradigms seemed necessary to galvanize efforts toward scientific study of prospective memory. But how do we set up an experiment in which we want subjects to remember but cannot explicitly instruct them at the moment to remember (so we do not lose the interesting and unique features of prospective memory)?

A Typical Paradigm

We have developed the following general approach for the controlled laboratory study of prospective memory (Einstein & McDaniel, 1990). To parallel the real world, we keep subjects busily engaged in an ongoing activity. While thus engaged, they are to try to remember to perform an unrelated action at some prescribed point in the experiment. Figure 1.3 displays the major elements of this paradigm. A critical feature is that the opportunity to perform the prospective memory task is completely embedded in the ongoing activities in which the subject is engaged. Within this paradigm, event-based, time-based, and activity-based prospective memory tasks can all be implemented.

For example, consider an experiment reported by Einstein, McDaniel, Richardson, Guynn, and Cunfer (1995). The ongoing task for engaging subjects was answering general-knowledge questions such as, "What is the slowest-moving land animal?" and, "How many hours will it take a person to walk twenty-four miles at the rate of three miles per hour?" To implement event-based prospective memory, subjects were instructed at the outset that we had a secondary interest in their ability to remember to press the F8 key (the prospective memory intention) whenever a question with the word *president* appeared. To implement time-based prospective memory,

1. Participants kept busy with an ongoing task (e.g., pleasantness rating).

2. At the outset, they are asked to perform another task whenever a designated target word (e.g., *spaghetti*) is mentioned.

3. They are given some distraction before the ongoing task starts so that prospective memory intention is not maintained in working memory.

4. Performance is measured by the proportion of trials in which participants remember to execute the prospective memory task.

Figure 1.3   An Event-Based Prospective Memory Paradigm

other subjects were instructed to remember to press the F8 key after 5-minute periods had elapsed. After these instructions, all subjects were given the distracter activity of a vocabulary task before beginning the general-knowledge-question task.

In the event-based prospective memory condition, the target event appeared six times during the course of the ongoing activity. Similarly, in the time-based prospective memory condition, there were 6 five-minute segments for which responses were recorded. Also, for the time-based task, subjects could press a key to get a display of elapsed time. These key presses provided an overt measure of clock monitoring in the time-based task (see Chapter 2).

Most laboratory paradigms of prospective memory are variations on this basic procedure. Now that we have established a working definition of prospective memory and presented the general features of the paradigms used to study prospective memory, we are ready to plunge into the core research issues, theories, and findings that are the focus of this book.

2

Monitoring in Prospective Memory

. . . it defines one of the challenges to explanations of prospective memory: What happens to allow recall to take place?

—Peter Morris, *Aspects of Memory*

The next three chapters consider the intriguing and central puzzle of how an intended action is activated at the appropriate window of opportunity. By definition, prospective memory tasks are those in which remembering to recall is the primary challenge. Existing models of recall and recognition based on laboratory studies of memory focus on the processes that occur once a person has been explicitly prompted to remember. Thus, these models do not consider and address the retrieval process of most interest in prospective remembering. We need other theoretical approaches to help us understand prospective remembering.

Fortunately, theorists have been fertile in developing ideas about how the cognitive system enables us to remember the intended action at the appropriate moment. These ideas fall into two broad classes: One class we will term *attentional monitoring* and the other we will term *spontaneous retrieval*. First we will describe the attentional monitoring approaches and

13

the associated evidence for these approaches. In the following chapter, we will consider the competing spontaneous retrieval approaches that account for prospective memory by more automatic, less strategic processes.

Attentional Monitoring

A widely embraced view is that in order for the intended action to be performed at the appropriate moment, the environment must be monitored or checked for a signal. A hallmark of this view is the idea that the monitoring process exacts an attentional cost. That is, some attentional resources must be expended to monitor for a signal that indicates the intended response is appropriate. Further, these attentional resources are deployed prior to the prospective memory response. In an informal and implicit sense, this is the view assumed when people draw negative conclusions about the conscientiousness of someone who forgets a prospective memory task. When a parent forgets to pick up his child from tennis practice, people wonder how the parent could be so irresponsible or lazy or care so little for his child. This aspersion is based on the assumption that the person opted not to devote the required attentional resources to the prospective memory task. In one formal view, these attentional resources would be directed by a Supervisory Attentional System (Shallice & Burgess, 1991). So in a sense the criticism directed at the parent is that some supervisory (cognitive) processes that could have been engaged for successful prospective memory have lapsed because of the "supervisor's" laziness or misplaced priorities.

Test-Wait-Test-Exit

One influential and seminal monitoring model was proposed by Harris (1984; Harris & Wilkins, 1982), a pioneer in prospective memory research. Harris reasoned that the attentional costs of monitoring are sufficient to discourage continuous monitoring. Instead, he claimed, people only periodically evaluate whether the conditions are right for performing the intended activity. The dynamics of this periodic monitoring are captured by a procedure known as test-wait-test-exit (TWTE) (Miller, Galanter, & Pribram, 1960). Figure 2.1 provides a schematic of the TWTE process. The idea is that people will initially evaluate (test) early because the cost of responding late is high. Taking cookies out of the oven too late results in ruined cookies; remembering to tell your roommate that his girlfriend called to cancel their date only after the roommate has left results in an embarrassed and possibly angry roommate. Once the test reveals it is too

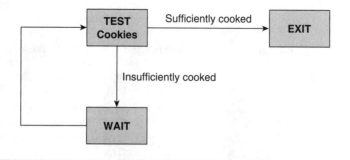

Figure 2.1   The Test-Wait-Test-Exit (TWTE) Model

early to perform the intended activity, a "wait" period follows, during which attention to events continues in a normal fashion. After some period of waiting, another test is initiated and so on, until a test confirms that it is appropriate to perform the intended action. At this point, the test-wait cycle is discontinued (exit).

Evidence for the TWTE process has been reported in laboratory prospective memory tasks in which monitoring can be explicitly identified and recorded by the experimenter. In these tasks, participants are engaged in an ongoing activity, and in addition they are required to make an intended response at a particular time of day or after a certain period of time has elapsed (time-based prospective memory). The laboratory tasks are designed to approximate everyday situations where people are involved in their daily activities, perhaps watching TV, and also have to remember to do something at a particular time (pick up a child from tennis practice at 5:00 P.M.) or after a period of time has elapsed (take cookies out of the oven in 10 minutes). For instance, in an experiment done by Harris and Wilkins (1982), participants watched a 2-hour movie, and in addition held a stack of cards on which designated times were printed (3 minutes or 9 minutes). Participants were instructed to hold up each card at the designated time and display it to a video camera. So, if a participant's first three cards indicated 9, 3, and 9 minutes, he or she was to wait 9 minutes and hold up the first card, wait 3 minutes and hold up the second card, and wait 9 minutes before holding up the third card.

The critical feature of these experiments is that the available clock is obscured so that checking the clock requires an overt behavior (Harris & Wilkins, 1982; see also Einstein, McDaniel, Richardson, Guynn, & Cunfer, 1995). Typically the clock is placed behind the participants so that they have to turn their heads to check the clock. These experiments show several important findings: First, they confirm that participants do periodically check the

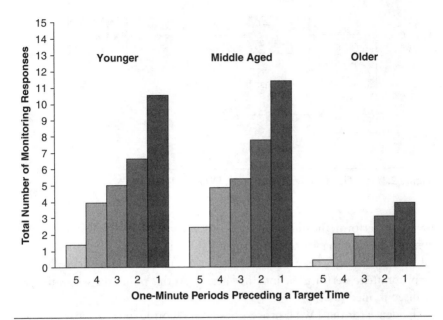

Figure 2.2   Mean Number of Monitoring Responses During the Five 1-Minute Periods Before the Target Time in an Experiment Performed by Einstein, McDaniel, Richardson, Guynn, and Cunfer (1995)

SOURCE: From Einstein, G. O., McDaniel, M. A., Richardson, S. L., Guynn, M. J. & Cunfer, A. R., Aging and prospective memory: Examining the influences of self-initiated retrieval processes. *Journal of Experimental Psychology: Learning, Memory, and Cognition, 21,* 996–1007. Copyright © 1995, American Psychological Association. Reprinted with permission.

clock. Second, the clock-checking behavior is generally strategic, at least for many participants. Participants will check the clock at a modest rate until a short period before the target time. As the performance time approaches, monitoring frequency will significantly increase, as shown in Figure 2.2.

Third, the accuracy of prospective memory performance is associated with the monitoring behavior. Figure 2.2 shows that younger and middle-aged participants monitored more often than older participants did. Especially noteworthy is that older participants did not significantly increase their rate of monitoring as the target time approached, whereas the other participants did. These monitoring patterns paralleled prospective memory performance: Relative to younger participants, older adults showed significant decline in performance of the intended activity within a reasonable interval following the target time. Figuratively speaking, the older adults were more likely to burn the cookies! Harris and Wilkins

(1982) tested a middle-aged group of women and in this experiment correlated the frequency of monitoring during the period just preceding the target time with the promptness of the prospective memory response. Again, when monitoring frequency increased near the target time, prospective memory responses were more likely to be right on time. Late responses were associated with very infrequent monitoring as the target time approached. A similar pattern has been observed with 10- and 14-year-old children (Ceci & Bronfenbrenner, 1985).

These results offer practical insight for improving prospective memory. One day one of the authors of this book was supposed to pick up his son from tennis practice at 4:00 P.M. Being a prospective memory researcher, he engaged the TWTE process and monitored the clock early in the afternoon. Feeling confident about his ability to remember to pick up his son, he began to monitor less frequently as the afternoon progressed. The intended action occurred to him only when his son called—well after 4:00 P.M.—to ask how the "memory expert" could have forgotten to pick up his son. If we want to improve our prospective memory accuracy, we need to initiate more frequent monitoring as the target time approaches.

More frequent monitoring, however, does not ensure perfect prospective memory. A fourth intriguing finding is that when Harris and Wilkins's participants forgot to respond on time, over a quarter of the time they had monitored the clock within 10 seconds of the target time! Sellen, Louie, Harris, and Wilkins (1997) report a similar finding in an experiment in which subjects performed a prospective memory task in their usual work setting. Apparently, absorption in an ongoing activity can quickly disrupt maintenance of the intention in awareness (see also McDaniel, Einstein, Stout, & Morgan, 2003). Perhaps the fragileness of the intention in awareness even with appropriate monitoring partly accounts for prospective memory lapses that are considered egregious.

Factors Involved in Initiating Monitoring

A critical question not addressed by the TWTE description is, what processes lead us to initiate a check in the first place? Researchers do not have a clear answer, but several possibilities are evident in the literature. One idea was introduced earlier: A supervisory executive system stimulates a check of the environment for the appropriate opportunity to perform the intended action. For the time-based prospective memory tasks discussed here, perhaps this executive process depends on judgments of time derived from biological and/or cognitive clocks (Coren & Ward, 1989).

In a similar vein, certain personality variables such as compulsiveness and conscientiousness might affect the degree to which the cognitive system is engaged in monitoring. Consistent with this idea, a preliminary study in our laboratory (conducted by Edwards and Hagood) found a significant correlation between obsessive-compulsive tendencies and the extent to which resources were allocated for monitoring for a prospective memory task. According to Goschke and Kuhl (1993), another individual-difference characteristic that relates to monitoring is whether people have a "state" or an "action" orientation. Individuals with a state orientation find it difficult not to think about future intentions over a retention interval and tend to ruminate about future goals. In contrast, action-oriented people do not experience these kinds of intrusive thoughts over the retention interval. According to this view, people with a state orientation (as measured by Goschke and Kuhl's Action Control Scale) are more likely in certain prospective memory situations to keep intentions for to-be-performed activities in a highly activated state.

Another possibility is that initiation of monitoring is not really self-initiated or dependent on executive control. Checking behaviors may be stimulated by sometimes direct and sometimes subtle cues in the environmental context. One of our students mentioned that an absent glance at a clock can remind her that she needs to perform a task at a certain time later that day. About a third of Harris and Wilkins's participants indicated that events in the film reminded them of the prospective memory task. These events included discussions of time and visual views of clocks. Morris (1992) also has reported evidence of this kind of reminding.

Finally, Wilkins (cited in Harris, 1984) suggests that monitoring is driven by a random-walk process in which one's "train of thought" wanders randomly through a multidimensional semantic space. The idea is that the prospective memory intention is stored as a representation in this multidimensional space. Thus, having to take cookies out of the oven (an everyday prospective memory task) is stored in a particular area in the space; similarly, having to press a key on the keyboard (a laboratory prospective memory task) is stored in its own area in the space. As the train of thought moves through the semantic space, it may move close to the area where the intention is stored. The closer the train of thought is to that area, the more likely it will be to jump to the intention and prompt clock monitoring. If the intention is in the train of thought at the time for the intended action, the action will be performed (the cookies will be removed from the oven). If the time is too early, the random walk may or may not again venture close to the area associated with the intention. This idea has remained relatively undeveloped, though random-walk processes are implicated in other cognitive tasks such as lexical decision (Ratcliff, Gomez, & McKoon, 2004). One recent naturalistic time-based study suggests that subjects' patterns of thinking about the intention prior to the target time are more consistent with a TWTE formulation than a random-walk process (Kvavilashvili & Fisher, 2007).

Preparatory Attentional Processes

For event-based prospective memory tasks, Smith and her colleagues (2003; Smith & Bayen, 2004) propose a more specified view that assumes that monitoring is fairly continuously engaged in order to support prospective remembering. Event-based prospective memory tasks are those in which the intended action is to be executed upon the occurrence of a particular environmental event. For instance, the intention to give your colleague a message must be activated when you encounter your colleague. Smith's preparatory attentional and memory processes (PAM) theory proposes that a capacity-consuming "preparatory" process is engaged to monitor events as possible prospective memory targets (appropriate occasions for performing prospective memory tasks). Memory processes are also involved in discriminating nontarget events from target events and in recollecting the intended action once a target event is encountered.

When the PAM theory is applied to the everyday prospective memory task of remembering to give your colleague a message, the idea is that a preparatory process monitors the environment as events are encountered. These preparatory processes ensure that a recognition check (the memory component of PAM) is initiated for the environmental event that signals the appropriateness of executing the intended action. Preparatory processes might also include rehearsing the critical target event (Smith & Bayen, 2004). This theory takes the strong stance that retrieval of the prospective memory intention is not possible without the preparatory monitoring process.

A possible objection to this theoretical idea is that the attentional and supervisory resources needed to implement prospective remembering would be too costly to allow smooth functioning in day-to-day ongoing activity. We will revisit this issue later, but initially two arguments counter this objection: First, costs are relative. According to the monitoring view, the cost of monitoring is small relative to the cost of performing the prospective memory task early or late. Consider our example of taking cookies out of the oven too late, which can make the cookies inedible. Relative to the brief use of attentional resources that would be expended for periodic monitoring, this mistake is costly. Time and ingredients must be spent remaking the cookies and baking them again (or one must cope with the disappointment of having no cookies). Second, the cost of monitoring is not clearly specified in most models, so it is uncertain how costly monitoring is (see, for example, Shallice & Burgess, 1991).

What does the experimental evidence show regarding the existence of preparatory processes? Note that the assumed preparatory attentional processes cannot be as directly tested as the TWTE process because, in the event-based prospective memory tasks to which the model has been applied, the prospective memory cue is embedded in the ongoing activity in which participants are engaged. Thus, for these tasks there is no discernible behavioral movement that reveals monitoring. (See Chapter 8 for discussion of neuroimaging studies that may offer some insights.) One experimental approach is to increase the attentional demands of the ongoing activity by adding another task. Increasing attentional demands should reduce attentional resources available for monitoring for the prospective memory target. Consequently, if prospective memory requires monitoring, prospective memory performance should suffer.

Increasing Attentional Demands of the Ongoing Activity

In one experiment, Marsh and Hicks (1998) increased the attentional demands of the ongoing activity by asking subjects to perform two ongoing activities. As anticipated, subjects in the "attention-demanding" condition showed more prospective memory failures than did subjects in the standard condition in which performance of just one ongoing activity was required. An interesting aspect of Marsh and Hicks's findings is that prospective memory did not always decline when subjects performed two ongoing activities. When the second concurrent ongoing activity engaged the articulatory loop of working memory—that is, subjects were asked to repeat several words (Baddeley & Hitch, 1994)—prospective memory did not suffer (see Otani et al., 1997, for a similar finding). Prospective memory did suffer when the second ongoing activity was to generate a random order of digits. These results can be understood by assuming that monitoring requires resources associated with a Supervisory Attentional System (as mentioned earlier in this chapter). Generating random digits heavily draws on this central attentional system, whereas a task involving the articulatory loop is thought to require few, if any, central attentional resources (Baddeley & Hitch). In favor of the monitoring view, a number of other studies have also demonstrated that adding a concurrent task to the ongoing task disrupts prospective memory performance (McDaniel, Robinson-Riegler, & Einstein, 1998; Park, Hertzog, Kidder, Morrell, & Mayhorn, 1997).

Though suggestive, these results are not conclusive. Increasing attentional demands might disrupt prospective memory processes other than monitoring. Processes involved in becoming oriented to the prospective memory target, retrieving the intended action, scheduling execution of the various tasks (the ongoing task, the additional-attention-load task, and the prospective memory task), and maintaining the prospective memory intention in mind could all be compromised by increasing attentional demands.

The Cost of Adding a Prospective Memory Intention to the Ongoing Activity

To gain additional leverage for her monitoring view, Smith (2003) focused on evaluating the cost of a prospective memory intention on performance of the ongoing activity. In the laboratory setting, the idea is that preparatory processes need to be engaged on nontarget trials (ongoing task trials in which the prospective memory cue does not occur, and which therefore require no prospective memory response) as well as on target trials (in which the cue does occur) for successful prospective remembering. Smith reasoned that if nonautomatic preparatory processes (monitoring) need to be active to support prospective memory, attentional resources that could otherwise be deployed for the ongoing activity will be siphoned off for monitoring on nontarget trials (as they would on target trials). When resources devoted to the ongoing task are reduced, performance of the ongoing task should suffer relative to performance of the ongoing task on trials in which subjects are not given a prospective memory intention. The critical feature here is that the cost of the prospective memory intention should be evident on nontarget trials. Research prior to Smith's either focused on target trials or included target trials in assessing costs. This approach was not decisive, because trials on which the prospective memory target occurs would be expected to exhibit slower ongoing-task responding regardless of whether monitoring is present (Marsh, Hicks, & Watson, 2002).

To test the monitoring view, Smith (2003) asked subjects to perform a lexical decision task. This involves presenting subjects with a string of letters and asking them to decide as quickly as possible whether the letters form a word. On some trials they do (for example, *river*) and on some trials they do not (for example, *rovul*). Subjects tend to be highly accurate on this task; thus the interest is typically in the speed of responding. Smith found that lexical decision times on nontarget control trials were significantly slower when a prospective memory task was included in the procedure than they were when lexical decision was performed in the absence of a prospective memory intention. Subsequent experiments have reported similar results with a range of ongoing tasks, including category judgment, sentence stem completion (Einstein et al., 2005), and color matching (Smith

& Bayen, 2004). Table 2.1 provides a summary of these findings. The costs to the ongoing activity evident in Table 2.1 imply that subjects were engaged in monitoring for the prospective memory target events.

These results alone, however, do not clinch the idea that monitoring is a requisite process for prospective memory. Even though subjects in these experiments were presumably monitoring, it could be that monitoring was not functionally related to prospective remembering—that is, was the monitoring in fact associated with prospective memory performance? To answer this question, Smith (2003) examined the lexical decision reaction times (on nontarget trials) for those subjects who were at or above the mean on prospective memory performance relative to those subjects who were below the mean. Table 2.2 shows the reaction times in Smith's nontarget trials for these two groups of subjects. The subjects who had demonstrated better prospective memory performance clearly took more time to respond in the lexical decision trials than did subjects who had demonstrated poorer prospective memory performance. The implication is that prospective memory performance increased as monitoring increased (as evidenced by greater costs to performance of the lexical decision task).

A Formal Measurement Model

To mount further support for the PAM theory, Smith and Bayen (2004, 2006) developed the first mathematical model of prospective memory. They used mathematical modeling to estimate and validate the involvement of the preparatory attention processes (designated P in the model) and the memory processes, which recognize targets and distinguish them from nontargets (designated M in the model), in prospective memory performance. In one experiment, the importance of the prospective memory task relative to the ongoing task (color matching) was varied (Smith & Bayen, 2004). One group of subjects (indicated by striped bars in Figure 2.3) was told that the prospective memory task was more important than the color-matching task; the other group (indicated by solid bars in the figure) was told that color matching was more important than prospective memory. As expected, prospective memory performance was better when it was considered more important. However, this result does not tell us what underlying cognitive processes mediated the importance effect.

The key finding hinged on the P and M values estimated by the mathematical model of PAM. According to Smith's theory, the importance of the prospective memory task could prompt someone to increase engagement of the preparatory attentional processes (monitoring) but possibly have little effect on the memory processes (that is, recognition of the target would not necessarily improve because of importance). As Figure 2.3 reveals, the value

Table 2.1   Experiments Finding Significant Costs to Response Latency in Ongoing Activity Due to Prospective Memory (PM)

Study	Ongoing Activity	Cost	PM target(s)
Einstein et al. (2005)	*Category Judgments*		
Experiment 1	High PM emphasis	90	one word
	High PM emphasis	410	one syllable
	Moderate PM emphasis	284	one syllable
Experiment 2	Moderate PM emphasis	198	one syllable
	Sentence Completion		
Experiment 3		322	six unrelated words
Experiment 4		192	one word
Guynn (2003)	*Continuous Detection Task*		
	Blocked control and PM trials	121	one category (fruit)
	Alternating control and PM trials	140	one category (fruit)
Marsh, Hicks, Cook, Hansen, & Pallos (2003)	*Lexical Decision*		
Experiment 1		87	one category (animal)
Experiment 3		229	eight unrelated words
		302	eight unrelated words
		216	eight related words
Smith (2003)			
Experiment 1		335	six unrelated words
Experiment 2		183	six unrelated words
Smith & Bayen (2004)	*Color Matching*		
Experiment 1	High PM emphasis	579	six unrelated words
	Moderate PM emphasis	371	six unrelated words
Experiment 2	High PM emphasis	641	six related words
	High PM emphasis	498	six unrelated words
	Moderate PM emphasis	333	six related words
	Moderate PM emphasis	249	six unrelated words

NOTE: Cost is the difference in reaction times (in milliseconds) on nontarget trials in the prospective memory condition minus the reaction times on matched trials in the control condition (no prospective memory task).

Table 2.2   Latencies for Ongoing Activity as a Function of Prospective
Memory (PM) in Two Experiments (Smith, 2003)

	Latencies (ms) for Ongoing Lexical Decision Task	
Study	*Subjects With PM Above Mean*	*Subjects With PM Below Mean*
Experiment 1	1,149	972
Experiment 2		
Orthographically Distinct Words	1,131	950
Orthographically Common Words	1,022	801

of P but not the value of M increased when the prospective memory task
was considered more important. (The error bars in Figure 2.3 represent
95% confidence intervals [Smith & Bayen, 2004].) These results support
Smith's theory and suggest that the effects of importance on prospective
memory performance are mediated through variations in the involvement
of the preparatory attentional processes. Converging with this assertion,
the cost to the ongoing activity on nontarget trials was greater when the
prospective memory task was deemed important than it was when the
ongoing task was deemed important (see Table 2.1 for means).

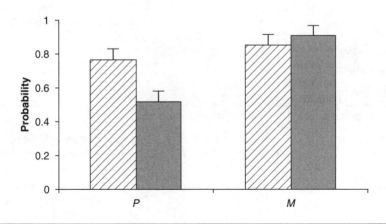

Figure 2.3   Estimates for Smith and Bayen's (2004) Experiment 1

SOURCE: From Smith, R. E. & Bayen, A., Multinomial Model of Event-Based Prospective
Memory, in *Journal of Experimental Psychology: Learning, Memory, and Cognition, 30.*
Copyright © 2004, American Psychological Association. Reprinted with permission.

To Monitor or Not to Monitor: When Is the Question

The PAM model takes the clear stance that nonautomatic preparatory attentional processes must be engaged during the interval prior to the occurrence of the target event. One straightforward interpretation of this model is that prospective memory requires that monitoring continuously occur between the formation of the intention and its subsequent execution. This account may apply in some laboratory circumstances, but we think it implausible that in everyday settings event-based prospective memory requires some level of nonautomatic monitoring of the environment for the occurrence of the target events (cf. Smith, 2003, p. 349). Many times the opportunity for executing the prospective memory intention is hours or days removed from formation of the intention. These kinds of intervals would not favor continuous monitoring. Maintaining a nonautomatic monitoring process over hours or days in the face of everyday demands would seem an insurmountable challenge for the cognitive system. Indeed, one general approach in cognition assumes that extensive reliance on conscious attentional processes is exhausting and that the cognitive system tends to rely on more automatic processes to mediate behavior (Bargh & Chartrand, 1999). Even in laboratory settings, when subjects must maintain a retrieved intention for up to half a minute before executing the intended action, expenditure of resources to maintain the intention in mind appears to wane after as little as 5 seconds (Einstein, McDaniel, Williford, Pagan, & Dismukes, 2003).

Moreover, we suspect that most people would find it unsatisfactory in everyday settings to exact a cost on important ongoing activities for the purpose of supporting a preparatory attentional monitoring process. The decline in performance of ongoing activities that would accrue over the course of the day would potentially be prohibitive. We think it likely that people prefer to allocate their attentional resources to the task at hand without also having to allocate attention to other demands such as monitoring to support prospective remembering. Therefore, if preparatory attentional processes had to be engaged in the interval after forming an intention for prospective remembering, prospective remembering in everyday circumstances would perhaps be a rare event. Based on these conjectures, other ideas about monitoring dynamics merit consideration. To finish our discussion on monitoring, we mention two approaches that have been suggested.

Strategic Allocation of Monitoring

Consider the prospective memory task of remembering to buy milk before returning home for the day. According to monitoring theory, this task would be accomplished by monitoring for opportunities to buy milk throughout the day. However, in everyday settings this task is more likely to be formulated as the intention to buy milk on the drive home from work. Now the intention to buy milk has been associated with a particular context that potentially restricts the window in which one needs to allocate resources for monitoring. Marsh, Cook, and Hicks (2006) suggest that people use these contextual associations for strategically allocating monitoring resources. The idea is that, rather than monitoring every event (or every trial in an experimental setting), one does not allocate resources to monitoring until one encounters the anticipated context for completing the prospective memory task. In our example, monitoring for a store to buy milk would only be initiated in the critical context associated with the intention—when in the car driving home. Thus, contextual markers may allow monitoring to be strategically deployed so that attentional resources presumably required for successful prospective remembering do not necessarily disrupt one's daily activities.

To test this idea, Marsh, Hicks, and Cook (2006) developed a new twist on the typical laboratory paradigm. Specifically, they performed an experiment in which the subjects' ongoing task was lexical decision and their prospective memory task was to press a designated key if they ever encountered an animal word. The new twist was that subjects were also told that the animal words would appear in Phase 3 of the experiment, Phase 1 being a series of lexical decision trials, Phase 2 a set of questionnaire tasks, and Phase 3 another set of lexical decision trials. Subjects in a control group were given no prospective memory instructions. Of interest was the costs to lexical decision (in terms of latency to respond) of adding the prospective memory task. Based on the findings reviewed above, one might expect that the prospective memory task would incur costs to the ongoing activity throughout the experiment.

On the other hand, if subjects given the prospective memory task used the phases of the experiment as contextual markers to strategically restrict monitoring to an appropriate context, costs to lexical decision would be restricted to Phase 3. This is exactly what happened. As can be seen in Figure 2.4, lexical decision latencies were equivalent for subjects in both the control and prospective memory conditions in Phase 1, whereas in Phase 3 lexical decision latencies were slower for subjects in the prospective memory condition. This pattern implies that subjects limited monitoring to an appropriate context—the context in which the prospective memory target event was expected to occur. In another series of experiments, Cook, Marsh, and Hicks (2005) reported the flip side: Prospective memory performance was significantly reduced when the moment for performing the prospective memory task did not occur in the expected context.

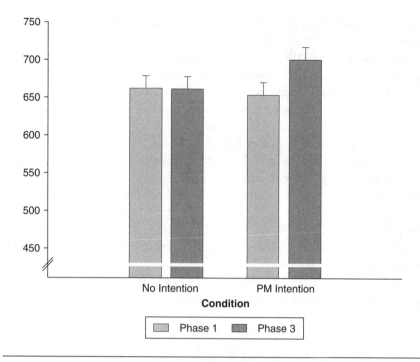

Figure 2.4   Reaction Times of Subjects in the No-Intention Control Condition and the Prospective Memory (PM) Condition in an Experiment Performed by Marsh, Hicks, and Cook (2006)

SOURCE: From Marsh, R. L., Hicks, J. L., & Cook, G. I., Task interference from prospective memories covaries with contextual association of fulfilling them, in *Memory and Cognition 34*, Issue 5, copyright © 2006, Psychonomic Society. Reprinted with permission.

The alert reader may note that tying monitoring to particular contexts does not completely account for prospective memory retrieval. In a sense, this view implicitly creates another prospective memory task—remembering to monitor when a target context is present. A person might begin to monitor for a store (to purchase milk) only during the drive home, but how does she remember to begin monitoring for the store once she starts her drive home? That is, how is the intention to monitor itself brought to mind during the specified context? In the next chapter, we approach prospective memory retrieval from a completely different perspective in order to gain leverage on this perplexing issue.

Prospective Memory Retrieval Mode

In Chapter 1, we mentioned that in laboratory retrospective memory tasks the experimenter's instruction to engage in recall or recognition stimulates the subject to adopt a retrieval mode. The retrieval mode is a hypothetical cognitive (or neurocognitive) set in which stimuli are treated as cues for retrieving information (Tulving, 1983). In contrast, we suggested that prospective memory tasks do not stimulate the adoption of a retrieval mode. There is not complete agreement on this point, however. Guynn (2003) has proposed that upon forming an intention, people put themselves in a prospective memory retrieval mode. Her view is that once a prospective memory intention has been formed, the cognitive system is placed in a set of readiness to treat stimuli as retrieval cues for the prospective memory intention. According to this view, being in a retrieval mode increases sensitivity to particular stimuli as cues for retrieving the prospective memory intention. The increased sensitivity might be achieved by utilizing resources to maintain the prospective memory intention at an increased level of subthreshold activation (cf. Mantyla, 1996; Yaniv & Meyer, 1987). It should be noted that in Guynn's model, the retrieval mode is one of two monitoring processes (the other process is checking of the environment for the target event).

Regardless of the exact mechanism, for present purposes the important point is that maintaining a prospective memory retrieval mode presumably would require relatively few cognitive resources. The basis for this claim hinges on research examining the effects of divided attention on encoding and retrieval in retrospective memory tasks (Craik, Govoni, Naveh-Benjamin, & Anderson, 1996). Unexpectedly, even though dividing attention at encoding reduced memory performance, dividing attention at retrieval produced little if any decline in retrieval performance relative to not dividing attention. During retrieval, however, there was some impairment in the accuracy of performance of the divided-attention task. One straightforward interpretation of this pattern is that maintaining a retrieval mode places only modest demands on limited-capacity resources. Turning back to prospective memory, the implication is that a retrieval mode would produce minimal disruption to ongoing activities (perhaps no disruption if the ongoing activity was not overly demanding). Consequently, such a mechanism might be a candidate for explaining how monitoring is mediated in everyday prospective memory tasks. We must emphasize that to this point little evidence has been marshaled for a prospective memory retrieval mode (for example, see Guynn, 2003). Doubtless, more extensive theoretical work on this issue will emerge as researchers devote more attention to monitoring processes in prospective memory.

Summary

A fundamental challenge in understanding prospective memory is specifying the cognitive processes that activate (recall) the intended action at the appropriate moment. One long-standing theoretical idea is that the cognitive system monitors the environment for the appropriate moment. Because attentional resources are assumed to be required for monitoring, this view regards prospective remembering as a resource-demanding process.

The test-wait-test-exit model is a description of a possible strategy that people adopt to efficaciously expend resources for monitoring. Under this view, continuous monitoring is too costly and fatiguing, and thus periodic checking is preferred. The TWTE description is consistent with overt clock-monitoring behaviors evidenced in laboratory time-based prospective memory tasks. An important and complicated theoretical issue is what processes stimulate the periodic checks (or monitoring) of the environment.

Monitoring processes are more covert in event-based prospective memory tasks (that is, subjects need not check a clock), and accordingly are not as easy to study. One experimental technique used to infer the involvement of monitoring in event-based prospective memory is to examine whether adding attention-demanding secondary tasks attenuates prospective memory performances. Some studies do report prospective memory decline under extra attentional load; however, interpretation of this pattern is potentially ambiguous. A more compelling experimental technique is to assess the costs of performing the ongoing activity when a prospective memory task is added. Much recent research has exploited this technique and frequently found that a prospective memory task produces significant costs to the speed at which the ongoing task is performed.

The above findings are marshaled to support a contemporary monitoring theory: the preparatory attentional and memory model. According to this model, on every trial subjects must devote attention to initiating a recognition check for the prospective memory target event. It is important to note that some theorists take the strong stance that prospective remembering is not possible without these preparatory attentional processes (Smith, 2003; Smith & Bayen, 2004). We examine this assertion directly in the next chapter.

3

Spontaneous Retrieval in Prospective Remembering

If I resolve in the morning to carry out a certain intention in the evening . . . it is not at all necessary that [the resolution] should become conscious throughout the day. As the time for its execution approaches it suddenly occurs to me and induces me to make the necessary preparation for the intended action. If I go walking and take a letter with me to be posted, it is not at all necessary that I . . . should carry it in my hand and continually look for a letter-box . . . I am accustomed to put it in my pocket and give my thoughts free rein on my way, feeling confident that the first letter-box will attract my attention.

—Sigmund Freud,
Psychopathology of Everyday Life

Freud's speculation suggests that retrieval of an intended action at the appropriate time depends on a relatively spontaneous, involuntary process. Our remarks at the end of the last chapter dovetail with this suggestion: At least for everyday event-based (or activity-based) prospective memory tasks, in which the delay between formation of an intention and the opportunity to carry it out is often hours or even days long, attentionally demanding monitoring is likely not the strategy used by most individuals. Instead, people presumably rely on less voluntary, less demanding processes to support prospective remembering in many everyday settings. These considerations raise, in our opinion, one of the most central and intriguing questions concerning prospective memory: If attentional monitoring processes are not deployed to achieve prospective memory, then what cognitive processes support relatively spontaneous prospective memory retrieval?

We will present some possible answers to this question, but first we need to demonstrate that our laboratory investigations of prospective memory can reflect such spontaneous processes. Laboratory paradigms of prospective memory involve a number of key components that arguably might predispose subjects to adopt monitoring strategies. The ongoing tasks are not typically extraordinarily demanding, and the delay between the prospective memory instructions and the opportunity to perform the intended activity is relatively short compared to delays accompanying everyday demands. If people are apt to monitor in laboratory situations, scientific study of prospective memory processes other than monitoring would require development of new paradigms—paradigms that might not even be tractable in the laboratory. As one anonymous commentator wrote, there is the "extreme challenge of trying to simulate a real life spontaneous prospective memory scenario in a laboratory setting." However, some existing laboratory paradigms do appear to capture the kind of spontaneous prospective memory retrieval processes most researchers agree play an important role in everyday prospective remembering. Let's turn to the relevant evidence.

Self-reports provide preliminary evidence of some sort of involuntary or spontaneous retrieval process in prospective memory. At the end of our laboratory experiments, we have asked subjects how they were able to remember to perform the intended action. Many responded that the intended action seemed to "pop" into mind while they were performing the ongoing activity (Einstein & McDaniel, 1990). Perhaps more convincing, Reese and Cherry (2002) probed subjects at various points during a prospective memory experiment and asked them to indicate what they were thinking about. Subjects mentioned the prospective memory task rarely—less than 5% of the time. (In contrast, they reported thoughts about the ongoing task about 69% of the time.) If subjects were relying on a strategic monitoring process rather than a spontaneous process, one would expect either (a) more frequent reports of thoughts of the prospective memory task or (b) in the face of infrequent reports, quite poor prospective memory. To the contrary, subjects evidenced respectable prospective memory performance (about 60%).

In evaluating the accuracy of self-reports for informing prospective memory processes, we note that self-reports of the phenomenological experience of memory retrieval have been fruitfully utilized in recent years to distinguish between qualitatively different retrieval processes in retrospective memory (see, for example, Gardiner, 1988; Tulving, 1983). Also, self-reports have provided the data for a seminal study on "mind-pops," a retrieval process in which information comes to mind spontaneously (Kvavilashvili & Mandler, 2004). This kind of process may be akin to retrieval processes involved in prospective memory. Accordingly, self-reports may hold some promise for revealing aspects of prospective memory processes. Self-reports will not supplant more objective behavioral data, however, and we now evaluate these data.

Costs of Prospective Memory: Always Present?

Consider the initial paradigms that have reported costs to the ongoing activity in the presence of a prospective memory task (viewed as a critical signal for monitoring processes in prospective memory [Smith, 2003]). In one major study, six words were used as prospective memory target events and each word was presented two times, giving a total of 12 prospective memory trials. The ongoing lexical decision task began immediately after the prospective memory instructions (and a recall check to ensure that subjects could remember the six targets). In the lexical decision task, the prospective memory target words appeared at short intervals (for example, 1.5 minutes apart [Smith, 2003]). It is perhaps not surprising that in this context subjects showed substantial slowing on the ongoing task (about 300 ms for a lexical decision process that normally takes about 750 ms), thereby giving evidence of monitoring for the prospective memory target word under these conditions.

In contrast, our overriding intent in developing laboratory-based prospective memory paradigms has been to structure tasks so that subjects are not disposed to adopt strategic attentional strategies. We assume that in many, if not most, everyday prospective memory situations, once an intention has been formed, people become completely engaged in ongoing activities. These ongoing activities occupy people's attention so that the prospective memory intention is not maintained in awareness.

To approximate this situation, we often interleave a distracter task between the prospective memory instructions and busily engage subjects in an ongoing activity in which the prospective memory target event can appear. We place only moderate emphasis on the prospective memory task. We often instruct subjects that we have a secondary interest in whether they can remember on their own to perform a task later in the experiment. We make the prospective memory task simple. There is one target item, it is presented relatively infrequently (for example, three times), and the subjects have a simple activity to complete (for example, press the F7 key) when the target item is encountered (Einstein & McDaniel, 1990; Einstein, McDaniel, Richardson, Guynn, & Cunfer, 1995).

We have reason to suspect that in this paradigm subjects are not monitoring. For instance, in the studies just cited, older and younger adults displayed equivalent performance on event-based prospective memory tasks (see also Cherry & LeCompte, 1999). Assuming that older adults have reduced resources, if subjects were monitoring, older adults would be expected to display lower prospective memory performance than young adults (cf. Maylor, 1996). However, because there was no index of performance on the ongoing task in the *absence* of the prospective memory task, these studies offer no direct basis for evaluating whether subjects were monitoring.

To test whether monitoring (as indicated by costs to the ongoing task) is absent in a paradigm with a single target item, Einstein et al. (2005) conducted the following study: For one group of subjects, six words served as prospective memory targets, and for the other group, one word served as the target. The ongoing activity was a sentence completion task. Subjects were given a sentence with a missing word replaced by a blank. At the end of the sentence a capitalized word appeared, and the subjects' task was to indicate whether the word meaningfully fit with the sentence. Subjects were told that the prospective memory target word(s) could occur anywhere in the sentence. Subjects performed the sentence completion task both in the presence and in the absence of a prospective memory task, and the response times for the sentence completion task were recorded.

On nontarget trials, the prospective memory task produced significant reaction time costs to the sentence completion task in the group with six prospective memory targets (a 323-ms cost on average) but not in the group with one target (a 94-ms cost on average). In a follow-up experiment using the one-target condition and over 100 subjects, the nonsignificant cost dropped to a mere 5 ms (Breneiser, 2004). These results must be interpreted cautiously, however, due to the relatively long response times needed for the sentence decisions (the average was just under 5 seconds) and the relatively slow pace at which the sentences were displayed (every 7.5 seconds). One might argue that with these processing times, subjects were able to sneak in monitoring during the sentence completion task without incurring a detectable cost. For performing other kinds of tasks such as remembering short lists of words, participants are known to sneak in controlled processes like rehearsal (Reitman, 1974).

However, the absence of costs associated with a prospective memory task has been reported in experiments involving more rapid ongoing-task response. Using a lexical decision task as the ongoing activity (as had Smith [2003]), Marsh, Hicks, Cook, Hansen, and Pallos (2003) found no cost to the ongoing task in nontarget trials involving a single prospective memory target word (see Einstein et al., 2005, Experiments 1 and 2, for similar findings with a category decision task). Table 3.1 provides a summary of studies examining the costs of performing a prospective memory task on the speed of ongoing task performance when there is a single focal target event. It is important to note that even with no costs, prospective memory performance was relatively high in all of these studies. This evidence strongly implies that laboratory prospective memory paradigms need not induce monitoring, and that prospective memory retrieval can be successful in the absence of monitoring.

To verify that the absence of costs signals an absence of monitoring and that prospective memory retrieval can occur without monitoring, Einstein and Larson tried to eliminate monitoring by emphasizing the importance of the lexical decision task through occasional feedback to subjects on the

Table 3.1   Summary of Studies Examining the Costs of Performing a Prospective Memory Task With One Target Item on the Speed of Performing the Ongoing Task

Study	Cost	N	Sig	PM
Breneiser (2004)	5 ms	128	no	83%
Einstein, McDaniel, Shank, & Mayfield (2002)	−73 ms	24	no	94%
Einstein et al. (2005)				
Experiment 1	47 ms	24	no	88%
Experiment 2	29 ms	24	no	93%
Experiment 3	94 ms	32	no	80%
Experiment 4	192 ms	104	Yes	94%
Einstein & Larson (unpublished)	13 ms	12	no	86%
Marsh, Hicks, Cook, Hansen, & Pallos (2003)	23 ms	32	no	93%

NOTE: N indicates number of subjects; Sig indicates whether cost is significantly greater than zero; PM indicates percentage of successful prospective memory trials.

speed of their responses (McDaniel & Einstein, 2007). Einstein and Larson's results showed a very minimal and nonsignificant cost (13 ms) of performing a prospective memory task. Nevertheless, subjects remembered to respond on the prospective memory trials 86% of the time. We are now in a position to approach even more central questions: What is the evidence that a more spontaneous retrieval process is operating in these paradigms, and what is the nature of these putative spontaneous processes?

Spontaneous Retrieval

> Do I ever cross your mind
>
> Darlin' do you ever see
>
> Some situation somewhere, somehow
>
> Triggers your memory
>
> —Ray Charles, "Do I Ever Cross Your Mind"

It is very challenging to obtain objective experimental evidence for the kind of spontaneous retrieval captured in Ray Charles's song (see Kvavilashvili & Mandler, 2004, for a self-report technique). To attempt to provide direct evidence of spontaneous retrieval processes associated with prospective memory, Einstein et al. (2005, Experiment 5) adopted the experimental strategy of examining behavior during phases of the experiment in which subjects were not intending to perform the prospective memory task. The unique feature of this novel paradigm is a lexical decision task interleaved between the prospective memory instruction and an ongoing image-rating task. Subjects were instructed to remember to press a designated key if they ever saw a target word in the context of an image-rating task. They were also told that in the middle of the image-rating task, they would receive a lexical decision task and that they should ignore the prospective memory task during lexical decision. The subjects were instructed to simply respond as quickly as possible during lexical decision. Once the lexical decision trials were completed, the image-rating task was resumed. During this portion of the image-rating task, sometimes the prospective memory target item was presented, and subjects were to execute the intended action at each such occurrence. The sequence of these tasks is illustrated in the left column of Table 3.2. There were 10 blocks of this sequence, and at the outset of each block subjects were presented with a new prospective memory target item. The critical aspect of the experiment is that for every block the prospective memory target word was presented during lexical decision.

The signature of a spontaneous process is that it occurs without intention. Thus, even in contexts where subjects are not intending to perform a prospective memory task (the lexical decision phase in this experiment), the presence of the prospective memory target might trigger involuntary retrieval processes. Einstein et al. (2005) assumed that spontaneous retrieval and attendant consideration of the elements of the prospective memory task would interfere with the speed of making a lexical decision when a target item is presented relative to when a matched neutral item (a word that is not a prospective memory target but is matched on dimensions known to influence lexical decision speed, such as the number of syllables) is presented (cf. Marsh, Hicks, & Watson, 2002). In contrast, response times for lexical decision regarding words presented previously (in the image-rating phase just before lexical decision), words not associated with an intention, might well be faster due to priming (facilitation). The lexical decision response-time patterns confirmed these predictions. Response times for prospective memory target items were significantly slower (631 ms) than they were for neutral words (604 ms), but response times for previously presented nontarget words were faster (576 ms) than those for neutral words.

Could subjects have been monitoring for the target during the lexical decision phase, and this monitoring perhaps be responsible for the slowdown in lexical decision response time for prospective memory targets? Einstein et al. (2005) assumed that subjects would not monitor for the prospective memory targets during the phase of the experiment (lexical decision) in which subjects did not need to implement the prospective memory task. In Chapter 2, we described evidence of monitoring from Marsh, Hicks, and Cook (2006) that is consistent with this assumption. Nevertheless, it would be more conclusive if we had evidence from the current experiment that subjects were not monitoring during the lexical decision phase.

To obtain such evidence, Einstein et al. (2005) included an additional 10 blocks of trials identical to the prospective memory blocks except that the prospective memory task was replaced by a retrospective memory task. The right-hand column of Table 3.2 provides a schematic of these 10 blocks. Of interest are the lexical decision response times for neutral words in the prospective memory blocks relative to the response times for neutral words in the retrospective memory blocks. Based on reasoning and results described in Chapter 2, monitoring in the prospective memory blocks would be signaled by a cost to lexical decision response time for the neutral words. However, the means show that there was no cost in the prospective memory blocks (604 ms) relative to the retrospective memory blocks (594 ms).

A possible criticism of this experiment is that subjects were constantly switching back and forth between the ongoing task and the lexical decision

Table 3.2   Sequence of Tasks in an Experiment Performed by Einstein et al. (2005)

Prospective Memory (PM) Block (x 10 Trials)	Retrospective Memory (RM) Block (x 10 Trials)
Target item presented for 2.5 seconds	Target item presented for 2.5 seconds
Imagery rating for 7 items[a]	Imagery rating for 7 items[a]
Lexical decision task involving 9 words and 9 nonwords of 3 critical types: PM target Previously presented Neutral	Lexical decision task involving 9 words and 9 nonwords of 3 critical types: RM target Previously presented Neutral
Imagery rating for 7 items[b]	Imagery rating for 7 items[b]

[a]Items were presented for 2.5 seconds each and participants rated the ease of forming an image.
[b]The target word occurred during the second set of imagery ratings in 4 of the 10 blocks.

task, and that this may have created confusion regarding the demands associated with each task. In a new experiment conducted by McDermott and Rusinko (reported by Einstein & McDaniel, 2005) for which the procedure was simplified, subjects were told about an ongoing image-rating task and then given the prospective memory intention of pressing a key whenever any one of two target events occurred in the ongoing task. Subjects were then interrupted with a "speed" task (a "living/nonliving" judgment task), and were told to ignore the prospective memory intention during this speed task. Each prospective memory target event occurred a total of four times across the living/nonliving judgment trials. This is a simpler procedure because subjects switched only once from the ongoing task instructions to the speed task and then began the ongoing image rating. Consistent with the results from the Einstein et al. (2005) experiment, response times were significantly slower (by 30 ms) for judgments regarding prospective memory target items relative to judgments regarding matched control items.

These convergent results lead to the conclusion that environmental and even internal events can trigger retrieval of associated memories. Often these retrieved memories are retrospective in nature. For example, as captured in the Ray Charles lyrics at the beginning of this section, seeing a stimulus can elicit a poignant memory—even when there was no intention to recover that memory prior to exposure to the stimulus. It is in the same way that we believe prospective memories are often retrieved. To give another example, one of our students related that she was returning to school from her mother's house in another state. Her mother, who was interested in knowing how far away the school was, had asked her to remember to look at the odometer upon arriving in St. Louis. Our student forgot to do this, but she retrieved the intention upon glancing at the speedometer several days after returning to school. We next consider the cognitive processes that underlie spontaneous retrieval.

Spontaneous Retrieval as a Reflexive Associative Memory Process

The examples above may remind many of you (perhaps spontaneously) of an often-studied retrospective memory task, that of paired associate recall. In the typical laboratory paradigm, the subject is given a list of paired items: a cue item and an item to be remembered (for example, *train—BLACK*). Then, during the test, the subject is provided with the cue (*train*) and prompted to try to recall the to-be-remembered item. Similarly, in a prospective memory task, a person pairs a particular anticipated event (for example, encountering a friend) with an intended action (giving a message). Later the individual encounters the cue event and must remember the associated intention. Laboratory prospective memory tasks seem even more similar to the associative cued-recall task. To perform the prospective memory task, the person must associate a cue and an intended action (for example, *rake—Press the F8 key*). Later the person is provided with the target cue (*rake*) and must remember to perform the target action (press the key). Thus, at first blush it seems that the processes underlying cued recall would be co-opted to support prospective memory retrieval.

There is a critical difference, however, between the cued-recall task and the prospective memory task. In cued recall, the experimenter requests that the subject try to remember the target words when presented with the list of cues, and recollection is stimulated by the request. In Tulving's (1983) terms, the experimenter's instruction to try to remember places the person in a retrieval mode. In carrying out the cued-recall task, the person is set to consider the ongoing information as retrieval cues and presumably strategically activates associative information to try to produce the target (for examples, see Guynn et al., 2005, and Jacoby & Hollingshead, 1990).

In contrast, for the prospective memory task there is no experimenter requesting a memory search during the ongoing activity, which includes presentation of the target cue (for example, *rake*). Thus, this target cue is processed while in the service of the ongoing task. The intriguing theoretical puzzle is, how does the cognitive system produce retrieval of the intended action when the individual is not in a retrieval mode (or not monitoring for the target) when the target event is encountered? Though no one has definitively solved this challenging puzzle, some fruitful leads are emerging. We describe several possibilities in the remainder of this chapter.

Moscovitch (1994) has proposed that memory includes a system that supports automatic associative retrieval. This system, which Moscovitch believes is located in the medial-temporal lobes and hippocampus, is designed to perform associative encoding and retrieval. It takes as input fully processed stimuli, and to the extent that a stimulus interacts with previously associated memory representations, the system delivers the contents of those representations to consciousness. Let's apply this theoretical idea to the cued-recall example above. When studying *train* and *black,* the system binds these two items together, and later at test, when processing the cue *train,* the system retrieves *black.* The key aspect is that the system is reflexive. Given a sufficiently strong associative interaction between the stimulus and memory representations, retrieval is rapid, obligatory, and achieved with few cognitive resources. Applying this theoretical process to prospective memory, assume that you give yourself the task of remembering to give your friend Lynn a message. If you form a sufficiently strong association between Lynn and the message and later encounter Lynn, the system will reflexively deliver the intended message into consciousness. In the laboratory, the idea is that subjects create an association between the target cue (*rake*) and the intended action (*Press the F8 key*) when initially forming a prospective memory intention. Later when the target event (*rake*) is encountered and fully processed, the automatic associative process will probably deliver the intended action (*Press the F8 key*) to consciousness in a reflexive, obligatory manner.

To test this idea, McDaniel, Guynn, Einstein, and Breneiser (2004) conducted an experiment in which they used preexperimental associations to vary the associative interaction between the target event and the intended response. The ongoing activity was to rate words on various dimensions, and the prospective memory task was to write down particular response words to each of two target words. For the strong-association condition, prospective memory target word–response word pairs were sampled from the set *spaghetti—sauce; steeple—church; thread—needle; eraser—pencil.* For the weak-association condition, the identical cue words were used, but they were paired with an action (a response word) with no strong prior association: *spaghetti—church; thread—pencil; steeple—sauce; eraser—needle*. A real-world analogue for these conditions could be your intention to stop at the grocery store on the way home from work to buy bread (strong association between the cue and the intended action) versus your intention to stop at the grocery store to buy shoe polish (weak association between the cue and the intended action).

Prospective memory was better when the cue was strongly associated with the intention (85%) than it was when the cue–response pair was minimally associated (56%). This pattern is in accord with the idea that prospective memory retrieval can be supported by a spontaneous associative retrieval process, because reflexive associative retrieval would be more probable if subjects were in the strong-association condition than it would be if they were in the weak-association condition. Alternative explanations can be ruled out as well: Because the target cues are identical for the strong- and the weak-association conditions, the accuracy of prospective memory produced by a monitoring process checking for the target cue should be equivalent for both conditions.

Perhaps monitoring performance was equivalent but in the low-association condition subjects could not successfully remember the associated action (a retrospective memory failure), thereby producing relatively poor prospective memory performance. To investigate this possibility, at the end of the experiment McDaniel, Guynn, et al. (2004) gave subjects a recall test to gauge their memory of the cues and associated actions. When prompted to report the details of the prospective memory task, all but two participants correctly recalled the prospective memory cue words and their assigned action words. Removing these two participants from the analyses did not change the prospective memory patterns. Thus, the advantage conferred by the strong cue–response association was apparently not due to better retrospective memory for the prospective memory targets and associated actions.

McDaniel, Guynn, et al. (2004) also tested the reflexive associative retrieval theory's implication that minimal cognitive resources should be required for prospective memory retrieval. They asked subjects to perform the prospective memory task under different attentional loads. In the normal-load condition, subjects simply performed the ongoing word-rating task. In the demanding-load condition, subjects also had to monitor an audio stream of digits for two consecutive odd digits. Of most interest was the effect of this high attentional load on subjects in the strong-association condition, because this condition is the one for which the spontaneous associative retrieval process should be most prominent. In line with the idea that prospective memory retrieval was reflexive and relatively automatic for subjects in this condition, prospective memory performance was not reduced when the attentional load was demanding relative to when it was normal (see Guynn & McDaniel, in press, for a related finding).

The results from the weak-association condition are also noteworthy. For this condition, there was a significant prospective memory decline when subjects were given a demanding attentional load (66%) relative to when they were given a normal attentional load (82%). Thus, reflexive associative retrieval processes are likely not the only processes involved in prospective memory. Other processes considered below may also at least partially support spontaneous retrieval.

Spontaneous Noticing

Familiarity

One way to describe prospective remembering is to say that a person recognizes an event as a cue to perform a prospective memory task. Invoking the well-researched memory process of "recognition" does not, however, necessarily overcome the puzzle discussed earlier. Recognition is studied in the laboratory by requesting that subjects make a judgment regarding whether target stimuli have previously occurred. Again, there is an external request to remember that places the person in a retrieval mode, a state of affairs not present in a prospective memory task. Mandler (1980), however, noted that even though memory researchers have not addressed it, in everyday memory we experience the phenomenon of *context-free* recognition. An example of context-free recognition that may be similar to one of your own experiences is what might occur when a person gets on a city bus. The person, of course, is not in a context in which she is trying to recognize people, as she is not expecting to see someone she knows. Nevertheless, while walking down the aisle amid a set of unknown faces, she experiences a feeling of familiarity upon encountering a particular face. This feeling of familiarity stimulates the person to engage in consideration of the source of the familiarity—that is, she may try to retrieve the episodic context in which she encountered the face. Upon doing so, she may recollect that the face belongs to the neighborhood butcher.

McDaniel (1995; Einstein & McDaniel, 1996) suggested that recognition of a target event as a prospective memory cue might be based on somewhat similar context-free recognition processes. The idea is that while we are busily engaged in ongoing activities (and not monitoring for a prospective memory cue), when we encounter an event that has been previously encoded as the appropriate moment for executing an intended action, what that event is may be processed more fluently than it ordinarily would. Consequently, we may spontaneously experience a sense of familiarity for that event, which in turn prompts further consideration of the event and subsequent retrieval of the intention to perform an action. For example, when forming an intention to give my colleague a message, I think about that colleague and activate relevant cognitive representations. These thoughts of my colleague support more fluent processing of who he is when I encounter him by chance the next day (note that fluency need not be restricted to perceptual levels of analysis [Jacoby, Kelley, & Dywan, 1989]), creating an unexpected level of familiarity (or accessibility). I may then consider what seems so familiar, which may stimulate retrieval of my intention to give him a message.

It is important to understand that a context-free recognition process would not produce completely spontaneous prospective memory retrieval. Upon the experiencing of a sense of familiarity, further consideration of the event and subsequent retrieval of the intended action would be engaged, and these are processes that might well require controlled cognitive resources (for example, see Craik, Govoni, Naveh-Benjamin, & Anderson, 1996, and Marsh, Hicks, & Watson, 2002). The familiarity process would only support noticing of the target as something other than a stimulus for the ongoing activity, thereby obviating the necessity to monitor for the target item (or to invoke monitoring as a necessary process in noticing the target item as a prospective memory cue). Thus, attentionally demanding situations (such as divided-attention paradigms) could compromise the attention needed to further process the event and consider it sufficiently to retrieve the intention (Marsh, Hicks, & Watson).

One experimental strategy for illuminating these theoretical processes in prospective memory is to vary the familiarity of the target event. Guynn and McDaniel (in press) manipulated prior processing of the prospective memory target. Half of the participants had to repeatedly complete word fragments and anagrams of two words later introduced as the prospective memory targets. This preexposure to the targets presumably increased familiarity of the targets in the experimental context. The other half of the participants received no preexposure task, and thus no extra boost in familiarity of targets. In general, preexposure of the prospective memory target increased prospective memory performance relative to no preexposure.

Consistent with this result is an effect reported by Mantyla (1993) based on a category fluency preexposure task. In his experiment, participants generated instances from conceptual categories and then performed a prospective memory task in which half of the target events were exemplars from categories to which participants had been preexposed and half were not. Preexposure improved prospective memory for both younger and older adults. One interpretation of this effect is that generating instances from the targets' category increased the fluency of processing the target event during the prospective memory phase of the experiment, thereby spontaneously eliciting a feeling of familiarity (context-free recognition). This in turn prompted subjects to consider the significance of the cue.

Discrepancy Plus Attribution

Further theoretical considerations have stimulated another idea about how a prospective memory target event might be spontaneously noticed as a cue for implementing the intended action. Mandler (1980) incisively noted that the typical laboratory study of recognition is constrained to examining judgments regarding whether events have previously occurred. The above construct of familiarity is tied to such judgments regarding previous occurrence. However, the noticing of a prospective memory target event as a cue may not reflect a feeling of previous occurrence. Consider everyday situations that require prospective memory. Typically, the prospective memory target event will be familiar and encountered in familiar circumstances, and therefore any feelings of familiarity are not likely to cause special noticing. Proposing that a sense of familiarity must be required to initiate a search for a prospective memory intention may be too restrictive to explain performance of everyday prospective memory tasks.

Perhaps a more fruitful approach follows Mandler's (1980) observation that in everyday usage the term *recognition* can convey that an event is significant. To say that a prospective memory target event is *recognized* seems to imply that its significance is appreciated, rather than that it has been identified as having previously occurred. But how is significance spontaneously signaled? One idea that we have applied to prospective memory follows Whittlesea and Williams's (2001a, 2001b) discrepancy-attribution hypothesis. Their formulation suggests that people chronically evaluate the coherence and quality of their processing, and that such evaluations sometimes produce discrepancies between the expected dynamics of processing and the actual dynamics that are experienced.

For example, regular nonwords like *hension* are easily pronounced and thus tend to be processed more fluently than irregular nonwords like *stofwus*. In the context of a recognition test, the fluent processing of *hension* may be discrepant with the fact that it is an unknown item, and thus individuals may attribute that discrepancy to the familiarity of the item, which becomes the basis for a positive (and perhaps false) recognition response. In other words, because the processing of *hension* is surprisingly fluent (that is, discrepant with expectations for a nonword), subjects are more likely to falsely attribute that fluency to their having seen the item previously. More generally, discrepancy attribution is posited to serve a variety of purposes, including alerting individuals to important stimuli.

Extending this idea to prospective memory, we suggested that one basis for noticing of a prospective memory target event may be a discrepancy between the quality of processing expected for that event in a particular context and the quality of processing that actually occurs (McDaniel, Guynn, et al., 2004). This discrepancy may elicit a sense of significance (cf. Jacoby & Dallas, 1981) about the target event. In turn, the sense of significance stimulates allocation of attention to determine what the target event might signify (which probably involves probing or activating past experiences, such as previously formed intentions). In the context of a prospective memory task, the significance of the target event would be determined upon successful retrieval of the prospective component. Retrieval could entail recovering at the appropriate moment the general notion that something needs to be done (for example, "I need to pass some information along to this colleague") or complete remembering of the particular action that is intended ("I need to invite him to my party").

Note that the perception of discrepancy and the basis for the discrepancy will depend on the context in which the processing of the stimulus takes place. For example, consider a typical prospective memory paradigm. Participants are presented with a list of words to rate on various dimensions. Before they begin rating the words, they are instructed that if they ever encounter a particular word, they should remember to press a designated key on the keyboard. Participants are then presented with the rating task. During this task, they are presented with many nontarget words, all of which are novel to the experiment. Presumably there is a particular quality and coherence of processing associated with these words that sets the standard for what to expect during the rating task. According to the discrepancy-attribution formulation, the prospective memory target word, having been previously encountered during the instructions, creates a different quality of processing (perhaps increased fluency or decreased novelty) that is discrepant from the standard for that context. The discrepancy stimulates an attribution of significance to the target word—rather than familiarity (which might be the attribution were the subject taking a recognition test). The feeling of significance in turn stimulates attempts to determine that significance, and possibly prospective memory retrieval.

Can we develop experimental tests that provide evidence that this hypothetical process supports prospective memory retrieval? One way to do so is to manipulate prior exposure of the *nontarget* items in the ongoing rating task so that the quality of processing of the nontarget items creates a context relative to which the quality of processing of a particular prospective memory target becomes either more or less discrepant. In several experiments, the nontarget words were exposed in a word-list-learning task administered at the outset of the experiment (McDaniel, Guynn, et al., 2004). For this low-discrepancy condition, both nontarget words and prospective memory targets were processed prior to the word-rating task. The nontarget words were read once, then retrospective memory was tested; similarly, the prospective memory targets were read and subjects had to repeat (recall) the instructions to the experimenter. Here the coherence and quality of processing of the nontarget items would presumably be somewhat similar to that of the prospective memory target item. For the high-discrepancy condition, the word-list-learning task preceding the experiment included none of the nontarget words in the word-rating task. In this situation, the fluent, coherent processing of prospective memory targets (due to their previous presentation during the initial instructions) would presumably be discrepant with the standard of processing established by the nontarget items, none of which had previously been presented.

Prospective memory performance was better when subjects were in the high-discrepancy condition than it was when they were in the low-discrepancy condition. Interpretations of this effect based on the features of the prospective memory targets, the prospective memory responses, the cover activity, and the nontargets in the cover activity can all be ruled out because all were identical across the two conditions. The idea is that the presumed chronic evaluation of processing coherence more readily yielded a feeling of significance of the prospective memory target when the processing of the target was more coherent than the norm established by all of the nontargets (to which subjects in the high-discrepancy condition had not been preexposed).

One might correctly protest that these results alone do not compel acceptance of the discrepancy-attribution formulation because, for subjects in the high-discrepancy condition, the prospective memory targets were also more familiar than the nontargets (in the experimental context). To counter this objection, Breneiser and McDaniel (2006) created a high-discrepancy condition by requiring subjects to study the nontargets *four* times in the word-list-learning task prior to the prospective memory phase of the experiment. Here the prospective memory target would arguably be less familiar in the experiment context than the nontargets would be; if familiarity is the key factor, prospective memory ought to decline in this condition. However, under the discrepancy-attribution view, the processing of the prospective memory target (seen only once during the instructions) would be discrepant because it would be less coherently processed than the well-processed nontargets (which would set the expectation for high coherence). Consistent with this view, prospective memory was significantly better when subjects were in the high-discrepancy condition relative to when they were in the low-discrepancy condition implemented as described in the above paragraphs. Still, some might argue that the high-discrepancy condition did not enhance noticing of the target, but instead enhanced a recognition check of the target prompted by monitoring (cf. Smith, 2003; Smith & Bayen, 2004, 2006). More research will be needed to tease apart these interesting possibilities.

A final piece of support for the discrepancy-attribution view is an experiment conducted by Gao and Graf (2005). In their experiment, the ongoing task was to solve anagrams. The key manipulation was that solutions to the anagrams of the prospective memory targets were sometimes subliminally primed so that these anagrams were easier to solve than the nontarget anagrams (when solutions to the prospective memory targets were not primed, they were at about the same level of difficulty as solutions to the nontargets). According to the discrepancy-attribution view, the nontargets would create an expectation of a certain level of difficulty for the anagram task. Anagrams that were solved more fluently would create a sense of discrepancy that could be interpreted as being somehow significant, leading to further consideration of the item's significance (its being a prospective memory target). In line with this reasoning, prospective memory improved when the target items were presented as relatively easy anagrams.

Exogenous Determinants of Noticing

There are likely a number of dimensions of the target event that could stimulate noticing through exogenous *attentional* mechanisms. These mechanisms promote attention to a salient or unusual event through relatively involuntary orienting responses, rather than endogenously driven attentional mechanisms (for example, monitoring) (McDaniel & Einstein, 2000). Thus, prospective memory target events that are salient or distinctive will involuntarily capture additional attention. Further consideration of the stimulus, momentary disengagement from the ongoing activity, or both may then prompt retrieval of the intended action.

Laboratory studies of prospective memory that have manipulated the distinctiveness of the target events converge to give rise to the idea that distinctive targets stimulate involuntary attentional orienting that supports prospective remembering. First, this process provides a robust mechanism for prompting prospective remembering. Indeed, for perceptually distinctive target events, such as a word presented in uppercase letters among words presented in lowercase letters, prospective memory performance for events appearing in the focus of processing is nearly perfect for both younger and older adults (for example, see Brandimonte & Passolunghi, 1994; Einstein, McDaniel, Manzi, Cochran, & Baker, 2000; West, Herndon, & Crewdson, 2001). Similarly, for conceptually distinct target events, such as not very meaningful words presented in the context of meaningful items, prospective memory performance can be perfect (McDaniel & Einstein, 1993).

Second, it is very likely that involuntary attentional orienting stimulated by salient targets more reliably produces prospective remembering than other processes we have discussed. These other processes, which are required for nonsalient targets, are arguably more prone to fluctuation (for example, resource-demanding monitoring, described in Chapter 2, and probabilistic associative memory processes, described above). Uttl (2005) has demonstrated the importance of the physical salience of a prospective memory target. Uttl and his colleagues have developed a technique in which subjects perform an ongoing task with information appearing in the center of a computer screen. While doing this, pictures of objects of various sizes are presented in the corners of the screen. Occasionally a picture of the prospective memory target is presented. If subjects do not detect it on that trial, the picture is again presented a few trials later in a larger size. One finding is that more and more subjects are likely to notice and respond to the prospective memory target as it becomes larger or more salient. Other studies confirm that distinctive targets (uppercase words; not very meaningful words) produce consistently better prospective remembering than nondistinctive targets (lowercase targets in the context of lowercase stimuli; meaningful words in the context of other meaningful words) (Brandimonte & Passolunghi, 1994; Einstein & McDaniel, 1990; Einstein et al., 2000; McDaniel & Einstein, 1993; West et al., 2001).

A third implication is that involuntary attentional orienting process should be fairly immune to resource limitations imposed by the ongoing activity in which a person is engaged. Initial support for this idea comes from experiments in which distinctive targets (consisting of an uppercase word in the midst of lowercase words) maintained high prospective memory performance in the face of a secondary task, whereas the same targets presented nondistinctively (lowercase) did not (Einstein et al., 2000, Experiments 1 and 3).

These findings support the everyday strategy of ensuring good prospective remembering by implementing distinctive cues. For example, to remember to call the experimenter at an appointed time, one person placed his or her shoe on the table next to the telephone (Moscovitch, 1982). Certainly, in most households (except perhaps a college dorm room), a shoe sitting on the table is an unusual sight and thus should capture attention, stimulating one's memory to retrieve the intention to place a telephone call.

Summary

The case for spontaneous retrieval processes in prospective memory is based on several lines of evidence. The first hinges on observations of performance during the ongoing task. When people are faced with a prospective memory task, their accuracy and speed of responding in an ongoing activity are not necessarily compromised, and when probed, people report rarely thinking about the prospective memory task. Yet under these circumstances prospective memory performance can remain relatively high. The fundamental implication here is that attention-demanding monitoring processes are not required for prospective memory retrieval.

A second line of evidence suggests that prospective memory intentions can be spontaneously retrieved or activated in the presence of a target event previously associated with the intention, even when the intention to perform the task has been removed (Einstein et al., 2005, Experiment 5). Thus, prospective memory retrieval may be a relatively spontaneous cognitive process, in line with the phenomenological experience that people report of the intention "popping into mind" when a target event is encountered. We note that evidence that prospective remembering can be mediated by a spontaneous retrieval process resurrects the historical roots of Ebbinghaus (1885/1964) (who suggested that one type of memory is the spontaneous appearance of a mental state "without any act of will" that is recognized as having been previously experienced), Freud (1909/1952) (as noted at the beginning of this chapter), and Lewin (1961) (see opening quote of Chapter 5), and builds on more contemporary theory (Moscovitch, 1994; Whittlesea & Williams, 2001a, 2001b).

A third line of evidence is that under circumstances in which spontaneous retrieval is presumably operative, prospective memory performance is not reduced under divided attention (Guynn & McDaniel, in press; McDaniel, Guynn, et al., 2004, Experiments 2 and 3). These findings still leave unclear whether these posited spontaneous retrieval processes are completely automatic. Research to date has not established whether such processes satisfy criteria for classifying a cognitive process as automatic, and this is an important issue for further investigation.

In addition to experimental evidence, rational considerations suggest spontaneous retrieval in prospective memory. In everyday prospective memory tasks, the delay between formation of the intention and the opportunity to respond is typically substantial. It would seem necessary to have a system that allows spontaneous retrieval so as not to compromise performance of ongoing activities. This view is consistent with that of Bargh and Chartrand (1999), who argue that most of our behaviors are not initiated by conscious will over a broad range of situations but rather are automatically triggered in response to the presence of environmental stimuli. It is also consistent with their position that controlled processing (like monitoring) is a limited resource that is quickly exhausted. Thus, we believe that spontaneous retrieval processes underlie most of our prospective remembering in everyday life.

Research is just beginning to illuminate the fine-grained cognitive mechanisms supporting spontaneous processes in prospective memory retrieval. In this chapter, we have described some initial hypotheses and the supporting evidence for each. One idea is that a prospective memory event stimulates reflexive, associatively based retrieval of the intended action. Another broad idea is that the target event is spontaneously noticed as a prospective memory cue, perhaps through context-free recognition based on familiarity or chronic discrepancy attribution processes. Neither of these ideas acknowledges a third possibility that spontaneous retrieval could occur in the absence of a target cue (perhaps through a random-walk process, as mentioned in Chapter 2). Clearly, much research remains to be done.

The theoretical work is complicated by the possibility that there is not a single spontaneous process mediating prospective memory, but rather a host of such cognitive processes that come to the fore in different situations. The experimental research is challenged to find paradigms that can more decisively reveal these hypothetical processes. We believe that the expanding research on this topic will be especially exciting and informative, not only for understanding prospective memory but also for revealing involuntary memory processes that have long been suspected (for example, see Ebbinghaus, 1885/1964) but not readily investigated.

4

Multiprocess Theory of Prospective Memory

So, if I've accomplished nothing else in this talk, I hope at least that the next time you're tempted to consider parsimony as a desirable aspect of whatever you are doing, you'll give some thought to whether you really want to advocate a simplistic and nonexistent parsimony, rather than an appropriately complicated and meaningful psychology.

—William F. Battig

This concluding paragraph from Battig's presidential address to the Rocky Mountain Psychological Association on April 7, 1978, summarizes his basic point that if we want to understand psychological phenomena in general and memory in particular, we have to embrace the idea that the mind is complex and that the processes recruited in a given situation are context dependent. When this idea is applied to prospective memory, it suggests that the processes we use in a given situation and the effectiveness of those processes depend on things like the importance of the task, the salience of the target item, the inclinations of the rememberer, and so on. We'll get back to this theme shortly, but for now let's consider some real-life situations.

Imagine that your friend calls and asks you to pick up some limes at the grocery store on the way home. You are in the library studying for an important exam, and you will leave for home in about an hour. Or imagine that you are in speech class, it is your turn to speak in about a minute, and you have just thought of a new humorous introductory comment for your speech. It's a good one, and you want to remember to use it. How likely are you to remember these actions in these different situations? Will you strategically rehearse or monitor until it is time to perform the action? Will you rely on spontaneous retrieval processes and simply wait for target events to trigger the thought to perform the action? Or, will you use a different strategy for each situation? What are the benefits and the costs of each strategy?

As captured in Chapter 2, there is clear evidence that people engage controlled processes such as monitoring and/or rehearsal in prospective memory situations, and that such processes are functional in the sense of improving prospective memory (Smith, 2003; West, Krompinger, & Bowry, 2005). On the other hand, there is also ample evidence that prospective memory retrieval can occur spontaneously. Chapter 3 describes research showing that very good prospective memory retrieval can occur in the absence of any evidence of monitoring. Also, following the formation of an intention, the appearance of target cues in a context in which the prospective memory intention has been temporarily suspended (Einstein et al., 2005) or even completed (Holbrook, 2005) triggers spontaneous retrieval processes. So, there is good empirical support for both theories. Yet the theories are diametrically opposed. How do we find our way out of this theoretical quagmire?

In developing an answer to this question, it seems essential to consider the variety of our prospective memory demands. Self-reflection suggests that the likelihood of fulfilling a prospective memory intention, as well as the processes underlying retrieval, varies as a function of a host of variables, such as our busyness during the ongoing activities, the length of the retention interval, the presence and salience of the cue, and the importance of the task. Thus, a professor may be more likely to forget to announce a test at the beginning of class if she is interrupted when walking into the classroom. While driving to work, a realtor may forget to stop at the loan office to drop off paperwork if the loan office is in a small, hidden building off the road but not if it is in a large, distinctive building. And, a friend may fail to pass along a relatively unimportant message, whereas he will be highly reliable with a very important one. In light of the fact that everyday prospective memory demands are ever present and that their features vary greatly from situation to situation, an adaptive system would be one that relies on multiple mechanisms for prospective memory retrieval. Such a system would at times provide backup routes for prospective memory retrieval and also would take advantage of the ability of humans to analyze memory demands and flexibly develop an approach appropriate to each particular context (cf. Son & Metcalfe, 2000). For example, if you anticipate that you will encounter a highly salient retrieval cue for a prospective memory action, you are likely to rely on spontaneous retrieval processes and thereby not compromise processing of ongoing activities during the delay. With more subtle cues and briefer delays, however, you may rely on controlled monitoring processes (and perhaps notes and other devices).

In the following sections, we describe the multiprocess theory, which was developed to account for remembering of event-based prospective memory tasks. This theory assumes that the effectiveness of spontaneous retrieval processes varies across different situations and that people thus tend to use different strategies in different situations. In this chapter, we evaluate the theory and discuss the factors that affect both the success of spontaneous retrieval processes and people's choice of prospective memory strategies. We admit at the outset that we have a bias in favor of the multiprocess view over single-process theories that emphasize only spontaneous retrieval or only monitoring processes.

An Advantage of the Multiprocess Theory

A critical (and we believe fatal) problem with taking a single-process approach (emphasizing either monitoring or spontaneous retrieval) to prospective memory retrieval is that it has great difficulty accounting for the fact that certain variables (aging, divided attention, duration of retention intervals, etc.) have ostensibly inconsistent effects. For example, whereas most studies show that dividing attention during retrieval interferes with prospective memory (Marsh & Hicks, 1998), some studies show no effects of this manipulation (McDaniel, Guynn, Einstein, & Breneiser, 2004). According to the view that prospective remembering always requires central executive resources (that is, monitoring) or the view that it never requires central executive resources (spontaneous retrieval), this should not happen. According to the multiprocess theory, however, this pattern should be the norm. Specifically, dividing attention should interfere with prospective remembering more in situations in which monitoring is needed for prospective memory retrieval but less in situations in which spontaneous retrieval is sufficient.

We embrace Battig's (1978) and Jenkins's (1979) views (developed to explain retrospective memory results) that humans are complex organisms who use a variety of processes, and that the processes that come to the fore in a given situation are context dependent. Our view assumes that people also generally take good advantage of the array of processes available to them to solve the problem of prospective memory retrieval effectively and efficiently. Below, we describe the multiprocess theory of prospective memory retrieval (McDaniel & Einstein, 2000), and then we describe the factors that influence the use and effectiveness of spontaneous and controlled retrieval processes.

Multiprocess Theory

There are three general assumptions (summarized in Figure 4.1) of the multiprocess theory (McDaniel & Einstein, 2000; see also Einstein et al., 2005; McDaniel, Guynn, et al., 2004). One is that several different kinds of processes can support prospective remembering. As described in Chapters 2 and 3, these range from strategic monitoring of the environment for the target event (hereafter, we refer to these as monitoring processes) to spontaneous retrieval processes (for example, associative retrieval and discrepancy plus search) that respond more or less reflexively to the target event and cues associated with the target event.

In line with contextualistic views of memory (Jenkins, 1979), a second assumption is that the particular process that people rely on and the effectiveness of that process depend on the characteristics of the prospective memory task, the nature and demands of the ongoing task, and characteristics of the individual. Thus, for example, when people perceive that a given context is likely to encourage spontaneous retrieval, they will be less likely to engage in monitoring processes. If, on the other hand, they predict that spontaneous retrieval is unlikely, they will be more likely to monitor. This idea bears some similarity to the attentional allocation view recently proposed by Marsh,

---

1. Several different kinds of processes, ranging from strategic monitoring to spontaneous retrieval processes, can support prospective memory.

2. The process that is used in a given situation and the effectiveness of that process depend on a variety of dimensions, including the characteristics of the prospective memory task, the nature and demands of the ongoing task, and characteristics of the individuals.

3. There is a bias toward reliance on spontaneous retrieval processes.

Figure 4.1   Central Assumptions of the Multiprocess Theory

Cook, and Hicks (2006). Specifically, they believe that after learning about the task demands, people develop an allocation policy based on the perceived difficulty of performing the ongoing and prospective memory activities. For example, people who believe that the prospective memory task will be difficult will allocate more attentional resources to it (that is, they will be more likely to monitor), whereas those who perceive it to be easy will allocate fewer attentional resources to it (they will be less likely to monitor). Marsh, Cook, and Hicks believe that calibration of the allocation policy is dynamic and will vary in response to changing demands and changing beliefs about the difficulty of the prospective memory task (and also the ongoing task).

Direct evidence for this point comes from Marsh, Hicks, Cook, Hansen, and Pallos's (2003) experiment. The ongoing activity for all participants was a lexical decision task, and for one condition participants were given the prospective memory intention of pressing a key whenever they saw the word *dog*. For the other condition, participants were to press the key whenever they saw a word naming an animal. In the first condition, because the word *dog* had been clearly associated with the intention, participants would likely expect the target item to "pop out" at them. In the category condition, however, participants would likely believe that spontaneous retrieval would be more difficult and that they would need to search or monitor for the target item. Consistent with these expectations, Marsh et al. (2003) found no significant costs, or interference, of performing the prospective memory task on the speed of performing the ongoing task when subjects were in the single-word condition, but significant costs when they were in the category condition (relative to when they were in a control condition that did not involve a prospective memory task).

A third assumption of the multiprocess theory is that people have a bias against regular monitoring and toward reliance on spontaneous retrieval processes. Why, when it is clear that a monitoring process can enhance the chances of successful prospective memory retrieval in many situations (see, for example, Einstein et al., 2005, Experiment 1, and Smith, 2003), would people not routinely engage in monitoring for prospective memory targets? One major reason is that controlled monitoring processes exact substantial costs on the ongoing activities, and thus a monitoring strategy is maladaptive in the sense that it compromises performance of ongoing activities during the retention interval. In Smith's (2003, Experiment 1) research, for example, the response times for the ongoing task of making lexical decisions (deciding as quickly as possible whether a string of letters forms a word) increased by over 40% when participants were also performing a prospective memory task. Given that we often have multiple prospective memory demands and that the delay between formation of the intention and the opportunity to carry out the intended action is often substantial—especially in the real world—we assume that there is a bias against monitoring and incurring these levels of costs or interference to ongoing activities.

This third assumption converges with Bargh and Chartrand's (1999) compelling arguments that many, if not most, of our behaviors are set in motion through unconscious processes that are initiated by stimuli in our environment (rather than consciously and strategically determined). For example, Bargh (1994) and others (for example, Banaji & Hardin, 1996) have shown that stereotypical characteristics of a group are reflexively or automatically activated upon perception of group membership. Also, Bargh, Chen, and Burrows (1996) have shown that nonconsciously activating stereotypes related to a construct (such as rudeness) in an initial task biases subjects to the point that their subsequent behaviors are more likely to fall in line with that construct (for example, they are more likely to interrupt a conversation in order to ask about the next phase of an experiment). Bargh and Chartrand argue that these kinds of nonconscious processes guide our behavior in most situations.

Importantly, Bargh and Chartrand (1999) propose that there are severe limits to conscious self-regulatory behaviors (and we would classify active monitoring of the environment as a conscious self-regulatory behavior). Specifically, they believe that the capacity for conscious control over behavior is limited and quickly depleted, and that "conscious self-regulatory acts can only occur sparingly and only for a short time" (p. 476). There is good evidence in the social psychology literature that using up this capacity in an early stage of an experiment (by having to exert self-control, for example) affects peoples' ability to expend conscious effort in a later stage. Specifically, in one study subjects who had to exert self-control to *not* eat chocolate chip cookies available in front of them were later less likely to persist in trying to solve unsolvable puzzles (Baumeister, Bratslavsky, Muraven, & Tice, 1998). We embrace these ideas as they relate to controlled monitoring of the environment for target events. We assume that monitoring is typically a conscious self-regulatory behavior. Thus, we suggest that monitoring is not the preferred strategy, not only because it creates costs for ongoing activities but also because it is difficult to maintain consistently over extended retention intervals.

We present more evidence for these positions in the sections below when discussing factors that determine the use and effectiveness of spontaneous retrieval and monitoring processes. These factors include parameters of the ongoing activity, parameters of the prospective memory cues, the importance of the prospective memory task, individual differences and intra-individual differences, and planning.

Parameters of the Ongoing Task

According to the multiprocess theory, the nature and demands of the ongoing task affect the degree of processing of the prospective memory target event and thus determine the types of processes that support prospective memory retrieval and the likelihood of prospective memory success.

Ongoing Tasks and Focal Processing of the Target

We suggest that the extent to which the ongoing task encourages focal processing of the target event determines the likelihood of spontaneous retrieval. This conceptualization borrows strongly from the transfer-appropriate processing explanation of retrospective memory effects (see, for example, Morris, Bransford, & Franks, 1977, and Roediger, 1996). The central idea here is that successful retrieval is more likely to occur when the processing at retrieval matches that at encoding. For example, Morris et al. had one group of participants encode the phonological features of words and another group encode the semantic features. Later, the phonological group performed better on a rhyme recognition test (in which they were asked if a given word rhymes with a word they had encoded earlier). Conversely, participants who encoded the semantic features of items performed better on a standard recognition test (a test assumed to depend on semantic information). Thus, when there was a match between the processing performed at encoding and at retrieval, memory was enhanced (see also McDaniel, Friedman, & Bourne, 1978). Maylor, Darby, Logie, Della Sala, and Smith (2002) applied this concept to prospective memory and called it *task-appropriate processing*. Maylor, Darby, et al. showed that age-related differences in prospective memory performance were smaller when the ongoing task encouraged the same type of processing of the target event at both retrieval and encoding (semantic-semantic or nonsemantic-nonsemantic) than when it did not (semantic-nonsemantic or nonsemantic-semantic).

The multiprocess view extends these general ideas and assumes that spontaneous retrieval is more likely when there is high overlap between the information extracted from the target event at retrieval and the information considered about the target during intention formation (encoding). Thus, if the ongoing task encourages processing of features of the target that are similar to those processed at encoding, the probability of spontaneous retrieval increases. This idea of focal processing extends Maylor, Darby, et al.'s (2002) task-appropriate processing view in at least three ways. First, it specifically links this overlap in processing to the ease of spontaneous retrieval processes and consequently to the reduced need to engage in monitoring processes for successful retrieval. Second, it goes beyond the general notion that the type of processing (either semantic or nonsemantic) encouraged by the ongoing task should match that which occurred at encoding. Specifically, according to the multiprocess view, it is important not only to engage in the same type of processing at retrieval but also to process the same features as those processed at encoding. For example, if one initially encodes the target item *bat* as a nocturnal flying animal, successful prospective memory will depend on whether the ongoing task encourages the processing of the word *bat* at retrieval as an animal versus as a piece of baseball equipment—even though both interpretations involve semantic processing (McDaniel, Robinson-Riegler, & Einstein, 1998).

A recent and telling example highlights that it is critical to distinguish between the multiprocess specification of the *features* processed at encoding and retrieval and the task-appropriate processing specification of the general *domain* of processing at encoding and retrieval. Marsh, Hicks, and Cook (2005) presented subjects with an ongoing lexical decision task, but they included a couple of interesting twists. They manipulated effort toward the lexical decision task by presenting tones that signaled what speed and level of effort subjects should use when performing the task. Three high-pitched tones indicated that subjects should devote maximum effort to the ongoing task, and one low-pitched tone meant that they should respond at a slower and more relaxed pace in completing the ongoing task. Their prospective memory task was to press a key whenever they saw an item from a general category. Prospective memory was found to be poorer when more effort was given to the ongoing task. This agrees with the general finding that enhancing engagement in the ongoing task draws resources away from processes (presumably monitoring) needed to detect prospective memory targets. Marsh et al. (2005) also varied the ongoing task so that one type of task (lexical decision) oriented subjects to semantic features and the other type (determination of whether individual words contain two contiguous identical letters, *speech* and *march* being a positive and a negative example, respectively) oriented them to orthographic features. They also varied the prospective memory task so that it was either semantic or orthographic in nature. Subjects in the semantic prospective memory condition were asked to press a key when they saw any word naming an animal. Subjects in the orthographic prospective memory condition were asked to press a key when they saw a palindrome (a word such as *civic,* which is spelled the same whether it is read in a forward or a backward direction).

From Maylor, Darby, et al.'s (2002) task-appropriate processing perspective, prospective memory performance should be better when the processing domain of the ongoing task is the same as that of the prospective memory task. Thus, increased effort toward semantic analysis in the ongoing task should improve prospective memory when subjects are in the semantic prospective memory condition, whereas increased effort toward orthographic analysis in the ongoing task should facilitate detection when subjects are in the orthographic condition. Surprisingly, the opposite pattern emerged. Great effort given to analysis of semantic features in the ongoing task lowered detection of semantic prospective memory cues but had no effect on orthographic prospective memory cues. Similarly, great effort given to analysis of orthographic features lowered detection of orthographic prospective memory cues but not of semantic prospective memory cues. Marsh et al.'s (2005) interpretation of these results is that target detection in a prospective memory task is *less* capacity consuming when there is task-*inappropriate* processing, presumably because the resources needed to detect orthographic targets do not compete with the resources needed to analyze semantic features and vice versa.

These are interesting results because they demonstrate the importance of going beyond the general domain of processing at encoding and retrieval and accentuate the need to consider the specific features processed as a result of the ongoing task and how these overlap with the features processed when the prospective memory intention is encoded. Consider the nature of the prospective memory tasks used in this research. Certainly, determination of whether a string of letters forms a palindrome is not what is naturally extracted when one makes a lexical decision or even when one determines if there are contiguous identical letters. From the perspective of the multi-process theory, both of these conditions are low in focal processing (even though there is overlap in the general domain of processing in the nonsemantic-nonsemantic condition). Thus, both conditions require that sufficient resources be present for monitoring for the appropriate features for there to be successful prospective memory retrieval. As proposed by Marsh et al. (2005), the other consideration is that the monitoring resources for orthographic-cue detection may draw from a pool of resources different from that used for analyzing semantic features.

A third aspect in which the focal-processing view extends Maylor, Darby, et al.'s (2002) task-appropriate processing position is that it considers the extent to which the ongoing task directs attention to or focuses attention on the target event (see Einstein & McDaniel, 2005). Thus, if the ongoing task is to rate the pleasantness of items presented in the upper left corner of a computer monitor while words are simultaneously presented in other parts of the monitor, presentation of the target word in the lower right corner represents a nonfocal-processing situation and is unlikely to lead to spontaneous retrieval. To give you a better feel for this concept, in

Table 4.1 we have listed examples of ongoing task–target event relationships that we believe lead to low and high levels of focal processing.

Focal Processing

As noted in the section above, a central assumption of the multiprocess theory is that ongoing tasks that foster focal processing of the target event are more likely to lead to spontaneous retrieval through associative retrieval or discrepancy-plus-search processes. When ongoing tasks do not encourage focal processing of the target cue, retrieval will be more dependent on strategic monitoring of the environment for the target event. The evidence thus far is impressive in showing that people rely on spontaneous retrieval processes versus strategic monitoring to different degrees in different situations.

Einstein et al. (2005, Experiment 2) used a category judgment ongoing task in which subjects were presented with two words and had to decide as quickly as possible whether the lowercase word (for example, *tiger*) was a member of the category represented by the uppercase word (*ANIMAL*). The prospective memory task for the nonfocal group was to press a response key whenever the syllable *tor* appeared in any of the words presented in the ongoing task. Subjects in the focal condition were to press the key when they saw a single word (*tortoise*). Subjects in both conditions were told that their main goal was to make the category decisions as quickly and as accurately as possible but that there was a secondary interest in their ability to remember to do something later on. Thus, they were not specifically encouraged to monitor the ongoing-task items for the prospective memory item. Because the category judgment task does not encourage conscious awareness of syllables but rather of the entire word, it does not foster focal processing of the target *tor* but it does foster focal processing of the target *tortoise*. As might be expected, the proportion of correct prospective memory responses was significantly higher for the focal condition relative to the nonfocal condition (93% versus 61%).

An important question is, what strategies did people in these two conditions use to remember the prospective memory task? Because Einstein et al. (2005) measured the speed of performance of the ongoing task both when there was a prospective memory task and when there was no prospective memory task (control condition), they were able to examine the costs, or interference, associated with a prospective memory task. They found no significant slowing (only 29 ms) associated with performance of a prospective memory task when subjects were in the focal condition but significant slowing (198 ms) when subjects were in the nonfocal condition. The substantial slowing demonstrated by subjects in the latter condition indicates that they

Table 4.1 Examples of Task Conditions That Encourage Focal and Nonfocal Processing of the Target

Processing	Prospective Memory Intention	Ongoing Task	Reference
1A. Nonfocal	Respond when you see a particular background pattern (background pattern is changed every three seconds)	Memorizing items presented in the center of a computer monitor for recall tests that occur at unpredictable times	Park, Hertzog, Kidder, Morrell, & Mayhorn, 1997
1B. Focal	Respond when you see a particular background pattern (background pattern is changed every three seconds)	Keeping track of the number of occurrences of each background screen pattern	An experiment for this condition was not conducted.
2A. Nonfocal	Respond to items from the animal category	A lexical decision task	Marsh, Hicks, Cook, Hansen, & Pallos, 2003
2B. Focal	Respond to the word *cat*	A lexical decision task	Marsh, Hicks, Cook, Hansen, & Pallos, 2003
3A. Nonfocal	Respond to the syllable *tor*	Examining a pair of words to decide whether the word on the left is a member of the category on the right	Einstein et al., 2005
3B. Focal	Respond to the word *tortoise*	Examining a pair of words to decide whether the word on the left is a member of the category on the right	Einstein et al., 2005
4A. Nonfocal	Respond when you see the face of a person wearing eyeglasses	Viewing pictures of famous faces and naming each person	Maylor, 1993
4B. Focal	Respond when you see the face of person with the first name John	Viewing pictures of famous faces and naming each person	Rendell, McDaniel, Forbes, & Einstein, in press

were monitoring the ongoing-task items for the target syllable. Thus, Einstein et al. (2005) found, consistent with the multiprocess theory, that the extent to which the ongoing task encouraged focal processing affected whether participants adopted a spontaneous retrieval or a strategic monitoring approach to the prospective memory task. Moreover, it is interesting to note that the absence of monitoring by subjects in the focal condition was associated with nearly perfect prospective memory, thereby indicating that high levels of spontaneous retrieval can occur under the right conditions.

The importance of focal processing is also evidenced by research showing that modulations in working-memory resources primarily affect performance of prospective memory tasks that have nonfocal cues (that is, tasks assumed by the multiprocess theory to be dependent on monitoring processes). The idea here is that tasks that depend on strategic monitoring (those with nonfocal cues) should be highly affected by the availability of resources, whereas tasks for which spontaneous retrieval is more likely (those with focal cues) should be less affected by the availability of resources. This pattern was obtained in an interesting recent set of experiments that examined the effects of nicotine on prospective memory performance.

In one experiment, Rusted's (2005) subjects performed an ongoing lexical decision task, and the prospective memory task was to press a key either when a letter (nonfocal cue) or a word (focal cue) appeared. Some subjects received nicotine and some did not. According to Rusted, nicotine enhances the availability of working-memory resources and has been shown to improve concentration as well as effortful and strategic processing. Interestingly, nicotine improved prospective memory only in the nonfocal condition. This result is consistent with the multiprocess theory in showing that additional resources are most beneficial for prospective memory retrieval in situations with nonfocal cues (where retrieval is more likely to be dependent on strategic monitoring). Presumably, the nicotine had no effect on the prospective memory of subjects in the focal condition because spontaneous retrieval was the predominant retrieval process for this condition.

Because processing resources are thought to decline with age (Craik, 1986; Salthouse, 1991), the magnitude of age differences should also vary across different kinds of prospective memory tasks. A perplexing pattern in the literature on aging and prospective memory is that age differences are often observed (for example, see Maylor, 1993) and sometimes they are not (see Cherry & LeCompte, 1999). A potential explanation of the discrepant findings is that age differences are more pronounced in tasks that are low in focal processing (those that require resource-demanding processes) and smaller or nonexistent in tasks that are high in focal processing (those for which spontaneous retrieval processes are likely). In a recent meta-analysis,

Henry, MacLeod, Phillips and Crawford (2004) found a pattern that appears consistent with this expectation. Specifically, they observed a larger effect of the age variable for conditions of "high demand" relative to conditions of "low demand." In Chapter 7, we revisit this analysis to examine whether the pattern of age effects does in fact vary as a function of the extent to which the ongoing task encourages focal processing.

Ongoing-Task Absorption and Demands

At times we become deeply engrossed in ongoing activities, such as reading a book or navigating our car through a new city. Some ongoing activities, perhaps due to their nature, pacing, and interest value, are more engaging or demanding than others. And tasks that are more engrossing and demanding will allow fewer resources to be available for strategic monitoring. How will these variations in absorption affect prospective memory? This kind of absorption seems intuitively to be the cause of many of our prospective memory failures. One particularly embarrassing example happened to one of the authors shortly after he became chair of the department. Despite being fully prepared, after being called to the research lab and getting involved in solving a pressing problem, he forgot to attend his first meeting as chair of the department. According to the multiprocess view, decreased resources available for monitoring should interfere with prospective memory performance mainly on tasks with nonfocal cues.

Kvavilashvili (1987) presented evidence that more-engaging ongoing tasks lead to decreased thoughts about the prospective memory task. She gave subjects an intention and then manipulated the presence and interest value of the ongoing task. Specifically, some subjects had no ongoing task, some had a less interesting ongoing task, and some had a more interesting ongoing task. To assess the extent to which subjects were thinking about the prospective memory task, she probed subjects for their thoughts during the retention interval. As might be expected, she found decreased thoughts about the prospective memory task as the ongoing activities became more engaging (42%, 20%, and 8% of the subjects reported thinking about the prospective memory task in the nonexistent, less interesting, and more interesting ongoing-task conditions, respectively).

What are the consequences of this increased absorption for prospective memory? First, whether or not extra absorption interferes with prospective remembering seems to depend on the nature of the absorption. Marsh and Hicks (1998) showed that increasing the cognitive demands of an ongoing task by adding a concurrent task (that is, dividing attention) sometimes interferes with prospective memory performance and sometimes does not. They found that dividing attention with tasks that engage central executive resources lowered prospective memory performance but that dividing attention with tasks that mainly occupy the articulatory rehearsal loop or the visuospatial sketchpad did not. The prospective memory target in their research was nonfocal (subjects were to press a key when a member of the fruit category was presented), and the implication is that central executive resources in particular are needed for monitoring for a general prospective memory target (fruit).

Second, the general answer to the question of how increased absorption in an ongoing task affects prospective memory is that prospective memory suffers—at least when prospective memory tasks are nonfocal and thus more dependent on monitoring processes. For example, Marsh, Hancock, and Hicks (2002) varied the demands of the ongoing task and found that subjects who had the more demanding requirement of performing two ongoing tasks (determining if each given word has a long *e* sound and determining if the word represents something that is living) and being randomly switched between them had significantly poorer prospective memory than subjects who had the less demanding requirement of performing only one of these tasks throughout (see McNerney & West, in press, for similar findings). This is understandable, because the subjects' prospective memory task was to press a key whenever they noticed a word naming an animal. Because the target cues were words naming specific animals, processing these words would not necessarily bring to mind the category *animals,* and accordingly the task was relatively low in focal processing. Marsh, Hancock, and Hicks's interpretation was that frequent switching between different activities usurps working-memory resources from the prospective memory task in the service of the ongoing activities. According to the multiprocess theory, the great absorption required by the two-task condition would interfere with monitoring processes which are helpful when searching for *animals.*

Thus far, we have presented evidence that increasing the central executive demands of the ongoing task lowers prospective memory performance on prospective memory tasks with nonfocal cues. An important question is whether increased ongoing-task demands of this kind also produce interference on prospective memory tasks with focal cues. Generally, the research shows that increasing the attentional demands of the ongoing task lowers prospective memory performance on these kinds of prospective memory tasks as well (Einstein, Smith, McDaniel, & Shaw, 1997; McDaniel et al., 1998).

Although at first blush these results may appear problematic for the multiprocess view, they do not necessarily argue against it. It may be, for example, that dividing attention interferes with full processing of the target event, which is thought to be important for at least some of these spontaneous retrieval processes (for example, see Moscovitch, 1994). Also, the locus of the divided-attention effect may not be in retrieval of the intention but rather that working-memory demands are increased to the extent that participants have difficulty selecting the retrieved intention and scheduling the appropriate action while the intention is still activated in working memory (Einstein et al., 1997). At this point, what is needed to more clearly evaluate the multiprocess theory predictions (in contrast to the monitoring theory predictions) is to vary the degree of focal processing (using a specific word versus a category as the target item, for example) while also varying the demands of the ongoing task. The multiprocess theory predicts that the negative effects of divided attention will be more pronounced with nonfocal cues than they will be with focal cues. To our knowledge, this has not been systematically investigated.

There is some suggestive evidence, however, that with highly salient target items (items that are easily noticed), the effects of increasing the demands of the ongoing task are, as the multiprocess theory predicts, less pronounced. Einstein, McDaniel, Manzi, Cochran, and Baker (2000) asked subjects to read sentences and later to answer questions about them. The prospective memory task was to press a key whenever the target word *technique* was presented. In one experiment, the word *technique* was written in capital letters while all other words in the sentence were written in lowercase letters. In another experiment, both the target word *technique* and the other words were presented in lowercase letters. Attention was sometimes divided during reading of the sentences and sometimes was not. Einstein et al. (2000) found that performance was almost perfect regardless of whether or not attention was divided during reading when the target word was highly salient. Divided attention did interfere with prospective memory when the target word was less salient. Similarly, McDaniel, Guynn, et al. (2004) found no effect of dividing attention when the target cue and the intended action were highly associated. Thus, it is clear that some prospective memory situations are not affected by the demands of the ongoing task, and further research is needed to delineate these conditions.

In summary, real-world prospective memory situations vary in the extent to which they are low or high in focal processing. According to the multiprocess theory, prospective memory tasks with focal cues should be relatively unaffected by the degree to which the ongoing task absorbs resources. On the other hand, successful remembering for tasks with nonfocal cues should be highly dependent on monitoring and the availability of resources for engaging in such monitoring. Thus, given our earlier argument that we have a limited capacity for controlled processes like monitoring, it may be especially important to rely on external aids like calendars and alarms in demanding situations with nonfocal cues.

Parameters of Prospective Memory Cues

As described in Chapter 3, the characteristics of prospective memory cues critically determine whether prospective memory retrieval is likely to occur spontaneously or to be more dependent on monitoring. In this section, we review the dimensions of (a) distinctiveness and (b) the associativity of the target cue and the intended action. Understanding how these characteristics affect prospective memory retrieval has important implications for evaluating theoretical views on the processes that support prospective memory. From the perspective of monitoring theory, prospective memory retrieval always requires some level of monitoring. From the perspective of the multiprocess theory, some cues are more likely to lead to spontaneous retrieval than others. Thus, with powerful cues, monitoring may be unnecessary. Understanding these characteristics also has important practical implications for designing cues that are effective and reliable in improving prospective memory in real-world settings.

Target Cue Distinctiveness

As described in Chapter 3, target events that are distinctive or salient relative to our existing knowledge or to the existing context produce very high levels of prospective memory performance relative to nondistinctive versions of these cues. Examples include target cues presented in uppercase letters when other words in the ongoing task are in lowercase letters (Brandimonte & Passolunghi, 1994; Einstein et al., 2000), meaningless target words presented in the context of meaningful words (Einstein & McDaniel, 1990; McDaniel & Einstein, 1993), and physically large pictures presented in the context of smaller pictures (Uttl, 2005). As discussed in Chapter 3, presenting target cues of this type will cause attention to be spontaneously and involuntarily captured and lead to noticing. This noticing is likely to lead to giving of extra attention to the target item and/or disengagement from the ongoing task, both of which should benefit prospective remembering.

Associativity of the Target
Cue With the Intended Action

Targets vary in the extent to which they are associated with the intended action. Sometimes the target cue and action are highly associated and sometimes they are not. For example, the target cue *campus coffee shop* is highly associated with the action of getting a latte. On the other hand, the coffee shop is only weakly associated with the action of getting change. Assuming we form these two intentions on different mornings and then walk by the coffee shop on the respective afternoons, are we likely to remember one intention more than the other?

Evidence from the laboratory is that spontaneous retrieval is especially likely when the cue and action are highly associated. Research has shown not only that prospective memory performance is good under these conditions but also that prospective memory performance is not diminished when attention is divided (McDaniel, Guynn, et al., 2004). McDaniel, Guynn, et al.'s explanation is that under these conditions, processing the cue leads spontaneously and relatively automatically to retrieval of the intended action. Thus, monitoring in these situations is unlikely to be of much help. When there is not a strong relationship between the cue and the target, however, processing of the target cue is less likely to lead to reflexive retrieval of the intended action. In this case, monitoring of the environment for the target is likely to produce substantial benefits for prospective memory. This analysis is consistent with the overarching theme of the multiprocess theory, which is that the processes that come to the fore in a given situation are context dependent.

Recent research by Loft and Yeo (in press) strongly supports the interpretation that prospective memory retrieval can occur without monitoring when there is a strong association between the target cue and the intended action. In contrast, a straightforward monitoring view (Smith, 2003) anticipates that monitoring should always be related to prospective memory performance. To test these views, Loft and Yeo presented subjects with a prospective memory task involving either highly or minimally associated word pairs. In the high-association condition, subjects learned word pairs like *mouth—wash,* and their prospective memory task was to press a key and type the second member of the pair (*wash*) when they saw the first member (*mouth*). In the low-association condition, subjects received unrelated pairs like *mouth—actress.* The ongoing task in this experiment was a lexical decision task.

Based on Marsh, Hicks, and Cook's (2006) view that our attention to a prospective memory demand waxes and wanes over the course of a retention interval (see also West & Craik, 1999; West, Krompinger, & Bowry, 2005), Loft and Yeo (in press) carefully examined the speed of lexical decisions for items presented immediately before prospective memory targets. They reasoned that slowed lexical decisions for items preceding a target (relative to control items) would be indicative of monitoring, whereas no slowing on these items would be indicative of no monitoring. They were interested in how these fluctuations in monitoring would affect prospective memory performance when pairs were minimally associated versus when they were highly associated. They found that slowed lexical decisions for items immediately preceding a target were associated with better prospective remembering when pairs were minimally associated but not when they were highly associated. That is, in the high-association condition, subjects remembered to perform the prospective memory response regardless of whether or not they had been thinking of the prospective memory task immediately prior to occurrence of the target. These results indicate that spontaneous retrieval can occur, and that it is more likely to occur when the target and action are highly associated.

Importance of the Prospective Memory Task

It seems intuitively reasonable to think that we more often remember important prospective memory tasks than less important ones. Because this is a common assumption, Winograd (1988) proposed that people often judge how important we consider a prospective memory task by whether or not we remember it. This certainly was the case in the household of one of the authors of this book recently, when his daughter criticized him for failing to remember to wash her red shirt for "red-shirt day" at school the following day. She was upset because he apparently did not consider the washing to be as important as she did.

Most studies have shown higher prospective memory performance under conditions in which successful performance of the prospective memory task has been emphasized (for example, see Ellis, 1998; Kvavilashvili, 1987, Experiment 2; Meacham & Singer, 1977) although some have not (Kliegel, Martin, McDaniel, & Einstein, 2001; Kliegel, Martin, McDaniel, & Einstein, 2004). According to the multiprocess theory, there should generally be benefits of such monitoring, but the benefits in prospective memory performance should be more pronounced with nonfocal cues. The idea here is that spontaneous retrieval is more likely with focal cues, and thus the additional monitoring will have less effect than it would under conditions in which spontaneous retrieval is less likely.

There appears to be good empirical support for the predictions of the multiprocess theory. Kliegel et al. (2001) found that emphasizing the importance of the prospective memory task improved prospective memory for a timed-based task but not for an event-based task high in focal processing. In more recent research, Kliegel et al. (2004) directly compared the effects of task importance (by telling subjects that the prospective memory task was more important than the ongoing task or vice versa) on performance of event-based tasks that were either low or high in focal processing. Subjects in the nonfocal condition were asked to press a key when they saw a *p* or a *q*, and subjects in the focal condition were asked to press a key when they saw the word *house* or *conversation*. The ongoing task was to rate words on various dimensions. Consistent with the multiprocess theory, emphasizing the prospective memory task improved prospective memory when subjects were in the nonfocal condition but had no effect when subjects were in the focal condition.

This effect was recently replicated by Einstein et al. (2005, Experiment 1). The basic design was very much like Kliegel et al.'s (2004), but Einstein et al. (2005) also examined the effects of the importance instructions on the speed of performing the ongoing task (categorizing words). They found that high emphasis (relative to moderate emphasis) on the prospective memory task significantly slowed the ongoing-task performance of subjects in both the focal and nonfocal conditions. Thus, it appears that instructions emphasizing the prospective memory task led to increased monitoring by subjects in both of these conditions. Yet, consistent with the results of Kliegel et al. (2004), this increased monitoring significantly improved prospective memory for subjects in the nonfocal condition and not for those in the focal condition. Taken together, this research indicates that emphasizing the importance of the prospective memory task in the laboratory increases monitoring in prospective memory tasks and thus tends to improve prospective memory performance. It is important to note, however, that the benefits of increased importance and monitoring seem to be more pronounced when task conditions do not encourage spontaneous retrieval.

Prospective memory researchers are increasingly realizing that instructional emphasis either toward or away from the prospective memory task can affect the allocation policy that subjects use in a prospective memory task. Because of this, at the 2005 International Conference on Prospective Memory in Zurich, Switzerland, there was good agreement that researchers should take great care in determining the instructional emphasis on the prospective memory task relative to the ongoing task, and also that they should present these instructions verbatim in their published papers.

We have focused in this section on the influence of the importance of the prospective memory task on monitoring. It should be noted, however, that importance can also affect other processes, such as planning (for example, we are probably more likely to spend time anticipating conditions that can trigger prospective memory retrieval when the task is highly important than we are when it is less important) and the use of external aids (like alarms and planners). We discuss the effects of planning in a later section and more fully in Chapter 6.

Length of the Prospective Memory Retention Interval

Let's say that you get the thought to tell a funny story to your friend. In one scenario, you expect to see her within a few seconds. In another, you expect to see her when she returns from her semester abroad in 4 months. Or, imagine that you want to buy a loaf of French bread at the local grocery store for dinner. In one scenario, you think about it as you get into your car and decide that you want the loaf of bread for dinner that evening. In another, you want to buy the loaf of bread in 1 week for a dinner party you are having. Do the dynamics of prospective memory retrieval differ in these situations? Will the retrieval cues operate similarly with short and long delays? Will your strategies for remembering be the same?

The multiprocess theory assumes that the choice of a strategy and the effectiveness of that strategy will vary with different retention intervals. First we will give an overview of the effects of delays on prospective memory performance, and then we will discuss multiprocess theory predictions. Because there has been little work examining the effects of very brief delays (on the order of seconds) between the formation of an intention and the occurrence of a target event, we describe research examining the effects of short delays in the context of delay-execute tasks (tasks in which there is a delay between *retrieval* of the intention and the opportunity to perform the intended action; see Chapter 7). With this type of prospective memory task, there is evidence that even very brief delays tend to lower prospective memory performance. McDaniel, Einstein, Stout, and Morgan (2003) had subjects read three sentences making up a paragraph, then perform synonym problems or take a brief break, then answer two trivia questions, and then answer two questions about the paragraph. Subjects went through this sequence of events for 20 different trials. In one experiment, subjects' prospective memory task was to press a key whenever they saw the word *TECHNIQUE*. This experiment was similar to the one performed by Einstein et al. (2000) in that the word *TECHNIQUE* appeared in capital letters whereas all the other words were typed in lowercase letters. As you might expect with such a distinctive target item, prospective memory performance of subjects in this "immediate" condition (that is, subjects could respond as soon as they saw the word *TECHNIQUE*) was quite high for both younger adults (97%) and older adults (93%). In another experiment, subjects were again asked to press a key when they saw the word *TECHNIQUE,* but they were asked not to make their key press until they got to the trivia questions, which occurred 5 to 15 seconds later ("delay" condition). We assumed here that, because of the highly distinctive target item, subjects would think of the intention when *TECHNIQUE* appeared, and thus we could examine how quickly the intention was lost. Introducing a delay created some forgetting for younger adults (a drop of about 12%) and precipitous forgetting for older adults (a drop of about 47%). As we describe in Chapter 7, the evidence indicates that when we are asked to briefly delay an intended action after retrieving the intention, we try to actively maintain the intention in working memory (at least under some conditions), and that older adults especially have great difficulty keeping the intention activated over these relatively brief delays. To date, the research shows that longer delays (15 and 30 seconds) do not produce greater forgetting than shorter ones (5 and 10 seconds), but the range of delays that have been tested with this paradigm has been limited.

Most of us can appreciate this rapid loss of an intention after a few seconds. For example, while in the bedroom we may form the intention to go to the kitchen to take medication, but on the way we may notice a drooping plant and decide to water it—and forget to take our medication. As discussed in Chapter 9, a way to avoid this potential problem is to perform the action as soon as you think of it (go to the kitchen right away and water the plant afterward) (see McDaniel et al., 2003).

With the more typical prospective memory paradigm (in which subjects form an intention and then experience a delay before there is an opportunity to respond to a target), researchers have varied the length of longer delays (on the order of several minutes or more). The findings from this research are more complex. In the retrospective memory literature, the classic forgetting pattern is greater forgetting with longer retention intervals. This result, however, is rarely found with prospective memory tasks. Although Brandimonte and Passolunghi (1994) have found declines in prospective memory over a 3-minute delay, Einstein, Holland, McDaniel, and Guynn (1992; see also Guynn, McDaniel, & Einstein, 1998) found no differences between a 15- and a 30-minute interval, and Hicks, Marsh, and Russell (2000) consistently found *better* retention with longer delays. We suggest that some of the discrepant findings may be understandable from the perspective of the multiprocess theory. As noted earlier, the multiprocess theory assumes that controlled self-regulatory behaviors are limited in capacity and depleted rather quickly (see Bargh & Chartrand, 1999). Thus, in situations in which spontaneous retrieval is unlikely and monitoring processes are needed for successful retrieval (that is, cues are nonfocal), there should be declines in prospective memory with increasing delays. However, in situations in which spontaneous retrieval is likely (that is, cues are focal), the length of the retention intervals should have less of an effect. In an initial study investigating this prediction, Einstein et al. (2005, Experiment 2) found this exact result. Subjects in their study performed a word categorization ongoing task and were given a prospective memory task that was either nonfocal (subjects were to press a key when they saw a word containing the syllable *tor*) or focal (subjects were to press a key when they saw the word *tortoise*). Subjects also performed the ongoing task in a control block without performing a prospective memory task, and this enabled the experimenters to examine the extent to which subjects were monitoring for the prospective memory targets.

When subjects were in the nonfocal condition, there were significant costs of performing a prospective memory task (presumably due to monitoring), but these costs decreased over quarters of the experiment. Consistent with the view that monitoring is needed for prospective memory retrieval when cues are nonfocal and that monitoring requires resources that are limited in nature (cf. Bargh & Chartrand, 1999), prospective memory detection also declined over quarters of the experiment. Thus, with nonfocal cues, subjects were unable to maintain monitoring at the same levels throughout the experiment and prospective memory suffered with longer delays. In contrast, when cues were focal, there were no significant costs of performing a prospective memory task, and costs tended to vary somewhat haphazardly across quarters of the experiment. These different patterns of costs for nonfocal and focal targets can be seen in Figure 4.2. Also, prospective memory performance was constant across all quarters of the experiment when cues were focal. Thus, in a condition in which prospective memory retrieval was more dependent on spontaneous retrieval

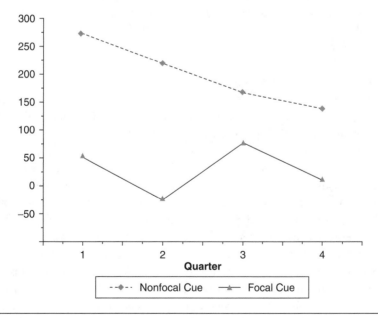

Figure 4.2   Costs (in milliseconds) of Performing a Prospective Memory Task Over Quarters of an Experiment Involving Focal and Nonfocal Target Events (Einstein et al., 2005)

processes, subjects showed no evidence of monitoring and there was no decline in prospective memory performance with longer retention intervals.

Although there are likely to be many factors that affect whether or not declines in prospective memory occur over longer retention intervals, the results above suggest that these declines will be more pronounced for tasks that are more dependent on monitoring processes. Further research is needed to determine what would happen over the much longer retention intervals (hours, days, and weeks) characteristic of many real-world prospective memory situations. (See Chapter 5 for more discussion of retention of prospective memory intentions.)

Individual Differences and Intra-Individual Differences

The extent to which people rely on monitoring versus spontaneous retrieval is likely to depend on a host of cognitive, metacognitive, and personality variables. From the perspective of the multiprocess theory, these variables should interact with the nature of the prospective memory task. That is, to the degree that these variables influence people's ability or willingness to initiate and maintain a monitoring process, they should have greater effects on some types of prospective memory tasks (those with nonfocal cues) than they have on others (those with focal cues).

Before discussing factors that could account for individual differences in how people approach a prospective memory task, it is interesting to consider recent research suggesting that people show a good deal of variability in their approach to the same prospective memory task. Einstein et al. (2005, Experiment 4) presented participants with sentences containing a blank and asked them to decide as quickly as possible whether the capitalized word following the sentence correctly filled the blank. There were two blocks in the experiment. In one block, subjects did not have a prospective memory task to perform, and in the other they did. The prospective memory task was to press a key on the keyboard whenever a target word (for example, *medicine*) was presented. Because subjects were asked to read every word in the sentence before making a decision and the target item was a specific word appearing in the sentence, we assumed that this was a case of focal processing of the target item, and therefore that there would be little need for monitoring. To our surprise, however, there was significant monitoring. To better understand these results, we adjusted each participant's sentence task response times for the prospective memory block and the control block by factoring in the speedup or slowdown associated with each person's counterbalancing condition. Our analysis of these adjusted response times suggested that some subjects were monitoring and others were not. In this particular experiment, 56% of the participants were slower on the prospective memory block than they were on the control block (suggesting that they monitored) and 44% were faster on the prospective memory block than they were on the control block (suggesting that they did not monitor). Interestingly, and consistent with the multiprocess theory prediction that monitoring is not essential for prospective memory retrieval with focal cues, prospective memory performance was high and almost identical in these two groups. Thus, it appears that different people will engage in different processes when they encounter a prospective memory situation. We turn now to cognitive and noncognitive variables that might affect which strategies are engaged.

Working Memory

Current thinking is that working-memory measures assess people's ability to maintain activation of a representation in the face of distraction (for example, see Engle, Tuholski, Laughlin, & Conway, 1999; Kane, Bleckley, Conway, & Engle, 2001), their ability to maintain an integrated representation of the current task concerns (Kimberg & Farah, 1993), and more generally their resources available for processing and storing current information (Baddeley, 1986). From the viewpoint that monitoring is always required for prospective memory retrieval, one would expect to consistently find correlations between working-memory capacity and prospective memory. The reasoning here is that people with higher working-memory capacity have the resources they need to monitor for target events while simultaneously performing the ongoing task. From the viewpoint of the multiprocess theory, however, strong correlations between working-memory capacity and prospective memory should occur when task conditions encourage monitoring (for example, when cues are nonfocal) and not when they encourage reliance on spontaneous retrieval processes (for example, when cues are focal). Thus far, studies have not been conducted to directly test these predictions.

As it is, the few studies that have examined the relationship between working memory and prospective memory yield a confusing and inconsistent pattern. Some studies have found a reliable correlation between working-memory capacity and prospective memory (Cherry & LeCompte, 1999; Einstein et al., 2000, Experiments 1 and 2; Kliegel, Martin, McDaniel, & Einstein, 2002; Reese & Cherry, 2002; Smith, 2003, Experiment 3; West & Craik, 2001) and some have not (Einstein et al., 2000, Experiment 3;

Kidder, Park, Hertzog, & Morrell, 1997; Park, Hertzog, Kidder, Morrell, & Mayhorn, 1997; West & Craik, Experiment 2).

Although it is tempting to try to make the results fit within the multi-process theory predictions, they simply do not neatly conform to the anticipated pattern. Experimental conditions that seem to demand monitoring, such as those involving a large number of prospective memory target events or the appearance of targets outside of the directed focus of the ongoing task, sometimes produce reliable correlations between working-memory ability and prospective memory (for example, see Smith, 2003, Experiment 3; West & Craik, 2001, Experiment 1) and sometimes do not (Kidder et al., 1997; Park et al., 1997). Also, some of the reliable correlations explain a very small percentage of the variance in prospective memory performance (for example, those reported by Cherry & LeCompte, 1999, and also Reese & Cherry, 2002, explain about 4% of the variance). A general difficulty in evaluating this pattern of results arises from the fact that the existing studies were for the most part designed simply to determine whether working-memory resources correlate with prospective memory, and thus comparisons among the studies are difficult to make because they differ on so many dimensions. It seems worthwhile in future research to go beyond asking whether or not a correlation exists between working memory and prospective memory, and to test for this relationship under conditions for which monitoring is and is not presumed to be needed for successful prospective memory retrieval. It seems important to consider other factors as well when examining the relationship between working memory and prospective memory performance. For example, the demands of the ongoing activity are likely to be relevant. Specifically, if the ongoing activity requires relatively few resources, then even with non-focal cues, individuals with smaller working-memory capacity could have enough resources to perform the ongoing activity and monitor.

Personality Variables

Researchers (Einstein & McDaniel, 1996; Meacham, 1988; Searleman, 1996; Winograd, 1988) have speculated that certain personality traits like conscientiousness and compulsiveness might affect prospective memory performance more than they affect retrospective memory performance. The idea here is that people in whom these characteristics are highly pronounced are more likely to monitor and generally more likely to remember in prospective memory situations than those who rely only on spontaneous retrieval.

Thus far, the evidence on this issue is sparse. According to Goschke and Kuhl's (1996) distinction between two personality types, people with a "state" orientation are thought to ruminate about unfulfilled intentions and to keep them more highly activated than people with an "action" orientation are. But, although Goschke and Kuhl generally showed that people with a state orientation have greater activation for intended actions than people with an action orientation have, there is no evidence of greater activation in situations in which people have to remember to perform actions on their own (that is, in prospective memory situations) (see Experiment 3). Salthouse, Berish, and Siedlecki (2004) conducted a large-scale study in which subjects completed the NEO Five-Factor Personality Inventory, which produces scores on the personality traits of neuroticism, extraversion, openness, agreeableness, and conscientiousness. Salthouse et al. also had subjects perform four different prospective memory tasks and tabulated a composite score representing performance over all of these tasks. The only trait that was significantly related to prospective memory performance was agreeableness, and this explained less than 3% of the variance in prospective memory performance. Perhaps the problem with detecting the relationship between personality traits and prospective memory is that Salthouse et al. used a composite measure based on the performance of four different tasks—tasks varying in the degree to which they encouraged focal processing of the target event. According to the multiprocess theory, the effects of these personality characteristics on prospective memory should be more prominent in performance of prospective memory tasks that require monitoring for successful retrieval (that is, tasks in which spontaneous retrieval is less likely).

Consistent with this thinking, a recent study by Jamison, Cook, Amir, Marsh, and Hicks (2006) found that people with untreated obsessive-compulsive disorder (OCD) performed more poorly than did control subjects on a nonfocal prospective memory task in which they were asked to press a key whenever they saw a word from a neutral category (for example, furniture). Jamison et al.'s explanation was that the OCD occupied working-memory resources and thus interfered with monitoring of the ongoing-task items for the target event. They did not include a focal condition in the study, but the prediction from the multiprocess viewpoint is that OCD would interfere less or not at all with performance of a focal prospective memory task. Interestingly, Jamison et al.'s OCD subjects did not exhibit a decrement in prospective memory performance when the target category (bodily fluids) was related to the source of their anxiety (hygiene), presumably because the obsession in this case directed attention toward the target events.

In a recent study conducted in our lab by Edwards and Hagood, fully functioning college subjects filled out a personality test that measured compulsive tendencies and then performed a prospective memory task that was either high or low in focal processing. The ongoing task involved categorizing words. The prospective memory task for the nonfocal condition was to press a key whenever the syllable *tor* was presented, and the prospective memory task for the focal condition was to press a key whenever the word *tortoise* was presented (see examples 3A and 3B in Table 4.1). Subjects performed only the ongoing task during one block of trials and the ongoing task along with the prospective memory task in the other block of trials. This design enabled us to examine the slowing on the ongoing task due to the presence of a prospective memory task, with more slowing indicating more monitoring. According to the multiprocess theory, subjects should be more likely to monitor in the "*tor*" condition than they would be in the "*tortoise*" condition. Consistent with this analysis, higher compulsiveness scores were related to greater costs to performance of the ongoing task when subjects were in the *tor* condition but not when they were in the *tortoise* condition. Thus, the personality variable of compulsiveness was related to monitoring only in the condition in which spontaneous retrieval was unlikely. Also, there was a reliable correlation between costs to performance of the ongoing task and prospective memory performance only in the *tor* condition. A possible explanation of why the effects of compulsive tendencies in this study differed from the effects found in Jamison et al.'s study is that compulsive characteristics were probably within the normal range in this study, as there was no attempt to screen for extreme tendencies.

The retrospective memory literature indicates that depression tends to interfere with memory for some types of tasks and less so or not at all for others. One explanation of this pattern is that individuals are less likely to self-initiate controlled processes that can lead to good memory but are capable of engaging in these processes if the task conditions obligate or force them to do so (Hertel & Rude, 1991). Consistent with this view, Rude, Hertel, Jarrold, Covitch, and Hedlund (1999) found that depressed individuals (relative to nondepressed individuals) performed more poorly on a time-based prospective memory task and also monitored the time less frequently. (As is the case for most time-based prospective memory tasks, there were no external cues prompting monitoring in this experiment.) Although this result is consistent with the multiprocess theory, it can also be explained by Smith's (2003) theory that prospective remembering always requires controlled resources. At this point, to test these views, more research is needed to compare the prospective memory performance of depressed and nondepressed individuals on prospective memory tasks that vary in the extent to which they rely on controlled monitoring versus spontaneous retrieval processes (for example, tasks that have nonfocal and focal cues). If Hertel and Rude's ideas about depression are correct, the multiprocess theory predicts that depression will result in larger deficits when tasks are nonfocal than it will when tasks are focal.

Thus far, there has not been a great deal of research examining the relationship between individual differences in personality and prospective memory. The results of the few existing studies suggest that examination of this relationship from the perspective of the multiprocess theory may be a fruitful avenue for further research.

Intra-Individual Differences

Given that some prospective memory situations depend on monitoring for successful retrieval, it seems likely that there are intra-individual differences that affect prospective memory performance. That is, other things being equal, we probably have moments when we are more likely to monitor or to keep the prospective memory intention active and others when we are less likely to do so (Marsh et al., 2005; West & Craik, 1999). Indeed, by measuring the costs of performing a prospective memory task on the speed of processing ongoing-task items, West, Krompinger, and Bowry (2005) showed fluctuations over trials in the extent to which subjects kept the prospective memory intention activated. They also showed that moments when decreased attention was given to the prospective memory task were associated with poorer prospective memory performance (that is, subjects tended to miss target items when they seemed not to be keeping the intention in mind). According to the multiprocess theory, these variations in attention given to the prospective memory task should have more pronounced influences on performance of prospective tasks that depend on monitoring. As mentioned earlier in this chapter, there is some preliminary support for this view, as Loft and Yeo (in press) have shown that waxing and waning of attention given to the prospective memory task has a reliable effect on prospective memory performance when there is little association between the target and the intended action and no effect when there is a strong association between the target and the action.

One variable that can reasonably be expected to affect our ability to maintain a monitoring strategy over the course of a retention interval is our optimal time of day. Zacks and Hasher (1994; see also May, 1999) have proposed that we are better able to inhibit distractions and thus maintain our cognitive goals at our optimal time of day. For example, when listening to a lecture at our nonoptimal time of day (and assuming that our goal is to process the lecture), we are more likely to be distracted by the teacher's polka-dot chartreuse tie, the breathing rate of our neighbor, noises in the hallway, and the asymmetrical nature of the holes in the ceiling tile. Therefore, we have more difficulty controlling our attention and maintaining it on the lecture. If this idea is applied to prospective memory, it might mean that when we are driving down the road and trying to actively maintain the intention to stop at the next gas station, our monitoring for a gas station is more easily disrupted by internal and external distractions at our nonoptimal time of day. For instance, we are more likely to meditate on the gait of a pedestrian crossing the street too slowly, and the funny slogan on the billboard may more easily trigger memory of a joke Uncle Joe recently told. Therefore, we are less likely to notice a gas station just off the road. If the intention is well encoded and the gas station appears directly in our line of view, however, it will probably be retrieved via spontaneous retrieval. Thus, if we take the multiprocess and time-of-day theories together, the prediction is that we will perform more poorly at our nonoptimal time of day on prospective memory tasks that require monitoring but not more poorly on those that do not require monitoring (those for which spontaneous retrieval is likely).

To date, no laboratory studies of which we are aware have examined the effects of being at one's optimal time of day on prospective memory performance (but see Leirer, Tanke, & Morrow, 1994, for initial evidence that time of day affects prospective memory in naturalistic settings). Thus, further research is needed to evaluate the effects of being at one's optimal time of day on prospective memory in general and, perhaps more interesting, on performance of prospective memory tasks that vary in their demands for controlled monitoring processes.

Fatigue has been shown to produce general decrements in attention and memory (Lieberman et al., 2005). Moreover, as described earlier in the chapter, Bargh and Chartrand (1999) believe that we have limited capacity for conscious control over behavior, and research has shown that using up controlled resources on one task leads to attenuated use of these resources on a subsequent task. Thus, it seems reasonable that we are unlikely to monitor when we are fatigued. If this is the case (see Einstein et al., 2005, Experiment 2, for some initial evidence), performance of prospective memory tasks that are more dependent on monitoring should suffer, whereas performance of prospective memory tasks for which spontaneous retrieval is likely should not suffer or should show smaller effects of fatigue.

There are probably a host of variables, like stress and the presence of ongoing concerns, that affect the extent to which we are willing and able to develop and maintain a controlled monitoring approach to a prospective memory task. According to the multiprocess theory, these variables should not have deleterious effects on all prospective memory tasks but mainly have those effects on prospective memory tasks for which monitoring is needed for successful retrieval. Thus far there has been little research examining the influences of these kinds of variables on prospective memory performance.

A Cautionary Methodological Note Concerning Research on Individual Differences

At present, the clearest pattern that emerges when correlations between cognitive and personality variables and prospective memory performance are examined is a pattern of inconsistency. As noted earlier, some of the inconsistency surely emanates from the great variation in task conditions from study to study. It is also likely, however, that some of the inconsistency is due to the lack of reliability of prospective memory measures that have been developed thus far. Schmidt, Berg, and Deelman (2001) have shown that the test-retest reliability for subjects performing a prospective memory task at one time and then again 5 weeks later was quite low (.24 relative to the benchmark standard of .80 for psychological tests). This is probably due to the fact that there are fewer opportunities to perform prospective memory tasks (typically, researchers present three to eight target items) relative to opportunities to perform retrospective memory tasks like recognition and recall, where often many items are tested.

Kelemen, Weinberg, Oh, Mulvey, and Kaeochinda (in press) have recently shown that the reliability of prospective memory measures can be improved substantially by increasing the number of targets appearing in the ongoing task from 6 to 30 (resulting in an increase in reliability from .12 to .62). Two concerns about this method of enhancing reliability are that presenting a target item 30 times across 200 trials can change the retrieval dynamics of the prospective memory task and that this dense appearance of target events seems unrepresentative of real-world prospective memory demands. Kelemen et al. also found that they could significantly improve reliability to .62 with six targets by using less salient target items. Using these types of targets reduces the number of people who are at the ceiling and increases the range of prospective memory scores, thereby allowing greater opportunities for obtaining a reliable measure of prospective memory across different occasions (see also Uttl, 2005). Thus, researchers interested in individual differences should take particular care to avoid ceiling problems.

Planning

What we do during encoding, or planning, of a prospective memory task may have important consequences for its later retrieval (Burgess & Shallice, 1997; Kliegel, McDaniel, & Einstein, 2000; Mantyla, 1996). Einstein et al. (1997) provided evidence for this assertion by showing that the prospective memory performance of both younger and older adults suffers when attention is divided during the encoding of the prospective memory intention. Thus, when there is little elaboration or planning of an intention, we are less likely to remember. But what is it that causes us to forget more often under these conditions?

In real-world settings, when we are rushed, we may be less likely to use external aids like calendars. But the research described above was conducted without the use of external aids, thereby indicating that a hurried or brief encoding decreases the likelihood that the appearance of a cue later on will initiate cognitive processes that lead to retrieval.

One likely factor is that thinking about the target cue strengthens its representation in memory and leads to greater discrepancy when the target is later processed. As described in Chapter 3, Whittlesea and Williams (2001a, 2001b) believe that we chronically evaluate the quality of our processing of items and that we are sensitive to the discrepancy between the actual and expected quality of processing. When we detect a discrepancy, we generate an attribution that depends on the context. The discrepancy can elicit a sense of significance, which can stimulate prospective remembering. Thus, prior thinking about the target item is more likely to lead to a discrepancy later on, which can then stimulate a search of memory in order to determine the source of the discrepancy. With a hurried encoding, there may be very little processing of the target cue and thus an attenuated discrepancy response when the target is processed at some later time.

Another likely factor is that a hurried encoding interferes with the development of a monitoring strategy. So, for example, when we are rushed or distracted, we may fail to consider that there will not be a good cue for the prospective memory demand coming up in a few minutes, and thus we may fail to initiate a monitoring strategy.

Good planning can also take the form of strengthening the link between intended actions and target cues, so that later processing of these cues more readily triggers retrieval of the intention, or of anticipating the cues that are likely to be present in the retrieval context. We develop these ideas more fully in Chapter 6.

Summary

The multiprocess view assumes that (a) prospective memory retrieval is supported by a variety of processes that can be roughly categorized as spontaneous retrieval processes and monitoring processes; (b) the use and effectiveness of these processes critically depend on the characteristics of the prospective memory task, the ongoing task, and the individual; and (3) people have a bias against monitoring and toward relying on spontaneous

Table 4.2   Some Task Conditions and Their Effects on the Likelihood of Spontaneous Retrieval and on the Strategy Subjects Adopt

Task Conditions for Which Spontaneous Retrieval Is Likely to Be Sufficient for Prospective Memory Retrieval	Task Conditions for Which Monitoring Is Likely to Be Required for Prospective Memory Retrieval
Focal cues	Nonfocal cues
Distinctive target cues	Nondistinctive target cues
Strong cue–target association	Weak cue–target association
Good planning (e.g., forming an implementation intention)	Poor planning
Test Conditions Favoring a Spontaneous Retrieval (nonmonitoring) Approach (strategy) to Prospective Memory Tasks	*Test Conditions Favoring a Monitoring Approach (strategy) to Prospective Memory Tasks*
Focal cues	Nonfocal cues
Demanding or absorbing tasks	Nondemanding and nonabsorbing tasks
Low importance of the prospective memory task	High importance of the prospective memory task
Long retention intervals	Very short retention intervals
Strong cue–target association	Weak cue–target association
Distinctive cues	Nondistinctive cues
Cognitive abilities (e.g., low working-memory resources)	Cognitive abilities (e.g., high working-memory resources)
Personality (e.g., low compulsiveness)	Personality (e.g., compulsiveness)
Extensive planning (e.g., forming an implementation intention)	Anticipation of absence of a good cue

retrieval processes (although people will strategically monitor under certain conditions to improve our chances of remembering). Table 4.2 summarizes the task conditions that are less likely to require monitoring for successful prospective memory retrieval and those that are more likely to require monitoring. Thus, some task conditions are likely to lead to spontaneous retrieval of the intended action and others are not. Also, some task conditions (for example, a focal cue, especially when there is a strong association between the cue and the action) and individual-difference characteristics are likely to encourage people to not adopt a monitoring strategy, whereas others will encourage monitoring. The multiprocess view assumes that we can use several cognitive processes for prospective memory retrieval and that in most situations we flexibly deploy these processes depending on the task conditions. For example, if it is critical not to forget and the delays are brief, we may be willing to sacrifice resources and monitor over the retention interval. When delays are longer and when we can predict that there will be a distinctive cue signaling the prospective memory intention, we are more likely not to devote resources to monitoring and instead to rely on spontaneous retrieval processes.

An important advantage of the multiprocess view is that it helps explain many of the inconsistencies in the prospective memory literature. As mentioned earlier in this chapter, aging sometimes produces decrements in prospective memory performance and sometimes does not. Also, dividing attention sometimes lowers prospective memory performance and sometimes does not. It is difficult to explain these results from the perspective of a uniprocess view that assumes controlled monitoring of the environment is critical for prospective memory retrieval. According to this view, if resources are compromised (due to aging or divided attention), prospective memory performance should suffer. According to the multiprocess view, however, compromised resources should have pronounced effects on performance of prospective memory tasks for which monitoring is needed for successful retrieval but attenuated effects on performance of tasks in which spontaneous retrieval is likely. Thus far, we believe that there is good support for the multiprocess theory, but as indicated throughout this chapter, further research is needed.

5

Storage and Retention of Intended Actions

The suggested intention slumbers on in the person concerned until the time for its execution approaches. Then it awakes and impels him to perform the action.

—Sigmund Freud, *Psychopathology of Everyday Life*

There exists . . . an internal tension-state which presses to carry out the intention. . . . The state of tension arising from the act of intending need not be continuously expressed in conscious tension-experiences. As a rule, it exists over long periods of time, only in latent form.

—Kurt Lewin, "Intention, Will, and Need"

These intuitions by two influential psychologists of the last century suggest that intended actions may enjoy special memory storage status or properties. In contemporary memory terms, the idea is more specifically that intended actions are stored in memory in a state of higher activation than are other memory contents (Goschke & Kuhl, 1993; Koriat, Ben-Zur, & Nussbaum, 1990; Marsh, Hicks, & Bink, 1998). It is easy to see that relatively highly activated representations of intended activities would be useful for supporting prospective remembering. With higher activation, intended actions would more likely be brought to awareness (retrieved) when an appropriate cue (for example, the person to whom you intend to give a message) is present (Mantyla, 1996; Yaniv & Meyer, 1987). Also, higher activation of intentions could lead to easily activated or more frequent thoughts of the intention during the retention interval—thoughts that could support or prompt monitoring. We will examine this possibility later in the chapter.

Further, theoretical mechanisms of memory provide straightforward ways to conceptualize special storage for prospective memory intentions. One prominent idea is that memory contents vary along a continuum of activation. Low levels of activation characterize much information in long-term memory, whereas relatively high levels of activation characterize information in conscious awareness (Anderson, 1983; Cowan, 1999; Yaniv & Meyer, 1987). There are intermediate levels of activation as well, levels that are not sufficient to bring an item into awareness but nevertheless closer to the activation threshold for conscious awareness than are items with low levels of activation in long-term memory. Items in this higher state of activation thus require less activation from related thoughts or environmental events to rise to awareness (Yaniv & Meyer).

With regard to prospective memory, the idea would be that intended actions are stored in this intermediate state of activation and are accordingly more sensitive to retrieval cues (either internal or external) than other memory contents are. That intended actions are more sensitive—that less activation is needed to bring them into awareness—carries the implication that they should be brought to mind more quickly than are other contents that are similarly cued. This implication provides the major basis for experimental work conducted to test the proposal that intended actions enjoy privileged storage status. To embellish Freud's metaphor, prospective memories are slumbering in a more agitated state, and are thereby more quickly awakened. Let's see if that's the case.

Goschke and Kuhl's Paradigm

Goschke and Kuhl (1993) developed a clever experimental paradigm to investigate whether intended actions are stored in memory in a more highly activated state. They generated short lists of actions (scripts) for the experiment. An example of one of the scripts is:

Setting a Table

Spread the tablecloth

Distribute the cutlery

Polish the glass

Fold the napkins

Light the candles

Subjects studied two of these scripts for a later recognition test. After each list had been studied, subjects were told that they would later have to (a) perform each action for one of the scripts (the *execute,* or the *prospective,* script) but not the other script (the *neutral* script) and (b) take a recognition test for both scripts. Informing subjects *after* they learn the scripts which one is to be performed later and which one does not have to be performed is a critical feature of this procedure. If subjects were informed prior to learning the scripts, any differences in later performance could be based on different strategies for studying the scripts. Goschke and Kuhl's procedure was designed to produce equal studying of both scripts. Thus, any differences in later performance would reveal differences in storage dynamics for memories of intended actions versus memories of information that would not be acted upon.

Next, subjects were given the recognition test. This test included the items in the execute script, the items in the neutral script, distracter items semantically related to the scripts, and unrelated distracter items. Of interest was how quickly subjects could confirm that a particular action was included in the previously studied list of actions. Let's pause and think about the expected pattern of results. The theoretical assumption is that memory representations of actions intended for later execution are stored at a higher level of activation than are other memory representations. If so, fully activating the execute-action representations on the recognition test should take somewhat less time than fully activating the neutral-action representations. That is, recognition latencies should be faster for actions in execute scripts relative to actions in neutral scripts.

Table 5.1 summarizes the results from several of Goschke and Kuhl's experiments. As you can see, recognition latencies were consistently faster for actions from the execute scripts than they were for actions from the neutral scripts. Goschke and Kuhl termed the activation advantage for intended actions the *intention superiority effect.* Yet these results alone do not conclusively demonstrate that intended actions are stored in a higher state of activation. There are alternative interpretations to the patterns in Table 5.1, and we need additional conditions to rule out the alternatives.

One possibility is that perhaps subjects quite rightly viewed the execute script as requiring free recall, a more difficult memory test than the recognition test expected for the neutral script. To adequately prepare for the additional memory demands, once the execute script was identified,

Table 5.1   Mean Recognition Latencies for Prospective and Neutral Words in Experiments Performed by Goschke and Kuhl (1993)

	Response Times	
Study	*Prospective*	*Neutral*
Experiment 1	900	955
Experiment 2	955	1010
Experiment 4 (imagery encoding)		
Nouns	930	975
Verbs	990	1025

NOTE: Response times are approximate, as they were originally reported in figures.

subjects may have recruited memory strategies to better remember the execute script. Goschke and Kuhl made several modifications to their paradigm to discourage subjects from using extra memory strategies for the execute script. First, subjects were told that they would have to recall both the neutral and the execute scripts at the end of the experiment. Second, immediately after a particular script was identified as the execute script, subjects were given a distracter activity to prevent extra rehearsal of the execute script. Items from the execute scripts were still recognized more quickly than items from the neutral scripts.

Another possibility is that the slower latencies for items from the neutral script reflect subjects' suppression of that information so as to permit fluid recovery of the script targeted for execution (cf. Bjork, Bjork, & Anderson, 1998). The idea here is that retrieval of the neutral actions might be relatively slowed. In other words, the activation of the execute actions might not be facilitated more than activation of any other information that subjects are expecting to use subsequent to the recognition test. To rule out this alternative interpretation, Goschke and Kuhl included another study group. Subjects in this group, after studying the two sets of script actions, were told that one of the scripts was going to be performed later by an experimenter and that they would have to say whether this script (termed the *observe* script) included all of the studied actions. Regarding the other (neutral) script, subjects were instructed as before.

The left portion of Figure 5.1 shows that the recognition latencies for items from these two scripts did not differ. That is, the neutral items did not produce especially slow recognition latencies relative to prospective items subjects knew they would be tested on later (but would not need to execute). However, recognition latencies for the neutral script were slower when the neutral script was paired with an execute script (right portion of Figure 5.1) than they were when it was paired with an observe script. This implies that there is some dampening of activation of items in the neutral script when it is paired with the execute script. Also, the recognition latencies for the execute scripts were faster than were the recognition latencies for observe scripts. This implies higher activation of memory representations for actions that *were* to be executed relative to actions that needed to be remembered for a later task but *were not* to be executed. (Though this comparison was not statistically significant in this particular experiment, both patterns have been reliably found across a number of experiments using this general paradigm [Goschke & Kuhl, 1993; Marsh, Hicks, & Bink, 1998].) Thus, the intention superiority effect as found in the Goschke and Kuhl paradigm appears to be a conjoint consequence of some dampening of activation of actions that have no special status (neutral-script items) and some higher activation of intended actions (execute-script items).

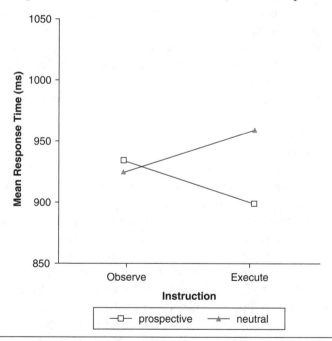

Figure 5.1   Mean Recognition Latencies for Prospective and Neutral Items in the Observation and Execution Conditions

SOURCE: From Goschke, T. & Kuhl, J., Representation of intentions: Persisting activation in memory, in *Journal of Experimental Psychology: Learning, Memory and Cognition, 19(5),* 1211–1226, copyright © 1993, American Psychological Association. Reprinted with permission.

Extending the Intention Superiority Effect

Some cognitive psychologists are skeptical of the assumption that recognition latencies provide a clear window into activation levels of information stored in memory. The concern is that recognition latencies might also involve strategic processes recruited to verify the initial retrieval, with differences in recognition latencies across conditions being produced by these strategic processes (postretrieval recognition checking) (see Keefe & McDaniel, 1993, and Potts, Keenan, & Golding, 1988, for details). To circumvent this concern, Marsh and his colleagues (Marsh, Hicks, & Bink, 1998) replaced the recognition judgments in Goschke and Kuhl's experiments with a more direct expression of activation—lexical decision (deciding as quickly as possible whether an item is a word). Lexical decision latencies show a pattern identical to the recognition latency pattern shown in Figure 5.1, thereby providing support for the idea that intended actions are stored in a more activated state than is other information.

Is higher activation of intended actions in memory something that persists over an extended period of time? We have very little information regarding this question. One of Goschke and Kuhl's experiments showed activation persisting nearly 15 minutes after encoding of the execute-script actions, provided the actions had not yet been executed. No research of which we are aware has examined this activation following intervals longer than 15 minutes. Certainly, given that real-world prospective memory demands often require that delays extend well beyond 15 minutes (see Chapter 9), if intention superiority is necessarily involved in prospective memory, the privileged activation of an intended action ought to persist for much longer than 15 minutes.

Logically, however, the cognitive system need not maintain higher activation of an intended action once the action has been performed. Confirmation of this expectation has been provided in experiments using the neutral, observe, and execute scripts from Goschke and Kuhl's paradigm and the lexical decision task to assess activation. In these experiments, the lexical decision task was given immediately after subjects had either performed the actions listed in the execute script or observed the experimenter performing these actions (Marsh, Hicks, & Bink, 1998). As Figure 5.2 clearly shows, after subjects observed performance of scripted actions, latencies for lexical decision regarding nouns and verbs from items in the observe script (for example, *fold* and *napkins* from the table-setting script) were identical to those for decisions involving the script listing neutral (not observed) actions. In contrast, after subjects performed intended actions listed in an execute script, lexical decision latencies for words from that script were significantly *slower* than they were for words from the neutral script. This is a striking finding, considering that subjects had learned the scripts to criterion initially and then just performed the actions; ordinarily, one might have thought that lexical decision latencies for the execute script would speed up relative to those for the neutral script. Instead, fulfilled intentions appear to be deactivated or inhibited. Deactivation of fulfilled intentions would be sensible, as one would not need the intentions to be activated subsequently. An interesting question for future research is whether similar deactivation occurs for a more habitual prospective memory task, such as taking medication.

What Produces the Intention Superiority Effect?

The ACT model. If we accept that intended activities are stored at a higher level of activation than other contents, another interesting theoretical question emerges: What produces the higher activation for intended actions? Anderson's (1983) adaptive control of thought (ACT) model provides a possible answer. In the ACT model of cognition, goals are presumed to be represented by special "goal nodes" that enjoy high and constant activation. Goal nodes are the only elements in working memory that sustain

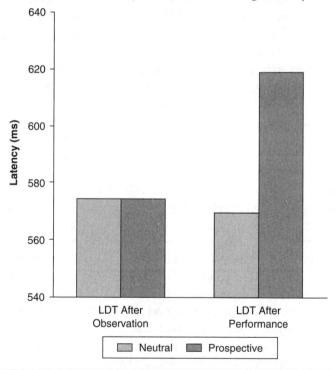

Figure 5.2   Lexical Decision Times (LDT) in an Experiment Performed by Marsh, Hicks, and Bink (1998)

SOURCE: From Marsh, R. L., Hicks, J. L. & Bink, M. L., Activation of completed, uncompleted, and partially completed intentions, in *Journal of Experimental Psychology: Learning, Memory and Cognition, 24,* 350–361, copyright © 1998, American Psychological Association. Reprinted with permission.

activation without rehearsal (pp. 118, 156). Intended actions can be viewed as goals, so in this model intended actions would be represented by special goal nodes. As such, activation for intended actions would be sustained without additional resources or stimulation.

One complication is that ACT explicitly limits this special node status to items in working memory. In contrast, the results from the experiments described above are presumably reflective of the activation dynamics of items in long-term memory. As we mentioned, some of the experiments introduced interference procedures, procedures that would be expected to exclude the target contents from working memory. Accordingly, the intention superiority effect may suggest a novel extension to the ACT model: Even for subthreshold levels of activation (in terms of working memory), there are special nodes that sustain activation longer than common nodes do. Thus, one possibility is that postponed intended actions are represented as these special nodes and are therefore activated for longer periods than other contents are (Goschke & Kuhl, 1993). Also, assuming that total activation in the memory system is limited (Anderson, 1983), the sustained activation for intended actions might be expected to concomitantly decrease activation to other representations. The slower latencies for decisions regarding neutral scripts in the intention superiority effect experiments is thus consistent with this interpretation.

An alternative more in line with the existing ACT model is that sustaining a higher state of activation for particular long-term memory contents will require at least sporadic use of resources (Anderson, 1983; Cowan, 1999). Perhaps this use of resources is linked to Guynn's (2003) proposal that the cognitive system activates a prospective memory retrieval mode during the retention interval (see Lebiere & Lee, 2001, for one formal model of the intention superiority effect within the ACT framework).

A motor encoding interpretation of the intention superiority effect. A very different idea is that intended actions are not stored only as a verbal code of what one intends to do, but that the verbal representation is translated into an action-based format (Freeman & Ellis, 2003; Koriat et al. 1990). The idea is that when a person forms an intention, motor information associated with performance of the intention is activated and stored in the representation of the intended action. Perhaps at some level, the cognitive system is simulating or imagining sensorimotor aspects of the action when the intention is formed. Importantly, research has shown that covert motor codes produce memory effects that parallel those produced when a motor action is actually performed. Much research has demonstrated that when subjects perform the actions described in verbal phrases (*knock on the table*), this information is better remembered than it is when the action phrase is simply studied (Engelkamp, 1998). Similarly, when subjects are told to encode simple noun-verb phrases for *future* enactment, they remember these phrases better than they do when the noun-verb phrases are encoded for verbal report on a recall test (Koriat et al.). The heart of the matter, though, rests on a study showing that performing a stated action speeds recognition of the action phrase relative to verbally encoding the action phrase (see Zimmer, 1986). The implication is that encodings enriched with sensorimotor information are more highly activated than are verbal encodings. Thus, the intention superiority effect could be based on the rich sensorimotor encoding presumably produced when an intention for future execution is formed.

Freeman and Ellis (2003) conducted a clever set of experiments to explore the possibility that the heightened activation of intentions is due to anticipated enactment. The novel feature of their study was that they manipulated (a) no enactment versus enactment of verbs (for example, *knock* and *bow*) during the encoding session and (b) the intention to perform at later testing versus the expectation to produce verbal recall at later testing. After encoding and before the final recall testing, Freeman and Ellis measured response latencies for recognition of the target verbs.

Consider first the two conditions in which subjects verbally encoded the verbs, with the subjects in one condition intending to later perform the actions signified by the verbs and those in the other intending to verbally recall the verbs. As expected, the recognition latencies were consistently faster when subjects intended to later execute the actions than they were when subjects expected a verbal recall test. This pattern is a conceptual replication of the intention superiority effect found in the experiments described above and establishes that the effect occurs despite variations in materials and experimental procedures.

Of special interest are the two conditions in which subjects enacted the verbs during the encoding phase. Here again, subjects in one of these conditions later intended to perform the actions and subjects in the other intended to produce verbal recall. Freeman and Ellis (2003) reasoned that if privileged activation of intentions is attributable to the status of that information as "actions to be executed later," we should again see a recognition latency advantage when subjects intend to later execute the actions relative to when they expect to later produce verbal recall. Alternatively, if the intention superiority effect is mediated by mnemonic benefits of enriched sensorimotor encoding, enactment of the verbs during the encoding phase even without intention to later execute the actions will be sufficient to speed recognition latencies to the level demonstrated when subjects also intend to later execute the actions. This expectation leads to two specific predictions: First, there should be no intention superiority effect when the two conditions requiring enactment encoding are compared. The bars on the right side of Figure 5.3 show that this is precisely the result that was obtained. Second, there should be a general "action superiority" effect, such that whenever the items must be enacted, either during encoding or at some future point, latencies will be roughly equal and faster than those accompanying verbal encoding and the expectation to produce verbal recall. By comparing the first bar of Figure 5.3 with the three other bars, we can see that Freeman and Ellis's results support this prediction as well.

The interested reader may note that this prediction contrasts with the assumption that intended actions have a special storage status independent of the mnemonic advantage of enactment during encoding. If so, the two effects should be cumulative, with enactment at encoding and intention to act combining to produce the most facilitation. Therefore, the leftmost bar of Figure 5.3, representing verbal encoding and verbal intention, should reflect the slowest response, and the rightmost bar, representing enactment at encoding and intention to act later, should reflect the fastest. This pattern was not evident in any of Freeman and Ellis's (2003) experiments.

The action superiority interpretation has further direct support from an experiment that introduced interference into the encoding phase. In this experiment, subjects were asked to learn lists of verbs for either a verbal memory test or an enactment test (Freeman & Ellis, 2003, Experiment 4). The key was that immediately after studying the lists, subjects were instructed to perform a verbal distracter activity (repeatedly count backward from 10) or a motor

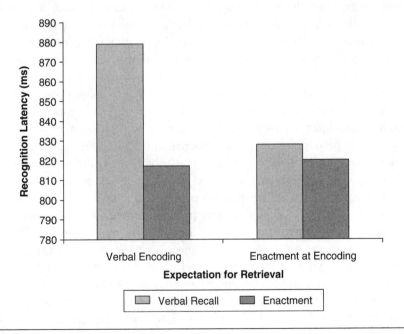

Figure 5.3   Mean Recognition Latencies for Prospective Items in the Verbal and Enactment Conditions (Freeman & Ellis, 2003, Experiment 2)

distracter activity (draw imaginary circles in the air). The idea here is that performing the distracter activity should interfere with storage of information in the specific dimension targeted by the distracter task. We know from other research that the mnemonic benefits of enactment encoding are reduced with motor but not verbal interference (Zimmer & Engelkamp, 1985). Therefore, if the intention superiority effect is based on covert sensorimotor encoding, the effect should be disrupted by the motor interference task but not the verbal interference task. On the other hand, if the intention superiority effect is mediated by privileged status of the represented intention, the modality of interference should not affect the intention superiority effect (cf. Goschke & Kuhl, 1993). Figure 5.4 shows that the intention superiority effect was eliminated after motor interference (the two rightmost bars) but not after verbal interference (the left-hand bars show the standard intention superiority effect).

Summary and Future Directions

The intention superiority effect is well documented in the literature. Subsequent research needs to address a number of critical issues. Perhaps the most central challenge is linking the intention superiority effect to prospective memory. There is a host of questions in this regard, and we mention only some here. First, the seminal Goschke and Kuhl (1993) paradigm did not actually embody a prospective memory task. Subjects knew that they would be cued to execute the intended script, rather than have to remember to initiate the actions on their own. Newer variations on the paradigm have investigated the intention superiority effect under conditions that are more like a prospective memory task. What remains is to directly link the intention superiority effect to prospective memory performance. Does the heightened activation as revealed by lexical decision and recognition latencies have a functional impact on prospective memory retrieval? What is the time-course of heightened activation—does it necessitate refreshing through conscious reflection? Is intention superiority ubiquitous or necessary for prospective remembering?

Another rich set of issues concerns the theoretical explanation of the intention superiority effect. One interpretation is that intended actions are maintained in a more highly activated state in memory. Departing from this interpretation, Freeman and Ellis's (2003) experiments converge with the idea that sensorimotor encoding for intended actions may underlie the intention superiority effect. Exploring this idea further, in one experiment Goschke and Kuhl (1993, Experiment 4) instructed subjects to imagine themselves performing the neutral and the execute script actions; these instructions would presumably stimulate sensorimotor encoding. Yet these instructions did not significantly diminish the intention superiority effect (see Table 5.1). So, whether sensorimotor processes are always involved in

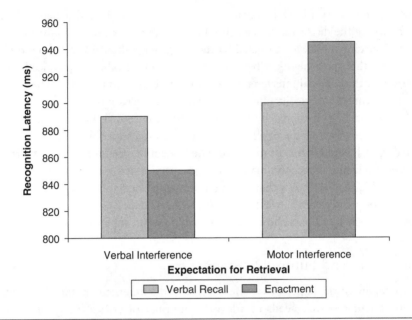

Figure 5.4   Mean Recognition Latencies for Prospective Items in the Verbal and Motor Interference Conditions (Freeman & Ellis, 2003, Experiment 4)

SOURCE: From Freeman, J. E. & Ellis, J., The representation of delayed intentions: A prospective subject-performed task? *Journal of Experimental Psychology: Learning, Memory, and Cognition, 29,* copyright © 2003. Reprinted with permission.

the intention superiority effect is as yet not certain. For instance, for some intentions the specifics of the intended actions are not necessarily known in advance or may be too rich for all of the actions to produce sensorimotor encoding. For example, the intention to take a trip encompasses intentions for a variety of activities such as packing, obtaining cash, and canceling mail delivery. People may or may not engage in covert motor encoding of detailed and rich activities involved in complex intentions.

Retention of Intended Actions Over Time: Immune to Forgetting?

Whatever the reason for intended actions' residing in memory with heightened activation, one possible consequence is that intended actions are more immune to forgetting than is other encoded information. The implication here is that prospective memory may not demonstrate the classic negatively accelerated logarithmic forgetting curve that is a prominent phenomenon in the retrospective memory literature. In support of this implication, one of the earliest experiments on prospective memory found no differences in prospective remembering when subjects were instructed to mail postcards back to the laboratory from 2 to 36 days later (Wilkins, 1979). Of course, subjects could have implemented external cues, such as writing the target mailing day on a calendar. Clearly, the use of external cues would compromise any conclusions about the dynamics of forgetting of intended actions (for example, see Meacham & Leiman, 1982, for the influence of external cues on reversing the negative effects of delay on prospective remembering).

Only several laboratory-based experiments have manipulated the length of the retention interval. Though limited to much shorter retention intervals, these experiments prevented the use of external aids, allowing for direct assessment of forgetting. Using an event-based prospective memory task, one experiment varied whether a prospective memory target event occurred 15 minutes or 30 minutes after the formation of the intention (Einstein, Holland, McDaniel, & Guynn, 1992), and another experiment examined 4-minute versus 20-minute retention intervals (Guynn, McDaniel, & Einstein, 1998). Both experiments found no significant difference in prospective memory as a function of retention interval length. Countering these findings are two other experiments in which prospective memory significantly declined as the retention interval lengthened (Brandimonte & Passolunghi, 1994; Loftus, 1971). In Chapter 4, we suggested a possible reconciliation of these mixed findings, the upshot being that retention of intended actions in long-term memory (as opposed to maintenance of intended actions in working memory, a process that the multiprocess theory assumes is required with nonfocal prospective memory cues) may indeed diverge from the salient forgetting functions we are used to seeing in retrospective memory. We now turn to a provocative finding that underscores this divergence.

One of the exciting aspects of science is that sometimes routine experiments uncover the most unexpected patterns, and so it was in a study conducted by Hicks, Marsh, and Russell (2000). Hicks et al. conducted a standard event-based prospective memory experiment focusing on two presumably straightforward issues: the effects of the depth of processing of the ongoing activity (a word-processing task) on prospective memory and the effects of the interval between when the prospective memory instruction was given and the point at which subjects began the ongoing task (in which the prospective memory target cues were embedded). In the short-retention condition, after receiving the ongoing-task and prospective memory instructions, subjects performed a distracter activity for 2.5 minutes before proceeding with the ongoing task. In the long-retention condition, subjects performed two distracter activities lasting 15 minutes, and then the ongoing task was presented.

The researchers had anticipated an effect of depth of processing of the ongoing activity, but there was no effect. More important for the present issue, they also thought that prospective memory would decline across the retention interval, or at best remain at constant levels for the short and long intervals. Remarkably, however, prospective memory performance significantly increased! In one version of the experiment, the proportion of times that subjects remembered to perform the intended action nearly doubled from 19% in the short-retention condition to 36% in the long-retention condition. Another version of the experiment also revealed a substantial increase in prospective memory performance from the short-retention condition (41%) to the long-retention condition (62%).

How can we interpret these findings? One possibility is that during the course of the retention interval, the intention is retrieved (activated from long-term memory), thereby making it more likely that the intention will be retrieved again (lessening forgetting). We know from the retrospective memory literature that retrieval is a potent potentiator of subsequent retrieval; that is, retrieval minimizes forgetting (Bjork & Whitten, 1974; McDaniel & Masson, 1985; Roediger & Karpicke, 2006). Concerning prospective memory, the idea is that more retrievals of the intention prior to the moment when the intended action is to be executed are possible as the retention interval increases. Assuming the effects of retrieval are cumulative (see Roediger & Karpicke, for related evidence in retrospective memory experiments), prospective memory retrieval at the moment the target event appears is more probable after longer intervals.

However likely this interpretation is of the Hicks et al. (2000) findings, that study produced no direct evidence of retrieval of intentions during the retention interval. Indeed, two observations caution against unqualified acceptance of the idea that the long retention interval prompted more retrievals of the prospective memory intention: First, the distracter activities in the long-retention condition (the Remote Associates Test and Ravens Progressive Matrices) were arguably more demanding than the distracter activity in the short-retention condition (rating the humor of cartoons). It is unclear how self-remindings (retrievals of the intention) would increase in the face of a more difficult distracter activity. Thoughts about the intended activity seem to occur less frequently as the distracter activity becomes more challenging (Kvavilashvili, 1987). Second, during informal postexperimental questioning, subjects in both the short- and long-retention conditions reported thinking about the intention infrequently ("once or twice" [p. 1163]).

In sum, much remains to be done to examine the limiting conditions under which prospective memory improves over longer retention intervals. For example, it seems implausible that prospective memory would continue to improve over increasing delays. Work is also needed to develop and test explanations of this effect. We now turn to consider more direct evidence regarding the degree to which thoughts about the intention surface during the retention interval of a prospective memory task, and the factors that may underlie the occurrence of these thoughts.

Retrieval of Intentions During the Retention Interval

In one naturalistic study, college students were asked to state their intentions for the following several days, and then over the course of 3 days to record the number of times per day that they thought about these intentions (Marsh, Hicks, & Landau, 1998). Thoughts of the intentions were reported to occur relatively frequently, on average more than 18 to 20 times per day. In a laboratory-based study, Kvavilashvili (1987) instructed subjects to remember to hang up a telephone at a given moment later in the experiment. At the conclusion of the experiment, subjects were also asked whether they thought about the intention to hang up the telephone during the interval between the initial instruction and the moment at which the intention was to be executed. Some subjects did report thinking about the intention in the retention interval, and as noted earlier, these thoughts were more likely as the ongoing activity became less absorbing. Further, the occurrence of thoughts correlated with better prospective memory performance. Another feature of this experiment was that for different groups of subjects, the importance of remembering to hang up the telephone was varied in the instructions. For the group to which the task was important, more thoughts about the task tended to be recorded during the retention interval. These findings reinforce our own experience that prospective memory intentions do come to mind, and are also perhaps related to successful prospective remembering. We explore this issue in more detail later in the chapter.

But first, a fundamental question remains largely unanswered: How are intentions brought to mind (retrieved) during the retention interval? Two general answers have been suggested. One is that internal cognitive mechanisms support retrieval of the intention during the retention interval. According to one variation of this theme, people may periodically engage in self-remindings (self-initiated retrieval of the intention) (Hicks et al., 2000). (The alert reader may notice that this "answer" leads back to the critical question we raised earlier in this book—how is it that, without an external request to remember, such retrieval occurs?) Another variation on this theme is that random internal "wanderings" from time to time come across a sort of internal marker ("mental note"), or representation, that prompts retrieval of the intention. Consistent with this idea, work in neuroscience implicates a neurological default state that is predominant when the person disengages from ongoing activity (for example, see Buckner et al., 2005). This default mode is responsible for daydreaming, random thoughts (musing), and retrieval of memories, all of which could reflect internal wanderings that might prompt retrieval of our intentions.

The other possible mechanism appeals to external cues. The idea is that cues encountered in the environment during the retention interval prompt retrieval of the intended action (Kvavilashvili & Fisher, 2007; Sellen, Louie, Harris, & Wilkins, 1997). For example, upon creating the intention early in the week to telephone a friend on the weekend (when I have unlimited mobile-phone minutes), I might encounter innumerable external cues during the week that could prompt retrieval of my intention. Hearing a telephone ring, seeing a telephone, reading a passage that mentions memory, encountering the name of the state or city in which my friend lives—any or all of these could associatively cue retrieval of my intention. The richness of our lives allows fortuitous encounters with potential cues. One of the older participants in our experiments, upon reading the informed consent form indicating the experiment was about remembering to do things in the future, remembered that he had yet to take his heart medication for the day. Thus, being in an experiment itself prompted retrieval of an important prospective memory intention for our participant, who upon returning home did take his medication.

Laboratory studies of prospective memory have likely minimized the appearance of external cuing mechanisms for retrieving intended actions during the retention interval. In laboratory studies to date, to avoid confusing the subjects, the prospective memory target events are carefully excluded from the distracter activities that fill the retention interval. In addition, in laboratory studies, subjects' distracter and ongoing activities are much more limited in scope than are the activities involved in our everyday lives.

To provide an opportunity for both internal and external mechanisms of intention retrieval to emerge, a group of applied cognitive science researchers circumvented the limitations imposed by laboratory studies. They developed a clever semi-naturalistic study and conducted it at their own workplace over the course of a month (Sellen et al., 1997). To illustrate the potential of naturalistic paradigms for examining prospective memory and perhaps stimulate more work along these lines, we take a moment to describe the method. The study revolved around an electronic diary system already in use in that workplace. For this "Active Badge" system, special sensors had been installed throughout the building, at least one sensor being in every room (except the bathrooms). These sensors picked up infrared signals emitted every 20 seconds by lightweight badges (see Figure 5.5) that workers clipped to their clothing. As badge-wearers moved about the building, a detailed record

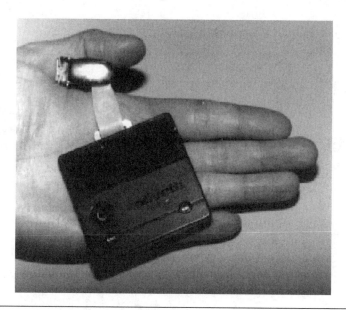

Figure 5.5   Example of an Active Badge

SOURCE: From Sellen, A. J., Louie G., Harris, J. E., and Wilkins, A. J. What brings intentions to mind? An in situ study of prospective memory, in *Memory,* 5(4), 483–507, copyright © 1997. Used by kind permission of Psychology Press, www.psypress.co.uk/journals.asp, 2006.

was automatically compiled of what rooms the people entered, the amount of time they spent in each room, and what other people (badge-wearers) were in the presence of a particular person. The badge also had a small button that, when pressed, produced a short recording. Some but not all workers ordinarily wore such badges at this workplace.

Before beginning the prospective memory tasks, all workers were instructed to wear their badges for a week to allow those who had not worn the badge to become accustomed to it. A time-based and an event-based prospective memory task were implemented on separate weeks, the instructions being provided on a Monday morning and each task lasting 5 consecutive workdays. For the time-based task, workers were instructed to remember to press the button on their badge three times at specified times throughout the day, the target times occurring every 2 hours. For the event-based task, workers were instructed to press the button on their badge three times whenever they entered the Commons, a public room in the building containing facilities (seminar room, kitchen, library). In addition, workers were to press the button once whenever the intention came to mind. Thus, the Active Badge system provided electronically recorded and reliable detailed environmental, contextual, and temporal information

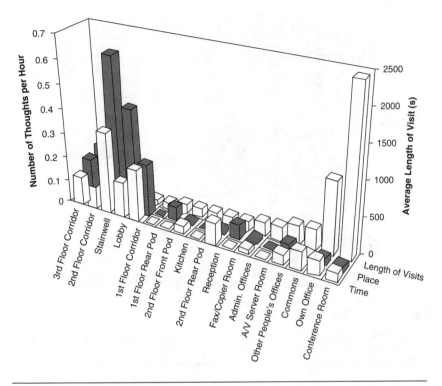

Figure 5.6   Number of Thoughts Per Hour as a Function of Location in a Study Conducted by Sellen, Louie, Harris, and Wilkins (1997)

SOURCE: From Sellen, A. J., Louie G., Harris, J. E., and Wilkins, A. J. What Brings Intentions to Mind? An in situ study of prospective memory, in *Memory*, 5(4), 483–507, copyright © 1997. Used by kind permission of Psychology Press, www.psypress.co.uk/journals.asp, 2006.

concerning retrieval of thoughts of the intention and actual prospective memory performance.

Of central interest were the dynamics associated with thinking about the intentions at moments other than when the prospective memory task was to be implemented. The findings suggested that the event-based and time-based tasks generally differed in the mechanisms that prompted thoughts about the intention. In the event-based task, the preponderance of thoughts about the intention occurred just prior to workers' entering the Commons, with 71% of the thoughts in the 2 minutes prior to the prospective memory response occurring within 30 seconds before entering the Commons. The implication is that the environmental cues associated with entering the Commons were quite influential in bringing the intention to mind. In contrast, in the time-based task, thoughts about the intention occurred fairly regularly throughout the 2-hour interval preceding the target time.

Participants indicated that they "made" themselves aware of the task—in our terminology, that they initiated thoughts of the intentions—and by doing so controlled the frequency of thoughts about the intention over the retention interval. Thus, this study provided evidence that both external-cue and internal self-initiated mechanisms play a role in bringing intentions to mind, with each mechanism's prominence perhaps depending on the nature of the prospective memory task.

Another salient pattern was that more thoughts about the intention occurred for both the time-based and the event-based task when workers were in transitional locations, such as the stairwell, a hallway, or a lobby. As you can see in Figure 5.6, thoughts about the intention were very rarely reported in the offices and work spaces (pods). This pattern suggests that when people have completed a task, or are taking a break from a task (Kvavilashvili, 1987), thoughts of intended actions are more likely to come into awareness. This finding is consistent with our theoretical ideas presented above, namely, that upon disengagement from a task, a prominent default state characterized by musings or retrieval of past events may allow the mind to wander to previously formed intentions.

The Sellen et al. (1997) finding appears to converge nicely with findings from the Hicks et al. laboratory study (2000). Hicks et al. filled long (15-minute) retention intervals with (a) several distracter tasks, in which 15-second breaks occurred for instructions, (b) a single distracter task with no breaks, or (c) a single task with several unfilled 15-second breaks. Prospective memory significantly increased when the retention interval contained breaks, and especially so when the breaks were unfilled (but see Finstad, Bink, McDaniel, & Einstein, 2006, for a different pattern). The idea is that the completion of the distracter tasks or the opportunity for breaks promoted retrieval of the prospective memory intention, with such retrievals supporting better subsequent prospective remembering.

Effects of Retrieval in the Retention Interval

The above studies do not directly address the issue of the impact of retrievals during the retention interval on prospective memory performance, and unfortunately, few existing studies do. We have already described one finding that correlated self-reports of the prospective memory task coming to mind with subsequent performance of the prospective memory task (Kvavilashvili, 1987). Another way to address this issue is to have the experimenter prompt subjects to retrieve during the retention interval. For instance, one study inserted brief breaks within the ongoing activity, and during each break half of the subjects were exhorted to "remember what to do if you see a target word" (Finstad et al., 2006, Experiment 1). The other subjects were simply allowed to relax during the breaks. The subjects prompted to retrieve the intention during the periodic rest breaks showed better prospective memory performance (75%) than did those who were allowed to relax during the rest breaks (60%). In this experiment, every break occurred within 20 words prior to the presentation of each target word, and sometimes the break was situated just 4 words prior to the target. Thus, this pattern reinforces the intuition that retrievals that are proximal to the appropriate moment for executing the intended action improve prospective remembering.

The effects of retrieval also depend on the particular information retrieved. Consider that a prospective memory intention typically includes encoding of the intended action itself and identification of a target event or time when it will be appropriate to execute the intended action. Sometimes, during the retention interval, retrieval of this information constellation might be partial. For instance, you might form the intention to reschedule a lunch meeting with a colleague when you see the colleague. Later, you might experience partial retrieval: You either remember that you need to reschedule the lunch appointment (the intention) or you think about your colleague (the target event). Does retrieval of partial information concerning the prospective memory intention improve prospective memory?

To answer this question, Guynn et al. (1998) prompted subjects approximately 1 minute prior to the appearance of each prospective memory target event to remember the several target words that were studied at the outset of the experiment (retrieve the prospective memory target events), remember the intended action (retrieve the action), or remember the targets and the action (retrieve the complete intention). Based on prospective memory performance in a control group with no retrieval prompts, target event retrieval, even though it was just 1 minute prior to the prospective memory task, had no positive influence on prospective memory performance. Retrieval of the complete intention produced robust improvement in prospective memory (from 31% in the control group to 82%). Action retrieval improved prospective memory but significantly less so than did complete retrieval. Thus, just having thoughts come to mind about features of the prospective memory task during the retention interval does not necessarily improve prospective memory. The contents of the thoughts are critically important.

A series of clinical studies with Alzheimer's disease (AD) patients has revealed that appropriately spaced retrievals prompted just after intention formation (and distal to the appropriate moment for performing the intention) can have powerful positive effects on prospective remembering (Camp, Foss, Stevens, & O'Hanlon, 1996). As you will see, the results of these studies are quite remarkable. The profound memory problems of individuals with AD include prospective memory problems, such as forgetting to keep appointments and forgetting to pay bills. Some will write notes to themselves or perhaps make notations on calendars to help them remember the intended activities, but often they will forget to consult these reminders or forget where the reminders are placed. Thus, the external reminders that many of us rely on are not as useful for people with AD.

Accordingly, Camp and his colleagues used a method of spaced retrievals to help individuals with AD remember to consult a calendar each day to see what tasks needed to be performed during the day. None of the participants had been able prior to the study to remember to consult the calendar, as determined in preliminary screening. During the initial training, participants were told that they should remember to look at a calendar each day (the location of the calendar having been selected for each participant) in order to find out the several tasks that needed to be accomplished that day. Twenty seconds after the participants were instructed to remember to check the calendar, the experimenter asked, "How are you going to remember what to do each day?" If the participant successfully retrieved the intention and responded, "Look at my calendar," the retrieval interval was augmented by another 20 seconds. Thus, 40 seconds later the participant was again asked to recall what he or she was going to try to do each day. After every successful retrieval, the interval was made 20 seconds longer than the last, until a 4-minute retention interval was successfully completed. If a participant failed to retrieve the intention, the intention was repeated to the participant, and the longest interval for which retrieval had been successful was again used. To illustrate, Figure 5.7 shows a hypothetical spaced-retrieval training session.

After the participant successfully completed the 4-minute retrieval, that week's training session was over. The experimenter left the participant a calendar having seven pages for each day of the current week, and each page had several tasks on it. One task was always to sign the page of the calendar, and another task was decided by the caretaker. Figure 5.8 shows an example of a page of a calendar used in the study. At the end of the week the experimenter collected the pages and supplied seven new pages for the participants. Successful prospective memory was defined as remembering to sign at least four of the seven pages and remembering at least four of the other seven tasks. When a participant demonstrated successful prospective memory for 2 successive weeks, the study was concluded for that participant. If prospective remembering was not evidenced, spaced-retrieval practice was repeated on following weeks, there being a maximum of 10 weekly training sessions.

The results were astonishing. With at most 10 training sessions, of the 23 AD participants, 87% were able to remember to tell the experimenter

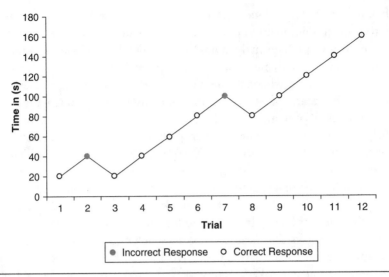

Figure 5.7   Hypothetical Performance During an Initial Spaced-Retrieval
Training Session

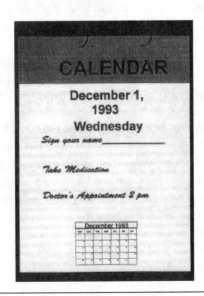

Figure 5.8   Sample Calendar Page From the Spaced-Retrieval Study

(upon his or her return at the beginning of the week) that they were supposed to look at the calendar each day. Of that 87%, 75% effectively used the calendar every week to perform the tasks displayed on the calendar pages. Recall that none of these participants had been able to remember to use the calendar before the study began. Similar studies with AD patients using the spaced-retrieval technique to remember different kinds of prospective memory tasks (other than remembering to look at a calendar each day) have been equally successful. These findings reveal the dramatic benefits of spaced retrievals of a formed intention on prospective memory. Further, the positive effects for AD patients underscore the potential of this technique for improving prospective remembering for individuals with a wide range of memory abilities. You may want to try spaced retrievals for your own prospective memory challenges.

Reminders During the Retention Interval

The previous section emphasized that events and physical locations (or objects) haphazardly encountered in the course of daily activities can prompt retrieval of the intended action during the retention interval, and thereby facilitate retention and prospective remembering. People can also purposely construct external cues to help remind them of the intended action during the retention interval. Tying a string around your finger so you remember to do something is a prototypical example of this kind of "engineered" external cue. For convenience, we will label environmental events specifically designed or constructed for the purpose of remembering the prospective memory intention *reminders*.

Some reminders that people use, such as alarms and pagers, are designed to alert them to perform the intended action at the appropriate moment. Other reminders, however, like tying a string around your finger, presumably serve to ensure that the intention is periodically retrieved or thought about during the retention interval, thus perhaps facilitating successful execution of the action at the appropriate moment. These kinds of reminders are noted in the earliest published paper touching on prospective memory, a paper published over 100 years ago. Colegrove (1899) surveyed more than 1,600 people (ranging from children to older adults), questioning them regarding the kinds of memory aids they used to remember to keep appointments. A variety of reminders was listed. Women changed rings or pinned paper on their dresses. Some respondents indicated that they turned chairs over or rearranged furniture. One man hid his hat to remind himself of an appointment. (The next morning, not finding his hat, the man selected another one to wear, but he did not remember why his usual hat was missing!) Clearly, people rely on reminders to facilitate prospective remembering. The question is, do such reminders work? Intuitively, one would think so. Let's see what the experimental evidence reveals.

In a pioneering study of prospective memory, Meacham and Leiman (1982) gave subjects who had completed a laboratory experiment on "several aspects of memory" a packet of postcards, and asked the subjects to mail the postcards to the laboratory at specified days distributed randomly over a 32-day period. Half of the subjects were also given a colored tag to place on their key chain as a reminder. The other half of the subjects were not given a reminder. The reminder produced a modest significant improvement in remembering to return the postcards on the specified days. In one experiment, subjects with the colored tag mailed 81% of the postcards on time, whereas subjects with no tag mailed 70% of the postcards on time.

Perhaps, however, the subjects not given the colored-tag reminder generated their own external reminders, thereby essentially undermining the no-reminder control. A follow-up questionnaire confirmed that 84% of all subjects tested in two experiments generated their own external reminders (using a calendar or placing the postcards where they would be frequently seen) to help them remember to mail the postcards. Thus, the true effects of the experimental reminder (colored tag) remain unclear.

Interestingly, a laboratory study that manipulated the presence of a reminder failed to find evidence of a facilitatory effect. In the context of a simulated air-traffic control task, subjects were instructed to remember to reroute designated airplanes that appeared on the radar after first completing tasks with other airplanes (Vortac, Edwards, & Manning, 1995). For some subjects, the symbol for the plane remained on the monitor during the retention interval as a reminder. For other subjects, there was no external reminder of the to-be-rerouted airplanes on the monitor. The reminders did not improve prospective memory.

One potentially important feature of these reminders is that they were continuously present throughout the retention interval or were not especially salient among the backdrop of many other symbols and radar blips on the monitor. Perhaps people become habituated to such reminders over the long term, thereby paying them little attention, and thus do not think about the prospective memory intention. Certainly, a reminder that is not attended cannot prompt retrieval of the intended action. For example, the daughter of one of the authors needed a floppy disk for her written homework and asked that he remember to pick one up that day. The father, being an expert in prospective memory, dutifully wrote himself a note to bring home the floppy disk and stuck it in his briefcase with other papers. As he periodically looked inside his briefcase during the day, the note appeared as just another sheet of paper and did not attract any attention. Needless to say, the reminder provided no help and the prospective memory task was not performed, much to the chagrin of both father and daughter.

Analysis of these examples suggests that reminders present during the retention interval can be helpful, provided they are relatively salient (see more about the characteristics of effective reminders in Chapter 9). The experimental evidence is consistent with this claim. Younger adults (college students) and older adults who were allowed to tape a note to the computer monitor during the course of an experiment (in which the ongoing task and the prospective memory targets were presented on the computer) showed substantially better prospective memory performance than did subjects not allowed to create an external reminder (Einstein & McDaniel, 1990, Experiment 1). In another study, after retrieving the intended action, subjects were instructed to briefly delay executing that action until the completion of the current ongoing activity (McDaniel, Einstein, Graham, & Rall, 2004). When that ongoing activity was interrupted by yet another task, execution of the prospective memory action was disrupted. The disruption was eliminated when a blue dot appeared in the corner of the computer monitor during the delay as a reminder to execute the prospective memory task. Note that the blue dot was not present during all of the experiment, but just during the delay over which the intention had to be maintained before the intended action could be executed. In this case, apparently, there was little habituation to the blue dot, and it was a potent reminder.

In everyday prospective remembering, external reminders do not always stem from inanimate external objects; reminders can also be generated by other people. For instance, it is not uncommon for spouses, administrative assistants, or friends to remind us to execute an intended action over the course of a retention interval. How do these reminders influence prospective memory? Note that verbal reminders generated by others over the retention interval differ cognitively from thoughts (or reminders) of the intended action generated within the person who has the prospective memory intention. When someone else reminds us, the intention is externally presented, whereas when we think of the intention ourselves, it is self-generated. Also, in the case of the former, the intention is essentially encoded again (additional study), whereas in the case of the latter the reminder is retrieved from long-term memory. Both of these differences could have important consequences for retention and subsequent retrieval of the intended action at the appropriate moment (cf. Marsh, Cook, & Hicks, 2006). Though these issues are potentially quite interesting, there are as yet no studies exploring them.

Summary

Our everyday prospective memory experiences suggest that it is not unusual for prospective memory intentions to periodically come to mind before we reach the opportunity to execute the intended action. Naturalistic and laboratory research confirm this observation. Further, theory and research have identified two general loci for thoughts of the intention during the retention interval (the interval between formation of the intention and execution of the intended action): Chance encounters with relevant external cues can prompt thoughts of the intention, and internal cognitive processes can initiate thoughts of the intention. Though these internal mechanisms are not yet well understood, it appears that people will sometimes make themselves aware of the intention through purposeful self-initiated processes; evidence also suggests that thoughts of the intention can spontaneously originate ("pop up") as well.

Thoughts of the intention during the retention interval might be expected to impact prospective memory performance. However, whether this is true remains largely unexplored in the literature and merits more investigation. The limited evidence suggests that this issue might hold some unexpected and interesting revelations. A few studies suggest a positive association between such thoughts and prospective remembering, but the association is not necessarily robust as indexed by correlational measures and experimental findings. Factors such as the recency of intention retrieval (relative to the opportunity for execution of the intended action) and the content of what is retrieved may play a critical role. For instance, retrieval of partial information about the intention, such as what target event signals the appropriateness of executing the action, seems to produce no benefit whatsoever to prospective memory, even when this information is retrieved proximal (one minute) to prospective memory execution.

To help ensure successful retrieval of intentions, people sometimes construct external cues or reminders. The research, which is again extremely limited, has revealed that external reminders are not always effective. Clearly, much remains to be learned about the dimensions of reminders that play a role in improving prospective memory performance.

6

Planning and Encoding of Intentions

Research often has been designed as though prospective remembering was a memory task, without attention to either the diversity of tasks or the multidimensionality of prospective remembering.

—Allen Dobbs and Barbara Reeves, *Prospective Memory*

Dobbs and Reeves's observation laments the relative exclusion in laboratory research of the study of important components of prospective memory, such as the formation of intentions and the construction of plans. Indeed, we have postponed discussion of planning and the encoding of intentions to this point in the book because of the paucity of experimental research on the topic.

Planning

Researchers acknowledge that planning is an important component of prospective memory (for example, see Dobbs & Rule, 1987; Rabbitt, 1996; Shallice & Burgess, 1991). The degree of planning involved in a prospective memory task likely varies widely, however, with characteristics of the prospective memory task and individual differences influencing the quality and quantity of planning involved. One characteristic of prospective memory tasks identified in the literature that possibly relates to the prevalence of planning behavior is the complexity of the prospective memory task (Kvavilashvili & Ellis, 1996). Some prospective memory tasks, such as mailing items to your daughter, may involve several steps. To accomplish this, you may need to construct a plan that involves taking the items to work, buying packing materials, and stopping by the post office on your way home from work. In contrast, the intention to give your colleague a message may be accompanied by very little planning—your expectation being that you will encounter him at work.

Second, some intentions, such as deciding to accept an invitation to go to dinner with friends when you already have a busy schedule, may require difficult decisions. Deciding to go to dinner will necessitate planning of how to accomplish your other tasks in concert with going to dinner, which in turn could require replanning of those tasks (cf. Marsh, Hicks, & Landau, 1998). On the other hand, intentions that require simple decisions, such as the intention to buy bread on the way home from the store, may not be accompanied by much planning.

Third, prospective memory tasks clearly differ in their importance. Remembering to pick up your girlfriend from the airport is likely more important than remembering to stop by the post office to buy stamps. It is likely that more planning is stimulated by important than by unimportant intentions.

Considering the examples above in relation to the typical laboratory prospective memory research described in previous chapters, it is easy to see that the laboratory prospective memory tasks are simple, neutral (not emotionally valenced), easily decided upon, and not centrally important to the participants. Likely, then, these tasks stimulate little planning—indeed, as Dobbs and Reeves (1996) noted, the planning component has essentially been obviated in most laboratory prospective memory research. Prospective memory research is rapidly evolving, however, and several recent laboratory studies have incorporated new features that stimulate planning. We next examine what this handful of studies reveals about planning and prospective memory.

In one set of studies, the prospective memory instructions provided specific information about the context in which the designated event or time for performing the prospective memory action would occur during the experiment. Specifically, subjects were informed that there were three phases of the experiment, and that the prospective memory target event (for an event-based task) or target time (for a time-based task) would appear in the third phase (Marsh, Hicks, & Cook, 2006). This feature of the experiment essentially allowed subjects to plan how they would remember to execute the intended activity. To understand the idea of this experiment, consider the difference between intending to buy milk before the day is over and intending to buy milk on the way home from work. The latter intention may let you plan to not worry about buying milk until you begin the drive home, at which time you will begin to monitor for the grocery store. Such a plan would minimize the costs of applying attentional resources to the prospective memory task during the day (that is, you would not need to remind yourself of the need to buy milk throughout the day) and restrict the costs of applying those resources (as discussed in Chapter 2) to the activity you are engaged in proximal to the time of execution.

Marsh et al.'s (in press) findings of the costs that the prospective memory task incurred on the response times to the ongoing activity are shown in Figure 2.4. These results clearly show that, when subjects were informed about the phase in which the target event would occur, the costs to the cover activity in the prospective memory condition (relative to the no prospective memory control condition) were limited to the third phase of the experiment (note that the target event was nonfocal, so it would be expected to require some monitoring; see Chapter 4 for full discussion). This finding implies that subjects may have formulated plans for how to approach and execute this prospective memory task.

In the real world, the situation becomes even more complicated than that reflected by the simple, isolated action studied in the above laboratory paradigm. We formulate multiple intentions, which often represent multiple subgoals, and sometimes these subgoals compete. One must associate cues or conditions that signal the appropriateness for performing the multiple intended actions, consider particular procedures for accomplishing these actions, and perhaps make decisions about when to terminate procedures (such as when there is a need to accomplish other intended actions) (Rabbitt, 1996).

To begin to investigate the planning processes that are presumably central to the rich, interrelated intentions found in everyday life, Kliegel and his colleagues (Kliegel, McDaniel, & Einstein, 2000; Kliegel, Martin, McDaniel, & Einstein, 2002) developed a prospective memory paradigm based on a laboratory subgoal scheduling task. In the subgoal scheduling task, subjects are given six open-ended tasks to work on in a fixed period of time. The six tasks represent two sets of three different tasks. For example, there may be two sets of word-finding problems (find the one word in a set of four: *conceil, concill, council, concel*), two sets of arithmetic problems, and two sets of pictures for which subjects generate appropriate labels. The only constraint placed on subjects in terms of the order in which they perform these tasks is that the two sets of the same task cannot be performed consecutively. The catch is that subjects are not given enough time to finish all of the tasks. Points are given such that the first items in each task are worth more than later items. The subjects' challenge is to schedule the order in which they work on the tasks, make sure that they work on every task, and not spend too much time on any one task. Thus, this six-element task is intended to be a laboratory analogue of complex real-world intentions that represent multiple subgoals, some of which have to be initiated and others of which have to be terminated for complex goals to be accomplished. Typically, performance on the six-element test is taken to be an index of subjects' ability to plan and execute plans (cf. Shallice & Burgess, 1991); however, performance on the six-element task blends planning, intention formation, and plan execution.

To disentangle the planning and intention-formation process from prospective memory performance and plan execution, Kliegel et al. (2000) developed the following procedure: Younger and older subjects were given instructions on the six-element task and were told that they needed to remember to perform this task when they encountered a questionnaire later in the experiment. To examine the planning process itself, subjects were asked to plan aloud how they would perform the six-element task (the plan was tape-recorded). To examine retention of the plan, subjects were next given unrelated experimental tasks lasting about 25 minutes, and were then asked to recall their plan. Later in the experiment subjects were presented with the questionnaire. When the questionnaire was presented, subjects who did not remember to initiate the six-element task were reminded to do so. Data were collected on the quality of subjects' plans, recall memory for the plans, whether subjects remembered to initiate the six-element task, performance of the six-element task, and the degree to which the intentions specified in the plans related to actual performance of the six-element task.

Several interesting findings emerged from this study. Memory for the plans was highly accurate for both younger and older adults. Strikingly, despite having excellent memory for their plans, when subjects performed the six-element task, only about 50% of the steps indicated in the plans were followed. Thus, the components included in a formulated plan in the context of a prospective memory task are not necessarily realized when the intended activities are being executed. Survey findings about people's daily prospective memory tasks converge with this laboratory finding. Execution of daily prospective memory tasks not infrequently diverges from the intentions as they were originally planned (Marsh, Hicks, & Landau, 1998).

A second major set of findings was that the quality of the plans varied across individuals, and importantly, plan quality was associated with the level of performance on the six-element task. Younger adults generated more complex plans than did older adults, including in their plans specific reasons for the order in which they intended to perform the six tasks and formation of cues for when to interrupt one task and move to the next. Thus, younger adults' plans seemed to more effectively incorporate components that would preclude spending too much time on any one task and concrete steps for initiating work on all subtasks. And younger adults did initiate more of the subtasks in the six-element task (which was the overarching goal) than did older adults. Finally, a greater number of younger than older adults remembered on their own to initiate the six-element task during presentation of the questionnaire. These results suggest that formulating detailed, more elaborate plans has a positive impact on prospective memory performance. Yet the pattern is correlational in nature, precluding a strong conclusion about causal influences of the contents of plans on prospective memory performance. People who show good prospective memory may also simply be good planners.

To establish a causal connection between plan quality and optimal execution of complex prospective memory intentions, Kliegel, Martin, McDaniel, Einstein, and Moor (2005) attempted to vary the quality of plans. Some younger and older subjects were provided explicit guidance in formulating plans for the six-element task. This guidance included instructions to explicitly consider the cue for initiating the six-element task (the questionnaire). The subjects in this condition (the "planning-aid" condition) were also advised that their plans might specify switching between subtasks after no more than two items in each subtask were completed. These subjects were expected to form relatively good plans. Other younger and older subjects in the control condition were not provided guidance in planning, and these subjects were expected to form plans that were not as good. The researchers reasoned that if the differential quality of plans was responsible, at least in part, for older adults performing more poorly than younger adults in the initial study, providing planning aids should improve older adults' prospective memory performance. To the extent that younger adults' plans were improved, their prospective memory performance should improve as well.

The results were precisely as expected. Subjects' plans were analyzed for two particular features: (a) whether the plan included explicit consideration of the cue for initiating execution of the six-element task and (b) whether the plan included specification of when to switch from one subtask to the next.

In the control condition, none of the older adults' plans and just 13% of the younger adults' plans included consideration of the cue for initiating the six-element task. The planning-aid instructions significantly increased the incorporation of this feature into younger and older subjects' plans. This in turn produced significant improvements for both younger and older adults in remembering to initiate execution of the six-element task at the appropriate point in the experiment. In general, only 30% of the control group remembered to initiate the six-element task, whereas 53% of the planning-aid group remembered to initiate the task. It is perhaps somewhat surprising that the planning aids did not result in higher prospective memory performance. This result becomes understandable in light of the fact that providing planning aids did not guarantee that the plans would incorporate the suggested feature. Only a third of the younger adults and just over half of the older adults in the planning-aid condition actually included consideration of the cue in their plan.

A majority of younger adults in the control condition spontaneously included the switching feature in their plans, and the planning-aid instruction did not increase this proportion. In contrast, older adults in the control condition generally did not spontaneously include a switching feature in their plans (only 7% did so), but a majority (53%) did so when they were given the planning instructions. These patterns of plan quality were mirrored in performance on the six-element task. For younger adults, planning-aid instructions did not increase the number of self-initiated switches from one subtask to another relative to the absence of planning-aid instructions. On the other hand, older adults, whose plans were improved by the planning aid, showed a significant increase in self-initiated switches when they had been given planning instructions as opposed to when they had received no hints on how to plan.

In summary, the findings confirm the expectation that planning during the formation of intended activities has important consequences for the success of prospective memory performance. Further, the success of providing planning guidance for older adults identifies it as a promising technique for intervention programs focused on memory (especially prospective memory) in the aging population. The surprising finding was that not all subjects in the planning-aid condition included critical features in their plans, despite instructions that encouraged them to do so. These results, taken in concert, indicate that prospective memory can be improved by appropriate planning, but that getting people to formulate appropriate plans may require more than general hints and conceptual tips. We next consider an important technique for specific encoding of prospective memory intentions so as to significantly reduce prospective memory failures.

Implementation Intentions

The road to hell is paved with good intentions.

—Traditional proverb

Intended activities that are prevalent in the real world have some characteristics not typically implemented in the laboratory. Many of them, such as the intention to exercise more often, are relatively general. Even the intention to take a vitamin supplement is somewhat vague, as it carries no specification of when or where the supplement will be taken. Real-world intentions also may be antagonistic to routine or long-standing behaviors.

Gollwitzer (1999) has developed a technique for improving memory and execution of intended actions that may overcome these obstacles. His technique hinges on encoding intentions using a particular formulation, termed *implementation intentions.* Implementation intentions take the form of, "When situation x arises, I will perform response y" (p. 494). The key features of an implementation intention are (a) clear specification of the situation (where and when) that will be a good opportunity for initiating the intended action and (b) linkage of these specific situational cues to the intended action. Thus, instead of forming the general-goal intention, "I will take my vitamins," Gollwitzer recommends forming the implementation intention, "At the breakfast table each morning, I will take my vitamins." The implementation intention technique is essentially a prescription for good planning. Do implementation intentions work?

First, consider the vitamin scenario. Sheeran and Orbell (1999) conducted a study investigating the use of implementation intentions to help people remember to take a vitamin C pill. In two experiments, subjects committed themselves to taking the vitamin C pill each day for the following 3 weeks and indicated that they were highly motivated to do so. Some of the subjects were encouraged to form the general intention of taking a vitamin C pill each day. Other subjects were instructed to form implementation intentions. These subjects had to plan when and where they would take the pill each day. In the first experiment, for the first 10 days there was little forgetting for any of the subjects; on average, subjects forgot to take the vitamin less than 1 time. For the last 11 days, however, subjects increasingly neglected to take their pill. Over this second half of the 3-week period, implementation intentions produced more successful daily intake of the vitamin supplement than did general intentions. In a second experiment, the implementation intention advantage was observed over the entire 3-week period, with 61% of the control subjects forgetting to take at least one pill and only 26% of the implementation intention subjects forgetting to take at least one pill.

Another study incorporated implementation intentions into a typical motivational treatment for getting people to engage in exercise (Milne, Orbell, & Sheeran, 2002). College students were asked to engage in vigorous exercise for 20 minutes during the upcoming week. One group was simply asked to form this intention. Another group was given motivational material for this exercise intention, including information on the severity of coronary heart disease, people's vulnerability to heart disease, and the association of exercise with reduced heart disease. A third group, in addition to being given the motivational material, was instructed to form implementation intentions to exercise. Only 29% of the students in the control condition exercised the following week. Stop reading now, and predict what effects motivational material and implementation intentions would have.

The results were dramatic. Providing motivational material did increase the proportion of subjects who exercised the following week, but only to 39%. Implementation intentions, however, increased the proportion of students who exercised to 91%.

Implementation intentions can also be remarkably effective when people find the intended actions unpleasant. One study involved women who completed a survey on their views of breast cancer and breast self-examination (Orbell, Hodgkins, & Sheeran, 1997), an important component of early detection of breast cancer. One group of women was instructed to form an implementation intention, and a control group was not so instructed. Over the next month, almost 66% of the women with the implementation intention reported performing a breast self-examination, whereas only 14% of the control reported performing a breast self-examination. Of particular interest were the women who indicated a priori that performing the breast self-examination was a strong goal for the upcoming month. None of the women with the goal who also formed an implementation intention neglected to perform a breast self-examination. In sharp contrast, even when the goal was strong, nearly half of the women in the control group failed to perform a breast self-examination during the next month. Of these women, 70% indicated that they had forgotten to act on their intention.

Another characteristic of implementation intentions that has both theoretical interest and practical benefits is their effectiveness with a variety of populations. Interestingly, these populations include people with memory impairments, such as individuals with schizophrenia (Brandstatter, Lengfelder, & Gollwitzer, 2001), frontal lobe patients (Lengfelder & Gollwitzer, 2001), and older adults (Chasteen, Park, & Schwarz, 2001; Liu & Park, 2004).

The evidence for the value of implementation intentions is impressive, so much so that last New Year's Eve one of this book's authors asked his friends about their resolutions for the upcoming year. When his friends gave answers like, "I want to get involved in more community service," or, "I want to exercise more," he told them that they were unlikely to remember these very general intentions and badgered them into forming implementation intentions. His enthusiasm was such that his wife thought he was a bit overbearing (maybe her exact description was "obnoxious").

Theoretical Mechanisms Underlying Implementation Intentions

Why are implementation intentions so effective? According to Gollwitzer (1999), encoding an intended action as an implementation intention has several cognitive consequences that improve the likelihood that the intended action will later be remembered and executed. First, the implementation intention produces an encoding with heightened accessibility. Second, linkage of the intended action to specific situational cues allows automatic triggering of the intention when the cues are encountered (see Chapter 3 for further discussion of this posited process). Third, initiation of the action is more efficient. That is, initiation of an intended action that is encoded as an implementation intention requires fewer cognitive resources and may even be executed swiftly with little or no conscious intent (see Bargh, 1997, for full development of this idea). Thus, strong theoretical assumptions have been assembled to explain the effectiveness of using implementation intentions in planning. Unfortunately, little research has been conducted to critically examine these assumptions. Evidence to this point has been largely indirect, but may offer some support for Gollwitzer's (1999) hypotheses.

Heightened accessibility. Consider first the idea that an implementation intention produces an encoding with heightened accessibility, thereby augmenting accessibility of the anticipated situation. It is interesting to note that instructions in typical laboratory paradigms testing prospective memory with specific target cues take the form of implementation intentions because they directly associate a target situation and a specific action (for example, "Press the slash key when you see the target word *dormitory*"). As the alert reader may recall, in Chapter 5 we presented evidence that laboratory-based intentions may be stored with heightened activation or accessibility (the intention superiority effect). Yet this idea does not perfectly map onto the implementation intention formulation. The intention superiority effect has been demonstrated when subjects expect to be told to perform scripted actions at a later point in the experiment (see Freeman & Ellis, 2003, for an exception); thus, in these experiments there is no direct association formed between a target situational cue and the to-be-performed actions. Therefore, implementation intentions may have heightened activation because an intended action is part of the content, not necessarily because the encoding takes the form, "When situation x arises, I will perform y."

Furthermore, the experiments on the intention superiority effect assess activation of the intended action, whereas Gollwitzer suggests that the situational target will also be more highly activated. To furnish support for the latter idea, Gollwitzer (1996) conducted a dichotic-listening experiment in which critical words reflecting the anticipated situational targets of an implementation intention were presented in the nonattending ear. The subjects' task was to repeat aloud (shadow) words presented to a particular ear through earphones. Shadowing was disrupted when the critical words relating to the implementation intention were presented to the nonattending ear. The implication here is that the critical words were in such a heightened state of activation that these words captured attention from the attending ear and disrupted shadowing performance. In a related study, Steller (1992) found that when a small partial geometric figure was included in an implementation intention, that figure was easier to detect when it was embedded in a more complex figure that subsumed the partial figure.

Automatic intention retrieval. The second assumption is that the linkage between specific target cues and an intended action allows people to rely on spontaneous retrieval of the intention cued by the occurrence of the target event (rather than requires them to rely on controlled monitoring of the environment for an appropriate moment or particular time for executing the intended action). Consistent with this assumption are findings in which such linkages provide good prospective memory in the face of reduced attentional resources. For instance, older adults are described as having reduced working-memory resources (Salthouse, 1991) but relatively intact automatic memory processes (Jacoby, Jennings, & Hay, 1996).

Liu and Park (2004; see also Chasteen et al., 2001) thus reasoned that if automatic memory processes underlie the success of implementation intentions, then older adults, despite their reduced working-memory resources, could improve their prospective memory for performing daily blood glucose monitoring by using implementation intentions. To foster especially strong linkages between cues and blood glucose monitoring behavior, Liu and Park required the implementation intention participants not only to specify where and when they would carry out the blood tests but also to visualize the surroundings that would be present at the test time, imagine the events leading up to the test time, and imagine performing the tests as events culminated at the test time. Other groups of older adults either rehearsed the intention ("I will test my blood sugar at 1:30") or deliberated on the pros and cons of monitoring blood sugar levels. As shown in Figure 6.1, the use of implementation intentions markedly increased the number of times that the participants remembered to test their blood sugar over a 3-week period. The implication is that this positive effect was mediated by automatic retrieval processes stimulated by the formation of implementation intentions.

As mentioned earlier, many typical prospective memory laboratory paradigms clearly specify a target cue, and thus in these paradigms the

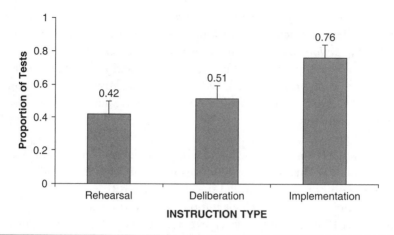

Figure 6.1   Average Proportion of Blood Glucose Tests Performed Correctly as a Function of the Type of Instruction Received in an Experiment Performed by Liu and Park (2004).

prospective memory intention already has the form of an implementation intention (Cohen & Gollwitzer, in press). Accordingly, results from these paradigms may help inform the assumption of automatic intention retrieval after formation of implementation intentions. In one study (described fully in Chapter 3), McDaniel, Guynn, Einstein, and Breneiser (2004) instructed subjects to perform an action that was either highly associated with the specific cue ("Write *sauce* when the word *spaghetti* appears") or had no prior association with the cue ("Write *steeple* when the word *spaghetti* appears"). Both conditions cause subjects to form an implementation intention; however, only the related cue-action pair produced prospective memory performance that was not negatively affected by high attentional load during the ongoing activity. Prospective memory in the low-association condition was significantly reduced by high attentional load during the ongoing activity. These results, along with those from Liu and Park's (2004) research using additional procedures to supplement implementation intentions, may suggest that forming an implementation intention does not per se create a linkage that supports automatic retrieval of an action in the presence of the specific cue. The implementation intention may provide the basis for a linkage, but perhaps additional processing (as described by Liu and Park) or prior experience (for example, an association between the grocery store and buying bread) may be necessary to create fully automatic retrieval. Clearly, much more work on this intriguing topic is warranted.

Efficient action initiation. In support of the assertion that implementation intentions produce reflexive, rapid initiation of the intention, Gollwitzer and Brandstatter (1997) observed how quickly subjects responded to racist remarks made by a confederate. Some subjects formed implementation intentions that included specification of good opportunities to make a response and particular counterarguments to the remarks. Other control subjects just identified good opportunities. The implementation subjects initiated their counterarguments more immediately upon presentation of the opportunities than did the control subjects.

The claim is that "implementation intentions create instant habit" (Gollwitzer, 1999, p. 499), such as pressing the gas pedal with no conscious intent when the light turns green. Aarts and Dijksterjuis (1999) contrasted the latency for initiation of an action after repeated and consistent performance of the action (formation of a habit) versus after formation of implementation intentions. In the habit-formation group, of course there was a speedup in action initiation. These fast latencies were matched by subjects who simply formed implementation intentions. The implication here is that forming implementation intentions produces an automatic initiation of the intended action that is not unlike that produced by a habit. We believe that this implication must be approached cautiously because, if implementation intentions mimic habits, one might expect to find no failures after forming implementation intentions. However, implementation intentions, though powerful, have not always produced perfect prospective memory in the studies reviewed above or in those typically conducted in the laboratory with specific cue-action pairs.

Individual Differences

Within the context of prospective memory, little is known about individual differences in planning intended actions. One study investigated plans that college students established for activities to be completed during the upcoming week (Marsh, Hicks, & Landau, 1998). A salient individual difference was that just over half of the students indicated using a daily planner to record their plans, whereas the other students did not use a planner. However, whether students used a planner or not, they indicated an approximately equal number of plans for commitments and appointments, intentions to study, and intentions to communicate with others. Also, use of a planner did not lower the rate of failures for completion of intended actions; regardless of planner use, students failed to complete about 25% of their plans.

What did differ was that students who used planners reported themselves to have poorer memory and concentration, and they performed more poorly on objective tests of memory and concentration than did students who did not use planners. Thus, planners may be used by individuals who believe that they will not remember to carry out their intentions unless they create external records of their plans. An interesting finding, however, is that those using planners thought about their intentions much less frequently throughout the week than those who did not use planners. Even though the number of intentions generated was equal with and without the use of planners, those using a daily planner thought about those plans three times a day fewer than those not using a planner. This correlation may suggest that recording intentions in a planner reduces the need to periodically review plans and intentions—that is, the act of recording the intention during planning is itself beneficial. The planner may not need to be subsequently consulted to ensure good prospective memory. More research on this possibility is clearly warranted.

Summary

In most laboratory prospective memory paradigms, the prospective memory task is quite constrained and embedded in a well-specified ongoing task. Consequently, in these paradigms, the planning and encoding processes that can occur in everyday prospective memory situations are excluded from study. Recently, a few studies have begun to examine planning processes in prospective memory by employing an unstructured laboratory task: the six-element task. Given that planning likely plays a critical role in everyday prospective memory, it is important to continue to develop laboratory paradigms for examining prospective memory planning processes. Fruitful paradigms might include tasks regarding which subjects have prior knowledge, such as cooking breakfast (see Craik & Bialystok's paradigm, 2006), and even manipulate the degree of prior knowledge subjects can bring to bear (Kliegel, Martin, McDaniel, & Phillips, in press). We believe it would also be profitable to continue examining how individual differences affect planning behaviors.

The most extensive research related to prospective memory encoding centers on implementation intentions. Forming implementation intentions to encode an intended action or goal can produce striking improvements in prospective memory performance. An attractive feature of this literature is that it includes a focus on many important health-related activities in naturalistic settings. The theoretical explanation of the effectiveness of implementation intentions suggests that relatively resource-free processes are involved in noticing the opportunity (event cues) to perform the intended action, triggering the intended action into awareness, and initiating the action. These provocative ideas await careful and thorough investigation, and more refined study of the functional components of implementation intentions is also needed.

7

Prospective Memory and Life Span Development

The developmental aspects of prospective memory have been studied for both the early stages of development—with children—and the later stages of development—with older adults. At both ends of the spectrum, a common assumption might be that prospective memory is relatively impaired. The research provides a somewhat different and in some cases surprising counterpoint to this assumption. We first examine the modest literature on children, then turn to the more extensive work with older adults.

Prospective Memory in Children

Even preschool-age children face prospective memory tasks such as remembering "to dress properly to go outside, to bring appropriate objects to games, to deliver messages, to carry out chores on a regular basis" (Meacham, 1982, p. 129). Some researchers have suggested that, more so than remembering in retrospective memory tasks, remembering to perform prospective memory tasks carries social rewards (Meacham,1982; Winograd, 1988). One could argue that these factors might stimulate rather rapid development of prospective memory skills (Kvavilashvili, Kyle, & Messer, in press). One avenue for examining this issue is to assess children's knowledge (metamemory) of prospective memory strategies.

In a seminal study, a survey was taken of children from four different grade levels: kindergarten (4 to 5 years), first grade (6 to 7 years), third grade (8 to 9 years), and fifth grade (10 to 11 years) (Kreutzer, Leonard, & Flavell, 1975). The children were prompted to think of and list strategies they could use to remember to take their skates to school the next morning, and strategies they could use to remember an upcoming event (for example, a friend's birthday). The responses revealed a range of strategies similar to those adults sometimes use (see Chapter 9). As displayed in Figure 7.1, two external strategies were mentioned: putting the skates in some visible location (by the door) and writing a note. The internal strategy of periodic rehearsal of the task was also listed (labeled "Self" in the figure), as was the

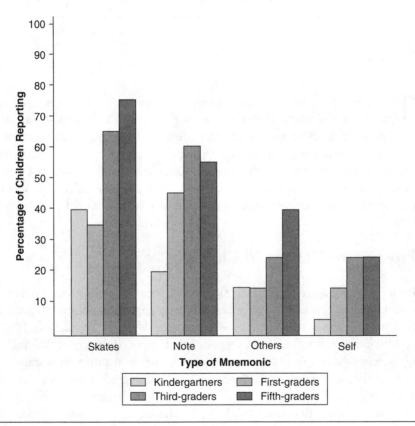

Figure 7.1   Percentage of Children in One Study Who Reported the Use of Different Types of Mnemonics

SOURCE: *The Development of Memory in Children* by Robert Kail. Copyright © 1979, 1994 by W. H. Freeman and Company. Used with permission.

strategy of asking others (a parent) to provide a reminder. These types of strategies were listed by every age group, though Figure 7.1 clearly indicates that the older children (third- and fifth-graders) listed more strategies and were more likely to mention each of the strategies than were the kindergarteners. Development of retrospective memory strategies in children displays a roughly similar pattern. By the third through fifth grades, children do recruit encoding strategies for trying to remember target material. By 7 years of age, using rehearsal to remember information emerges with some regularity, and more effective organizational strategies appear at about age 10 (fifth grade) (Kail, 1984). Therefore, these data do not compel us to conclude that prospective memory develops especially early on in children.

A related central question is whether children actually do marshal effective strategies for prospective memory. Time-based prospective memory tasks allow straightforward investigation of this question, because they tend to be dependent on strategic processes (see Chapter 2). Further, the strategic monitoring processes associated with time-based prospective memory (checking a clock) can be readily observed and recorded. In a now classic study, Ceci and Bronfenbrenner (1985) examined time-based prospective memory for 10- and 14-year-old boys and girls who were told to try to remember to take cookies out of the oven in 30 minutes or to remove a battery charger cable in 30 minutes. During the 30-minute interval, the children were encouraged to play a popular video game in another room, and were seated at the game with their backs to a clock. This allowed the researchers to clearly note the instances in which the children checked the clock.

For the most part, the children deployed strategic clock-monitoring strategies, with 10-year-olds showing patterns paralleling those of 14-year-olds. Further, the children showed varied strategies depending on the context in which the prospective memory task was presented. In one situation, the baking and battery-charging tasks were performed in the laboratory. Here, Ceci and Bronfenbrenner (1985) expected the children to be more anxious about performing the prospective memory task on time. To support good performance, many children increased the frequency of their monitoring as the target time approached. Kerns (2000) has reported a similar pattern of strategic monitoring for 7- to 12-year-old children.

In contrast, when the baking and battery-charging tasks were performed in each child's home with an older sibling conducting the experiment, the children adopted a strategy that maintained prospective memory performance and also freed up maximal time for playing the video game. Both 10- and 14-year-olds showed a U-shaped monitoring function. Monitoring started out at a moderate level, presumably for calibration of an internal clock, then decreased to very low levels until a period immediately preceding the target time. At this point, children substantially increased their rate of monitoring. These patterns indicate that children as young as 10 years of age can recruit strategic monitoring processes to meet their prospective memory objectives.

A handful of children (21 of 98) in Ceci and Bronfenbrenner's 1985 study displayed ineffective monitoring patterns, with frequency of monitoring progressively declining as the target time approached. These children also showed poor prospective memory performance. It is uncertain whether these children could not muster effective strategies or simply chose not to implement a more effective clock-checking strategy. Certainly, for younger children, the personal relevance of the task plays a major role in stimulating recruitment of effective strategies. For instance, when the prospective memory task is to remind a caretaker (typically the child's mother) to buy candy at the store (for the child) tomorrow morning, children (ages 2 to 4) show much higher levels of prospective memory performance (73% success with short delays of several minutes and 53% success with delays on the order of hours) than they do when the task is to remind the caretaker to bring in the washing after the nap (23% success with short delays and 17% success with longer delays) (Somerville, Wellman, & Cultice, 1983). There were remarkably high levels of prospective memory for tasks that were important to the children, even for those as young as 2 years of age (80% for short delays and 50% for longer delays).

Nevertheless, prospective memory dynamics begin to diverge across younger and older children. Several studies with event-based prospective memory tasks illustrate this general claim. One set of experiments found that the manner in which the prospective memory task was encoded differentially affected 7-year-old compared to 10-year-old children (Passolunghi, Brandimonte, & Cornoldi, 1995). The prospective memory task involved pressing a designated key when the word *boat* appeared in a list of words. In one encoding condition, the auditory instructions were supported by the presentation of a picture of a boat (visual encoding). In another encoding condition, auditory instructions were accompanied by practice at pressing the key (motor encoding).

Given the findings reviewed earlier on the relationship between enactment encoding and intention superiority (Freeman & Ellis, 2003), one might expect motor encoding to enhance prospective memory. Indeed, for 10-year-old children, remembering to respond substantially increased from 30% of the time after visual encoding to over 92% of the time with motor encoding. In contrast, for the 7-year-old children, visual encoding was substantially superior to motor encoding (resulting in remembering to respond over 50% of the time as opposed to 5% of the time). The researchers suggested that the 7-year-old children in the motor condition may have found it difficult to form an association between the prospective memory cue and the intended action. It is noteworthy that the 7-year-old children consistently outperformed the 10-year-olds in the visual encoding condition. To maximize prospective memory for children at these ages, communicating the intended activity at an age-appropriate level may be especially important.

Age 7 and Younger

At the outset, we raised the general issue of the extent to which even young children display strategic processes in prospective memory. There are only about half a dozen studies focusing on children younger than 7 years of age. With this limitation and the available findings in mind, we tentatively suggest that relevant strategic control processes for certain aspects of prospective memory performance have not been firmly established for children under 7. One such control process is effectively inhibiting the ongoing activity at the appropriate moment so that the intended action can be executed. In one condition, Kvavilashvili, Messer, and Ebdon (2001) obviated the need to interrupt the ongoing activity by placing the prospective memory target cue at a natural endpoint in the ongoing task. Children had to name stacks of pictures for Morris the Mole, because this mole did not see very well. The target picture for the prospective memory task (hide a particular picture from Morris) was placed either in the middle of each stack (interruption condition) or at the end of each stack (noninterruption condition). In the noninterruption condition, 5-year-olds performed the prospective memory task well (at almost 75%) and nearly at the level demonstrated by 7-year-old children (just over 75%). But when the ongoing activity had to be interrupted so the prospective memory task could be performed, the 5-year-olds' performance fell dramatically (to 25%).

In a study that more directly addressed strategic monitoring processes, Stokes, Pierroutsakos, and Einstein (2005) manipulated whether the prospective memory cue was focal or nonfocal to the ongoing activity (see Chapter 4 for a definition of focal and nonfocal cues). Following the general procedure of Kvavilashvili et al. (2001), 7- and 5-year-old children were given the task of naming a circled picture on a card on which three other pictures were also presented. The prospective memory task was to indicate when a picture of an animal appeared so that the experimenter could hide that card from Geoffrey the Giraffe, who was a bit afraid of other animals. For the children in the focal-cue condition, the target cue was the circled picture, and for the children in the nonfocal-cue condition, the cue was an uncircled picture.

According to the multiprocess theory (see Chapter 4), the nonfocal-cue but not the focal-cue condition should require strategic monitoring. Thus, if 5-year-old children have not developed certain strategic processes, they should show prospective memory declines primarily in the nonfocal-cue condition. Table 7.1 shows the prospective memory performance levels. As you can see, the substantial prospective memory decline for the 5-year-old children (relative to the 7-year-old children) with the nonfocal cue was significantly reduced when the prospective memory cue was focal. These patterns imply that children 5 years of age and younger have not developed strategic monitoring processes or do not have the attentional resources required to deploy these processes during engagement with ongoing activities. In a follow-up experiment performed by Stokes (unpublished), these results were replicated. Further, examinations of the speed of performing the ongoing task (measured only on nontarget trials) with and without a prospective memory task indicated that the older children but the not the younger children in the nonfocal condition slowed down when they were also performing a prospective memory task. This result strongly agrees with the interpretation that the 7-year-old children were strategically monitoring the cards for animals, whereas the 5-year-old children were not. Interestingly, performing a prospective memory task did not slow down ongoing-task responding in the focal condition.

Our analysis of prospective memory performances of younger children has focused on the joint consideration of (a) the degree to which successful prospective remembering requires strategic processes and (b) the degree to which the children have reached a level at which strategic processes (for

Table 7.1   Successful Prospective Memory (PM) Responses in Children in Several Experiments

Experiment	PM Condition	Correct Responses	
		5-Year-Olds	*7-Year-Olds*
Stokes, Pierroutsakos, & Einstein (2005)	Nonfocal	20%	92%
	Focal	67%	97%
McGann, Defeyter, Ellis, & Reid (2005)			
Experiment 1	Nonsalient	43%	73%
	Salient	61%	71%
Experiment 2	Nonsalient	49%	68%
	Salient	70%	60%

example, monitoring) have developed. In support of this analysis, McGann, Defeyter, Ellis, and Reid (2005, Experiment 1) had children, including 5- and 7-year-olds, name pictures. The prospective memory task was to help Rosie the Rag Doll collect food items for her picnic. Over the course of 80 picture-naming trials, four food items appeared as pictures, and the children had to remember to press a key to select that item for the picnic. The important manipulation was that food pictures were either presented in a salient fashion so that they stood out from the nonfood pictures (they were larger than the nonfood pictures) or were not salient (no size difference). In this experiment, salient but not nonsalient prospective memory targets should minimize the need for strategic monitoring, thus attenuating age differences in prospective memory performance. Confirming this expectation, prospective memory performance of 5-year-olds was significantly poorer than that of 7-year-olds when the target pictures were nonsalient but not when the pictures were salient (see Table 7.1).

A surprise, however, was that a second experiment showed no significant differences between the prospective memory performance of the 5-year-olds and that of the 7-year-olds, even when the targets were nonsalient (see Table 7.1). This result might be understood by noting that the ongoing activity was altered such that in addition to naming the pictures, the children sorted the pictures into categories. Now the prospective memory cue (a food item) was arguably focal to the ongoing activity of considering the category of each picture. Therefore, even for perceptually nonsalient pictures, prospective memory retrieval was not dependent on strategic processes, and 5-year-olds performed relatively well. Though other methodological differences between Experiments 1 and 2 and/or a lack of statistical power in Experiment 2 may have also contributed to the different age-related patterns (see Kvavilashvili et al., in press, for further details), at this point we believe that the multiprocess interpretation offers a fruitful direction for exploring variations in age-related differences in prospective memory in children.

Summary

Prospective memory research with children is only beginning to appear in the literature. The emerging developmental patterns, though admittedly preliminary, are consistent with the multiprocess framework (detailed in Chapter 4). Specifically, this theory acknowledges minimal involvement of strategic processes in some but not other prospective memory tasks and that children develop the capability for such strategic processes at a certain developmental level. Readers interested in a detailed review of this literature can consult Kvavilashvili et al. (in press).

Prospective Memory in Older Adults

Prospective memory has been studied most extensively with regard to its functioning in older adults (typically those over 60 years of age). Craik (1986) stimulated an early and abiding interest in examining prospective memory in older adults with his seminal framework on age-related memory deficits. Craik suggested that memory tasks could be ordered in terms of the amount of self-initiated processes required to retrieve the target information. Generally, the fewer the cues provided by the memory task, the more retrieval is dependent on processes initiated by the individual, such as generating possible cues, generating potential targets, and implementing any other strategies that will help bring the desired information to mind. For instance, as shown in Figure 7.2, recognition is considered to have low self-initiated retrieval demands, because the recognition task provides the target item. In this scheme, prospective memory is thought to have the highest self-initiated retrieval demands because not only is there an absence of cues, but also one has to remember to remember.

According to Craik's framework, because self-initiated retrieval presumably requires extensive processing resources and because processing resources decline with age, age-related deficits in memory should be a function of the amount of self-initiated retrieval required by the memory task. Because prospective memory is assumed to require the most self-initiated retrieval, this compelling theory makes the strong prediction that prospective memory tasks would be especially difficult for older adults. Let's see what the research shows.

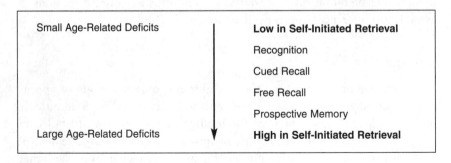

Figure 7.2   Self-Initiated Retrieval Processes

SOURCE: Adapted from Craik (1986).

Semi-Naturalistic Prospective Memory Tasks

One set of studies tested this idea in semi-naturalistic paradigms. Typically, subjects were instructed to telephone the experimenter at specified times over several days or to mail a postcard back to the laboratory on a certain day of the week for several weeks. As revealed in Table 7.2, these studies invariably found no deficit in prospective memory with age, and often reported better prospective memory for older than for younger adults. (See Rendell & Craik, 2000, Experiment 2, for another type of semi-naturalistic paradigm.) To determine the reasons for older adults' good prospective memory performance, some researchers asked subjects if they had used special strategies to help them remember the prospective memory task. Older adults usually indicated that they had implemented external cues, such as marking the scheduled times for calling the experimenter on a calendar (for example, see Moscovitch, 1982). In contrast, younger adults typically reported that they were confident about their ability to remember and thus had no need to implement an external cue. In some research, the experimenters asked older and younger adults not to use external aids, but even in this case, older adults persisted in using external aids and continued to outperform younger adults (Maylor, 1996; Moscovitch, 1982). Thus, in much of the semi-naturalistic research, the relatively good prospective memory performance of older adults likely has been due to their use of an external strategy. In terms of Craik's theory, the older adults were reducing their need for self-initiated retrieval.

In an attempt to circumvent this issue, Rendell and Thompson (1999) implemented complex time-based regimens designed to discourage the use of certain kinds of external cues. Also, Rendell and Craik (2000) explicitly prohibited the use of external aids. Older adults still consistently executed the prospective memory task significantly closer to the target time than did young adults. Nevertheless, it is not certain that older adults were absolutely prevented from using external cues. It is also uncertain that the pacing of ongoing activities was comparable for young and older adults.

To preclude older adults' use of external aids and strategies, many investigators have favored laboratory paradigms of prospective memory. Age effects have been examined with regard to both time-based and event-based prospective memory. The results regarding time-based prospective memory are more straightforward, and we turn to this topic first.

Time-Based Prospective Memory Tasks

As described in Chapter 2, in laboratory time-based tasks, subjects are given an ongoing activity to perform. For the prospective memory task,

Table 7.2   Prospective Memory (PM) Performance in Young and Older Adults in Semi-Naturalistic Experiments

Study	Experimental Condition or Segment	PM Task	Memory Aids Prohibited[a]	Memory Aids Used[b]		Percentage of Correct PM Responses	
				Young	Older	Young	Older
Devolder, Brigham, & Pressley (1990)	predict[c]	Call 8 times in 4 weeks[e]	no	no information	no information	56%	86%
	postdict[d]		no	no information	no information	57%	81%
Kvavilashvili & Fisher (2007)		Make a phone call at a particular time after 1 week	yes	no (except diary used to record all rehearsals)	no (except diary used to record all rehearsals)	68%	81%
Martin (1986)		Show up for appointments (last 8 years)	no	no information	no information	96%	99%
Patton & Meit (1993) Experiment 1		Return 4 postcards, each on a certain day	no	yes	yes	86%	100%
Patton & Meit (1993) Experiment 3		Return 4 postcards, each on a certain day	no	yes	yes	79%	100%

132

Study	Experimental Condition or Segment	PM Task	Memory Aids Prohibited[a]	Memory Aids Used[b] Young	Memory Aids Used[b] Older	Percentage of Correct PM Responses Young	Percentage of Correct PM Responses Older
Rendell & Craik (2000)[f]	regular[g]	Recite intended action into a recorder at certain points during the day[j]	yes	no	no	68%	83%
	irregular[h]		yes	no	no	51%	72%
	time[i]		yes	no	no	24%	36%
Rendell & Thompson (1993)	4 times	Press a button 4 times a day	no	no information	no information	44%	75%
	1 time	Press a button once a day	no	no information	no information	45%	77%
Rendell & Thompson (1999) Experiment 1[f]	same regular[k]	Press a series of keys on an organizer 4 times a day[i]	only for sequence of numbers entered in organizer	32%	20%	32%	67%
	same irregular[l]		no			40%	68%
	different regular[m]		no			36%	71%
	different irregular[n]		no			41%	69%
Rendell & Thompson (1999) Experiment 2	alarm[o]	Press a series of keys on an organizer 4 times a day[i]	no	yes	yes	60%	86%
	choice[p]		no	yes	yes	42%	78%

(Continued)

Table 7.2 (Continued)

[a]Indicates whether or not subjects were explicitly prohibited from using memory aids.

[b]Indicates whether or not subjects reported using memory aids.

[c]Subjects estimated what their scores on the ongoing retrospective memory task would be before they completed the task.

[d]Subjects estimated what their scores on the ongoing retrospective memory task had been after they completed the task.

[e]A response was considered correct if the participant called within 10 minutes of the appointment.

[f]These experiments included younger-old and older-old groups; older adult prospective memory performances reflect an average of the two groups.

[g]Intended actions were those that would happen the same way every day (e.g., taking medication).

[h]Intended actions were those that would change daily (e.g., calling the doctor at noon).

[i]In this condition, subjects did a time check after each of the irregular activities (e.g., 30 minutes after the first action).

[j]A response was considered correct if the participant performed the task within 5 minutes of the assigned time.

[k]Subjects were to press the button at regular intervals (every 4½ hours, starting at 8:00 A.M.) that were the same each day.

[l]Subjects were to press the button at irregular intervals (e.g., 4¼ hours, 3½ hours, and 4¾ hours) that were the same each day.

[m]Subjects were to press the button at regular intervals that differed each day.

[n]Subjects were to press the button at irregular intervals that differed each day.

[o]An alarm went off whenever the subject was supposed to press the button.

[p]Subjects chose the times for pressing the button to coordinate with regular daily events.

subjects are instructed to execute a particular action (such as press a key on the keyboard [d'Ydewalle et al., 1999]) after a particular amount of time (for example, 3 minutes or 5 minutes) has elapsed. This kind of task is akin to having to remember to take something out of the oven after a particular period of time. Typically, several prospective memory trials are implemented, as the subject is instructed to perform the designated action after a specified elapsed period of time several times over the course of the ongoing task. For instance, for an ongoing task lasting just over 20 minutes, the subject would be instructed to perform the prospective memory action at the 5-minute, 10-minute, 15-minute, and 20-minute marks of the ongoing task.

A key feature of these paradigms is that subjects must perform the prospective memory task without the advantages we sometimes have in everyday time-based tasks, such as using a timer or an alarm. Additionally, no clocks are in direct view and watches are removed from the subjects. Subjects can check a hidden clock, either by turning to view a clock placed behind them or by pressing a key on the keyboard to produce a brief display on the computer monitor. (As an aside, removing watches from the subjects places a prospective memory demand on the experimenter—remembering to return the watches to the subjects upon completion of the experiment. More than once, the experimenter—having missed the target cue—has ended up chasing one of the subjects out of the laboratory with the subject's watch in hand.)

Because no external cues are available to support prospective remembering in the time-based prospective memory paradigms, subjects must initiate retrieval of the intention in the absence of any environmental event signaling that the time is appropriate for performing the task. If subjects adopt a test-wait-test-exit strategy (see Chapter 2), they still must initiate retrieval of the intention to check the clock. Thus, at least in the laboratory, time-based prospective memory is heavily self-initiated, and thus robust age differences should be evident.

To measure accuracy of the prospective memory responses, a favored scoring procedure is to consider a prospective memory response on time if it occurs within a specified time window after the target time. The idea here is that if you remember to take the cookies out of the oven within, say, 15 seconds of the target time, you will be successful—that is, the cookies will not have burned. In an experiment performed by Einstein, McDaniel, Richardson, Guynn, and Cunfer (1995), responses were considered correct if they were within 1 minute of the target time, with the target time occurring every 5 minutes during an ongoing activity. Older adults (ranging in age from 61 to 76) were half as likely as younger adults to remember to perform the prospective memory activity. For middle-aged adults, those from 35 to 49, the news is better: They remembered to perform the prospective memory task at a high level. Using a much narrower response window (7 seconds), Park, Hertzog, Kidder, Morrell, and Mayhorn (1997) found similar significant declines in time-based prospective memory in older adults. Researchers who have examined a range of time windows have found no change in this pattern (see Park et al., 1997). Table 7.3 provides a more exhaustive summary of the published results. As you can see, in every case except one (Patton & Meit, 1993), older adults did show a decline in performance relative to younger adults. A meta-analysis of these effects confirms that the size of the age deficit is substantial (Henry, MacLeod, Phillips, & Crawford, 2004).

These results are consistent with the view that age-related declines in resources that support self-initiated retrieval underlie relatively poor time-based prospective memory performance for older adults. Note, however, that other interpretations are possible as well. One hypothesis is that older adults are less accurate in time estimation than are younger adults. The idea here is that older adults retrieve the prospective memory intention and remember to monitor a clock, but fail to do so in a timely fashion because of faulty time estimation. To test this idea, Mantyla and Carelli (2005) had subjects estimate stimulus durations of between 4 and 32 seconds. Time estimation errors increased for longer durations, but older adults were as accurate as middle-aged and younger adults on this task. Moreover, people's time estimation accuracy was at best weakly related to clock-monitoring performance in a time-based prospective memory task. That is, effective monitoring of time for a prospective memory task is not tied to time estimation accuracy, and moreover, time estimation accuracy does not appear to decline with age.

Effective monitoring of time does appear to decline with age, though. As discussed in Chapter 2, clock monitoring in a time-based prospective memory task typically reflects a strategic pattern, becoming significantly more frequent just prior to the target time (see Figure 2.2). It is important to note that this strategic monitoring pattern is not typically found with older adults. Older adults clearly monitor—indeed, they tend to monitor at least as frequently as younger adults in the intervals distal to the target time. But, as Figure 7.3 shows, in the interval just prior to the target time, older adults do not increase their monitoring frequency as do younger adults. It seems likely that the depressed monitoring just prior to the target time is the cause of older adults' less accurate performance on the time-based prospective memory task. What remains unclear is the reason that older adults exhibit less strategic monitoring. It could be that age-related deficits in self-initiated retrieval ability preclude older adults from increasing their monitoring. However, given that older adults monitor as frequently as younger adults at intervals distal to the target time, it may not be that older adults have problems with self-initiated retrieval of the intention to check the clock.

Table 7.3 Prospective Memory (PM) Performance in Laboratory Time-Based Experiments

Study	Experimental Condition or Segment	Significant Main Effect and/or Interaction	Ongoing Task	PM Task	PM Trials	PM Window	Correct PM Responses	
							Young	Older
d'Ydewalle, Luwel, & Brunfaut (1999)	questions	age, task	Answer trivia questions	Press a key at 4, 9, and 12 minutes	3	1 minute	87%	68%
	faces		Name famous faces	Press a key at 3, 8, and 10 minutes	3		97%	88%
Einstein, McDaniel, Richardson, Guynn, & Cunfer (1995) Experiment 1		age	Learn words presented on screen and recall last 10 words at unpredictable intervals	Press a button every 10 minutes	2	1 minute	83%[a] 100%[a]	50%[a] 75%[a]
Einstein, McDaniel, Richardson, Guynn, & Cunfer (1995) Experiment 3		age	Answer trivia questions	Press a button every 5 minutes	6	1 minute	65%	32%

(Continued)

137

Table 7.3 (Continued)

Study	Experimental Condition or Segment	Significant Main Effect and/or Interaction	Ongoing Task	PM Task	PM Trials	PM Window	Correct PM Responses	
							Young	Older
Martin & Schumann-Hengsteler (2001)	low complexity[b]	age, complexity, age by complexity	Play Mastermind and record protocol	Change protocol sheet every 3 minutes	6	+/- 90 seconds	92%	67%
	medium complexity[c]				6		75%	50%
	high complexity[d]				6		65%	2%
Park, Hertzog, Kidder, Morrell, & Mayhorn (1997) Experiment 2		age	Monitor words and recall last three at unpredictable intervals	Press a button every 1 or 2 minutes	6 or 12[e]	+/- 1 second	81%	40%
						+/- 3 seconds	89%	62%
						+/- 9 seconds	95%	79%
Patton & Meit (1993) Experiment 1		no main effect	Watch a video	Turn video off after 30 minutes	1		26.33[f]	20.35[f]

[a]This study examined performance on each trial separately.

[b]Easy game of Mastermind.

[c]Moderately difficult game of Mastermind.

[d]Difficult game of Mastermind.

[e]This study only reported means collapsed across these two trial densities.

[f]Given means indicate the amount of time in seconds that passed after the target time before the PM task was executed.

This observation leaves open the possibility that age-related deficits in laboratory time-based prospective memory task performance are related to ineffective monitoring strategies adopted by older adults.

Understanding the factors that influence monitoring behavior may well be a key in explaining the remarkable discrepancy between the robust age deficits seen in laboratory time-based prospective memory tasks and the absence of age deficits seen in semi-naturalistic time-based prospective memory tasks. Earlier we noted that semi-naturalistic studies allow older adults to engineer external reminders for time-based tasks (for instance, a shoe placed by the telephone as a reminder to call the experimenter), thereby obviating the need for extensive self-initiated retrieval or monitoring. Yet some semi-naturalistic studies take care to preclude the use of intentional external reminders, and older adults still perform as well or better than young adults (Rendell & Thompson, 1999; Rendell & Craik, 2000). To reconcile the disparate findings across laboratory and semi-naturalistic paradigms, Kvavilashvili and Fisher (2007) proposed an intriguing alternative to the assumption that time-based prospective memory relies heavily on self-initiated retrieval.

Kvavilashvili and Fisher's (2007) major premise is that outside the laboratory, between the formation of the intention and the time to perform the intention, there are chance encounters with cues that stimulate retrieval of

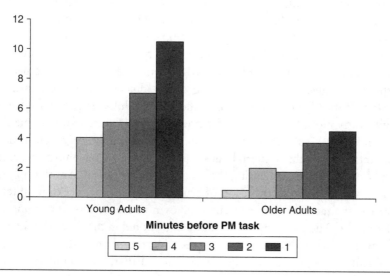

Figure 7.3   Clock Monitoring in Time-Based Prospective Memory in an Experiment Performed by Einstein, McDaniel, Richardson, Guynn, and Cunfer (1995)

the time-based intention. For instance, a week before your mother's birthday, you decide to call her on Monday between 11:00 A.M. and 1:00 P.M. (when she'll be home for lunch). During the week, you might encounter someone talking about a birthday, see a gift being wrapped at a store, or simply look at the telephone. These chance encounters may remind you that you intend to call your mother on her birthday, producing further rehearsal of the intention, which in turn may promote more spontaneous retrieval of the intention with subsequent cues and more frequent checking to see if the appropriate time (or date) is at hand. According to this formulation, in everyday contexts where ongoing activities allow encounters with cues relevant to the intention, even time-based prospective memory hinges on relatively spontaneous retrieval and rehearsal rather than predominantly on self-initiated retrieval (see also Rabbit, 1996). Because spontaneous retrieval appears to be unimpaired in older adults (McDaniel, Einstein, & Rendell, in press), this perspective provides a straightforward explanation of why older adults' time-based prospective memory performance outside the laboratory is not impaired relative to that of young adults.

To obtain evidence for their view, Kvavilashvili and Fisher (2007, Study 2) gave young and older adults a typical semi-naturalistic prospective memory task with a new twist. Subjects were instructed in the laboratory on a Monday that they were to try to remember to call the experimenter the next Sunday at an appointed time. The novel aspect of this study was that during the retention interval, subjects made an entry in a diary whenever the intended action came to mind. The entry included the place where the reminder occurred, the activity in which the subject was engaged, accompanying thoughts, and any evident external cues. The typical pattern for prospective memory performance in a semi-naturalistic setting was obtained: 81% of the older adults remembered to telephone on time, whereas 68% of the young adults telephoned on time.

More critically, for both young and older adults, reminders occurred significantly more frequently in the presence of a chance external cue than they did as a result of an incidental internal thought or a self-initiated plan–related thought. External cues included seeing a telephone, hearing a telephone ring, or even hearing the word *memory* spoken. Another notable finding was that the distribution of remindings over the weeklong interval reflected the familiar J-shaped curve (shown in Figure 7.4) for young and older adults. The frequency of reminders (as noted in the diaries) evidenced an upward scallop as the time for executing the phone call became more imminent. Kvavilashvili and Fisher speculated that, as reminders activate the intention, thereby fostering rehearsal of the prospective memory task, the representation of the intention and the designated time gains higher levels of activation. The higher activation further sensitizes the individual to encounters with cues as the week progresses, producing more spontaneous retrievals of the intention.

Note that in laboratory time-based tasks, the opportunity for chance encounters with environmental cues is minimized by a single, circumscribed ongoing activity. In further research, it will be important to examine whether semi-naturalistic contexts provide environmental support (sufficient chance cues) for a variety of time-based prospective memory tasks or whether the telephone-calling task used by Kvavilashvili and Fisher was especially well suited for this process (because, for example, the external cues—telephones and telephone ringing—are ubiquitous in our society). For instance, semi-naturalistic time-based tasks involving remembering to do something after a relatively brief period of elapsed time may prove more problematic for older adults than for young adults because there is limited opportunity for chance encounters with related cues. An example is remembering to take cookies out of the oven in 12 minutes. During this interval, it seems unlikely that the person's ongoing activity will produce encounters with related cues (especially if he or she leaves the kitchen), and accordingly, older adults may evidence impaired prospective remembering.

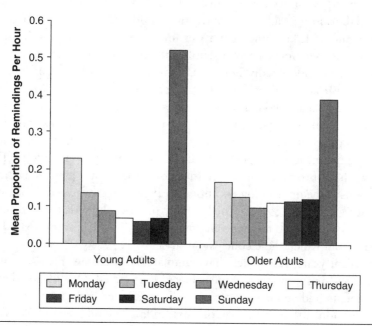

Figure 7.4   Distribution of Remindings in a Weeklong Study Conducted by Kvavilashvili and Fisher (2007)

SOURCE: From Kvaviliashvili, L. (2005, July). *Automatic or Controlled? Rehearsal and Event-Based Prospective Memory Tasks.* 2nd International Prospective Memory Conference. Zurich, Switzerland. Used with permission.

Another possible explanation for the good time-based prospective memory performance evidenced by older adults, however, is that in semi-naturalistic settings older adults have more control over the pace of ongoing activities and therefore have more resources available for internally initiated reminders or monitoring (see discussion of an experiment performed by McDaniel et al. [in press] later in this chapter). More work is needed to follow up these possible explanations, but for now they offer some possibilities for reconciling the opposing age-related patterns in laboratory versus semi-naturalistic time-based prospective memory tasks.

Event-Based Prospective Memory Tasks

The age-related patterns in event-based prospective memory mirror those in the time-based prospective memory literature: Taken as a whole, laboratory event-based tasks but not semi-naturalistic event-based tasks find substantial declines in prospective memory performance in older adults relative to young adults (Henry et al., 2004). But an additional intriguing puzzle emerges for event-based tasks. Table 7.4 summarizes over 80 event-based laboratory conditions contrasting young adults' and older adults' performances. Take a moment to examine the pattern of results to see whether the experiments reveal significant age-related differences.

What you undoubtedly noticed is that a number of experiments have found significant declines for older adults relative to younger adults, reinforcing the conclusion held by some researchers that "prospective memory failure generally increases with age" (Craik, 2003, p. 13). Yet you probably also noticed that some experiments have found equivalent or not significantly different levels of performance for older and younger adults. These findings have prompted the alternative conclusion that "prospective memory seems to be an exciting exception to typical age-related decrements in memory" (Einstein & McDaniel, 1990, p. 724). How can we reconcile these conclusions and the opposing findings from the laboratory-based paradigms from which these conclusions arise?

In recent years, researchers have animatedly discussed this issue among themselves, and a number of ideas have been offered. One idea is that the experiments finding no age differences have sampled more highly functioning older adults than have experiments finding age differences. Consistent with this idea, Cherry and LeCompte (1999) found that older adults with relatively high working-memory capacity exhibited prospective memory performance at levels equal to those of younger adults, whereas older adults with low working-memory capacity showed significantly worse prospective memory than did the younger adults. Another provocative idea rests on the

(Text continues on page 157)

Table 7.4   Prospective Memory (PM) Performance in Younger and Older Adults in Event-Based Laboratory Experiments

Study	Experimental Condition or Segment	Significant Main Effect and/or Interaction	Ongoing Task	PM Task	PM Task Type	PM Trials	Correct PM Responses	
							Young	Older
Cherry & LeCompte (1999)	low ability[a]	low/high ability	Recall words from a list	Press button when target word appears	focal	6	65%	40%
	high ability[b]				focal	6	68%	69%
Cherry et al. (2001) Experiment 1	specific	age, specificity	Recall words from a list	Press button when target word appears	focal	3	90%	50%
	generic			Press button when target category appears	nonfocal	3	54%	29%
Cherry et al. (2001) Experiment 2	specific	specificity	Recall words from a list	Press button when target word appears	focal	3	53%	62%
	generic			Press button when target category appears	nonfocal	3	43%	27%
Cherry et al. (2001) Experiment 3	typical specific[c]	age, specificity	Recall words from a list	Press button when target word appears	focal	3	86%	61%
	typical generic[d]			Press button when target category appears	nonfocal	3	67%	44%

(Continued)

Table 7.4 (Continued)

Study	Experimental Condition or Segment	Significant Main Effect and/or Interaction	Ongoing Task	PM Task	PM Task Type	PM Trials	Correct PM Responses Young	Correct PM Responses Older
	atypical specific[e]			Press button when target word appears	focal	3	78%	75%
	atypical generic[f]			Press button when target category appears	nonfocal	3	44%	28%
Cohen, West, & Craik (2001) Experiment 1	related[g]	extent of relatedness, age by extent of relatedness	After studying picture-word pairs, give word when shown picture	State intended action (could not actually be performed in the laboratory)	focal	24	92%	78%
	unrelated[h]				focal	24	73%	52%
Cohen, West, & Craik (2001) Experiment 2	related pair[i]	format, extent of relatedness, age, format by age	After studying picture-word pairs, give word when shown picture	State intended actions paired with either picture-word pairs or just words	focal	24	96%	85%
	related word[j]				focal	24	74%	54%
	unrelated pair[k]				focal	24	91%	83%
	unrelated word[l]				focal	24	73%	34%

Study	Experimental Condition or Segment	Significant Main Effect and/or Interaction	Ongoing Task	PM Task	PM Task Type	PM Trials	Correct PM Responses	
							Young	Older
d'Ydewalle, Luwel, & Brunfaut (1999)	questions	age, task	Answer trivia questions	Circle item number if question is about a certain topic	focal	3	81%	42%
	faces		Name famous faces	Circle item number if face belongs to a man wearing a bow tie	nonfocal	3	92%	73%
Einstein & McDaniel (1990) Experiment 1	external aid[m]	external aid	Recall words from a list	Press button when target word appears	focal	3	83%	69%
	no external aid[n]			Press button when target word appears	focal	3	47%	47%
Einstein & McDaniel (1990) Experiment 2	familiar words	familiarity	Recall words from a list	Press button when target word appears	focal	3	28%	36%
	unfamiliar words				focal	3	83%	94%

(Continued)

Table 7.4 (Continued)

Study	Experimental Condition or Segment	Significant Main Effect and/or Interaction	Ongoing Task	PM Task	PM Task Type	PM Trials	Correct PM Responses	
							Young	Older
Einstein, Holland, McDaniel, & Guynn (1992) Experiment 1	short delay,° one target word	number of target items, age, age by number	Recall words from a list	Press button when target word appears	focal	3	58%	53%
	short delay,° four target words			Press button when any of four target words appears	focal	3	58%[p]	19%[p]
	long delay,° one target word			Press button when target word appears	focal	3	42%	61%
	long delay,° four target words			Press button when any of four target words appears	focal	3	47%[p]	11%[p]
Einstein, Holland, McDaniel, & Guynn (1992) Experiment 2		age	Recall words from a list	Press button when any of four target words appears	focal	3	53%[p]	14%[p]

Study	Experimental Condition or Segment	Significant Main Effect and/or Interaction	Ongoing Task	PM Task	PM Task Type	PM Trials	Correct PM Responses	
							Young	Older
Einstein, McDaniel, Richardson, Guynn, & Cunfer (1995) Experiment 2	specific	specificity	Learn words presented on screen and recall last 10 words at unpredictable intervals	Press button when target word appears	focal	8	85%	83%
	general			Press button when target category appears	nonfocal	8	56%	47%
Einstein, McDaniel, Richardson, Guynn, & Cunfer (1995) Experiment 3		no age main effect	Answer trivia questions	Press button when target word appears	focal	6	93%	86%
Einstein, Smith, McDaniel, & Shaw (1997) Experiment 1	high demand	age, demand	Rate words and detect specific digits among other digits	Press button when target word (a word which has appeared in yellow previously) reappears	focal	3	58%[p]	25%[p]
	low demand		Rate words		focal	3	71%	53%

(Continued)

Table 7.4 (Continued)

Study	Experimental Condition or Segment	Significant Main Effect and/or Interaction	Ongoing Task	PM Task	PM Task Type	PM Trials	Correct PM Responses	
							Young	Older
Einstein, Smith, McDaniel, & Shaw (1997) Experiment 2	high R/low E[q]	age, demand at encoding, demand at retrieval	Rate words only (low demand) or rate words and also detect specific digits among other digits (high demand)	Press button when target word (a word which has appeared in yellow previously) reappears	focal	3	64%[p]	38%[p]
	low R/high E[q]				focal	3	47%[p]	54%[p]
	high R/high E[q]				focal	3	55%[p]	17%[p]
	low R/low E[q]				focal	3	66%	58%
Kidder, Park, Hertzog, & Morrell (1997)	2 words[r]/ 1 target background	age, number of words (demands of ongoing task), age by number of words[s]	Recall words from a list	Press button when target background appears	nonfocal	6	98%	98%
	2 words[r]/ 3 target backgrounds			Press button when any of three target backgrounds appears	nonfocal	6	97%	85%
	3 words[r]/ 1 target background			Press button when target background appears	nonfocal	6	82%	69%
	3 words[r]/ 3 target backgrounds			Press button when any of three target backgrounds appears	nonfocal	6	90%	63%

Study	Experimental Condition or Segment	Significant Main Effect and/or Interaction	Ongoing Task	PM Task	PM Task Type	PM Trials	Correct PM Responses	
							Young	Older
Mantyla (1993)	typical,[t] primed[u]	age, typicality, priming, age by typicality by priming	Perform cued recall using subject-generated associates as cues	Draw X on any page containing word(s) from one of four categories	nonfocal	8	85%[p]	75%[p]
	atypical,[t] not primed[u]				nonfocal	8	80%[p]	50%[p]
	atypical,[t] primed[u]				nonfocal	8	80%[p]	30%[p]
	atypical,[t] not primed[u]				nonfocal	8	47%[p]	25%[p]
Mantyla (1994)	typical[t]	age, typicality, age by typicality	Perform cued recall using subject-generated associates as cues	Draw X on any page containing word(s) from one of four categories	nonfocal	16	79%[p]	65%[p]
	atypical[t]				nonfocal	16	65%[p]	26%[p]
Marsh, Hicks, & Cook (2006) Experiment 1		no age main effect	Decide which category each given word belongs to	Press button when target word appears	nonfocal	8	62%	62%

(Continued)

Table 7.4 (Continued)

Study	Experimental Condition or Segment	Significant Main Effect and/or Interaction	Ongoing Task	PM Task	PM Task Type	PM Trials	Correct PM Responses Young	Older
Marsh, Hicks, & Cook (2006) Experiment 2		no age main effect	Decide which category each given word belongs to	Press button when target word appears	nonfocal	8	55%	63%
Maylor (1993)	Block 1	age, block, age by block	Name faces	Circle slide number if face is wearing glasses; cross out slide if face is smoking	nonfocal	2	80%	67%
	Block 2				nonfocal	2	83%	66%
	Block 3				nonfocal	2	88%	69%
	Block 4				nonfocal	2	93%	70%
Maylor (1996)	Block 1	age	Name faces	Circle slide number if face is wearing glasses; cross out slide if face is smoking	nonfocal	2	57%	26%
	Block 2				nonfocal	2	65%	25%
	Block 3				nonfocal	2	67%	27%
	Block 4				nonfocal	2	60%	28%

Study	Experimental Condition or Segment	Significant Main Effect and/or Interaction	Ongoing Task	PM Task	PM Task Type	PM Trials	Correct PM Responses	
							Young	Older
Maylor (1998)	Block 1	age, block	Name faces	Circle slide number if face is wearing glasses; cross out slide if face is smoking	nonfocal	2	68%	30%
	Block 2				nonfocal	2	75%	25%
	Block 3				nonfocal	2	80%	28%
	Block 4				nonfocal	2	88%	32%
McDaniel, Einstein, & Rendell (in press) Experiment 1	focal	focality	Give occupation of person whose face is pictured	Circle slide number if face belongs to a politician	focal	8	88%	84%
	nonfocal			Circle slide number if face is wearing glasses	nonfocal	8	45%	40%
McDaniel, Einstein, & Rendell (in press) Experiment 2	focal	focality	Decide which category each given word belongs to	Press button when target word appears	focal	4	92%	90%
	nonfocal			Press button when target syllable appears	nonfocal	4	64%	52%

(Continued)

Table 7.4 (Continued)

Study	Experimental Condition or Segment	Significant Main Effect and/or Interaction	Ongoing Task	PM Task	PM Task Type	PM Trials	Correct PM Responses	
							Young	Older
Park, Hertzog, Kidder, Morrell, & Mayhorn (1997)	6 trials	age	Monitor words presented on changing backgrounds and recall last three words at unpredictable intervals	Press button when target background appears	nonfocal	6	94%	71%
	12 trials				nonfocal	12	92%	87%
Rendell, McDaniel, Forbes, & Einstein (in press) Experiment 1	focal	age, focality, age by focality	Name famous faces	Circle slide number if face belongs to a person named John	focal	8	90%	78%
	nonfocal			Circle slide number if face is wearing glasses	nonfocal	8	87%	55%
Rendell, McDaniel, Forbes, & Einstein (in press) Experiment 2	standard task	age by task	Name famous faces	Circle slide number if face is wearing glasses	nonfocal	8	78%	40%
	simple task		Guess ages of faces		nonfocal	8	73%	70%

152

Study	Experimental Condition or Segment	Significant Main Effect and/or Interaction	Ongoing Task	PM Task	PM Task Type	PM Trials	Correct PM Responses	
							Young	Older
	slow task		Name famous faces (pictures stay on screen longer)		nonfocal	8	64%	70%
Tombaugh, Grandmaison, & Schmidt (1995)		age	Work on LAMB tests	When a designated word or phrase has been encountered, say it out loud	focal	6	87%	60%
Vogels, Dekker, Brouwer, & de Jong (2002)	letters block 1	block	Read aloud letters appearing on one side of screen	Remember to use +/- (which appears occasionally) to determine which side to read	indeterminate	12	81%[p]	81%[p]
	letters block 2						91%[p]	88%[p]
	letters block 3						94%[p]	97%[p]
	word	age	Press specific button depending on category of each given word pair	Press button if words are of same letter case or appear in same color	nonfocal	20	94%	68%

(Continued)

Table 7.4 (Continued)

Study	Experimental Condition or Segment	Significant Main Effect and/or Interaction	Ongoing Task	PM Task	PM Task Type	PM Trials	Correct PM Responses	
							Young	Older
	picture	age	Press specific button depending on category of each given picture	Press button when target object appears	indeterminate	35	84%[p]	69%[p]
	letter strings, feedback for prospective memory responses	no age main effect	Press button when certain letters appear	Press button if any letter appears three times in a row	indeterminate	8	88%[p]	87%[p]
	letter strings, no feedback for prospective memory responses	no age main effect			indeterminate	8	84%[p]	87%[p]

Study	Experimental Condition or Segment	Significant Main Effect and/or Interaction	Ongoing Task	PM Task	PM Task Type	PM Trials	Correct PM Responses	
							Young	Older
West & Craik (1999)		age	Press specific button depending on category of each given word pair	Press button if words are of same letter case or appear in same color	nonfocal	40	95%	79%
West, Herndon, & Crewdson (2001)		age	Press a button if word pairs are related; press a different button if word pairs are unrelated	Press button if both words are capitalized	nonfocal	40	95%	83%

(Continued)

Table 7.4 (Continued)

[a]Subjects had low educational levels and verbal ability.

[b]Subjects had high educational levels and verbal ability.

[c]Target cue was a well-known word.

[d]Target cue was any word in a given category, but only the third-most-common exemplar from the category was presented.

[e]Target cue was a less frequently used word.

[f]Target cue was any word in a given category, but only the fifteenth-most-common exemplar from the category was presented.

[g]Target action was related to the picture cue.

[h]Target action was unrelated to the picture cue.

[i]Target cue was a picture-word pair related to the target action.

[j]Target cue was a word related to the target action.

[k]Target cue was a picture-word pair unrelated to the target action.

[l]Target cue was a word unrelated to the target action.

[m]Subjects were allowed to create their own reminders for the prospective memory task.

[n]Subjects were not allowed any external reminders for the prospective memory task.

[o]*Delay* indicates the interval between the instructions and the beginning of the prospective memory task.

[p]Data were not included in the focal versus nonfocal analyses (see Chapter 7).

[q]R indicates demand at retrieval; E indicates demand at encoding.

[r]Subjects were to recall the indicated number of last words presented.

[s]This interaction just failed to meet standard levels of significance ($p = .06$).

[t]*Typical* indicates that the target was a typical exemplar of a given category; *atypical* indicates that the target was a less typical exemplar of a given category.

[u]*Primed* indicates that the category serving as the prospective memory target had been used by subjects, prior to the ongoing activity, in an exemplar-generation task

observation that, when tested at their optimal time of day but not at their nonoptimal time of day, older adults often perform memory tasks as well as young adults (Intons-Peterson, Rocchi, West, McLellan, & Hackney, 1998; May, Hasher, & Stoltzfus, 1993). There is some evidence that prospective memory performance varies across the day (Leirer, Tanke, & Morrow, 1994; Wilkins & Baddeley, 1978). Perhaps experiments finding no age differences in prospective memory performance have tended to test older adults at their optimal time of day (mornings), whereas experiments finding age differences have tested them at their nonoptimal times (Maylor, 2005). These ideas merit consideration, but three explanations for the disparate age-related patterns seem most compelling:

Prospective memory difficulty and age differences. One explanation is based on the long-standing idea that age differences in cognitive performance are a function of the difficulty of the cognitive task. For present purposes, the idea is that age differences in event-based prospective memory become more prominent as the prospective memory task becomes more difficult. A more specific variant of this idea is that easier prospective memory tasks are associated with ceiling effects, which precludes the emergence of age differences (Uttl, 2005). A way to evaluate the difficulty of tasks and the plausibility of the ceiling-effect explanations is to correlate the age difference in prospective memory performance with the level of performance of the older adults across experiments. A significant negative correlation would be consistent with these explanations. Using a set of 133 experimental conditions, Uttl reported a correlation of −0.64. We computed the correlation using the set of experiments shown in Table 7.4, and also obtained a significant negative correlation (−0.67). These relatively high correlations lend currency to the interpretation that diverging age differences in event-based prospective memory are related to the difficulty of the prospective memory task. Easier tasks may either not be subject to age differences or simply not reveal age differences because of ceiling effects.

Yet the correlations may not provide a complete explanation of the varied age-related patterns. Inspect Table 7.4 again, and you will see there were several experiments in which subjects remembered to make the prospective memory response just over 50% of the time, yet age differences were not found (Einstein, Holland, McDaniel, & Guynn, 1992; Einstein et al., 1995, Experiment 2). Even when prospective memory performance dropped below 50%, there were instances when older adults perform as well as younger adults (Einstein & McDaniel, 1990, Experiments 1 and 2). In these experiments, performance is not at ceiling, nor is the prospective memory task particularly easy (as determined empirically by levels of performance). These findings stimulate another explanation for varied age effects in event-based prospective memory, an explanation based on the multiprocess theory and findings presented in Chapter 4.

The multiprocess theory and age differences. Recall that according to the multiprocess theory, prospective memory retrieval can be accomplished by resource-demanding self-initiated processes (for example, monitoring) or by relatively spontaneous retrieval processes that demand few resources. According to this view, age differences are expected in performance of event-based tasks in which resource-demanding self-initiated processes are engaged. Age differences are not expected when spontaneous retrieval is prominent in supporting prospective remembering.

Certainly there are a number of factors that influence whether event-based prospective memory will require self-initiated processes (monitoring) versus more spontaneous or reflexive retrieval processes. Characteristics of the target event itself are undoubtedly important. For instance, as the target event becomes more frequent, retrieval may become more reflexive. In line with this idea, Vogels, Dekker, Brouwer, and de Jong (2002) reported no age differences in an experiment with frequently occurring target events, but they did report age differences in an experiment in which the target event was infrequent. Another apparently important characteristic of target events is the number of them. For instance, as noted above, Einstein et al. (1992) found no age differences despite relatively low prospective memory performance (53% to 61%); in these conditions, the intended action was to be performed upon the occurrence of one particular target word. In the other conditions, the intended action was to be performed upon the occurrence of any one of four words, and here substantial age differences appeared.

A more stringent evaluation of the fruitfulness of the multiprocess explanation is based on its prediction that the relationship of the target event to the ongoing task is a prominent factor in determining age effects in event-based prospective memory (McDaniel & Einstein, 2000). As described in Chapter 4, the target event can be focal to the processing engaged by the ongoing task. That is, the anticipated features of the target event are the very features that are processed because of the ongoing activity. An example of a situation involving a focal cue would be one where you encounter and pause to converse with the friend to whom you intended to give a message (see Table 4.1 for other examples). Here, the friend's physical features, name, and so on are likely activated when you intend to give her a message, and when you encounter her later on, these features are likely activated as part of the encounter. With focal cues, prospective memory retrieval is posited to be spontaneous (Einstein et al., 2005; see also Chapter 4), and thus age differences are not expected.

In contrast, processing of the target event may be nonfocal to the processing required by the ongoing task. In this case, the features of the target event are not activated by the ongoing activity. An example of a nonfocal cue would be a grocery store (at which you intended to buy bread) located a bit off the road when you are traveling in rush hour traffic. With nonfocal target cues, resource-demanding processes such as monitoring are assumed to be required, and for these cues, age differences are expected. Another way to phrase these ideas is within the transfer-appropriate processing terminology from retrospective memory research (for example, Morris, Bransford, & Franks, 1977; Roediger, Weldon, & Challis, 1989). Within this framework, age differences in prospective memory are attenuated as the degree of overlap increases between the type of information processing required by the ongoing task and the processing needed to identify the critical features of the prospective memory target cue (Maylor, Darby, Logie, Della Sala, & Smith, 2002).

To help evaluate the multiprocess explanation, Table 7.4 provides for each experiment a description of the ongoing task, the prospective memory target event, and our determination of whether the target event is focal or nonfocal to the ongoing task. Because cognitive theories are incomplete regarding how items are processed for certain tasks, for a few experiments we were not confident in making a designation. Those experiments are given the designation *Indeterminate*. Consistent with the multiprocess analysis, the magnitude of age-related differences is linked to whether the target event is focal or nonfocal to the ongoing activity. The average age-related difference in prospective remembering was nearly twice as large when cues were nonfocal (23%) as it was when cues were focal (12%)—a statistically significant difference. A similar analysis by Henry et al. (2004) classified the event-based laboratory prospective memory studies into those that seemed to impose higher levels of controlled strategic demand and those that were supported by more spontaneous processes. Henry et al. found that the prospective memory tasks they associated with higher strategic demand showed large age-related decline, whereas the tasks thought to be supported by more spontaneous processes showed minimal age-related decline.

Could it be that focal prospective memory tasks simply produced higher levels of performance than did the nonfocal tasks? If so, the patterns just discussed might still be interpreted within the difficulty explanation presented above. This possibility is ruled out by inspecting the performance dynamics of the focal and nonfocal experiments in Table 7.4. The average prospective memory performances for older adults across focal and nonfocal tasks were nearly identical (65% for focal tasks and 59% for nonfocal tasks). Further, the ranges of performance were virtually the same (36% to 94% for focal tasks and 27% to 98% for nonfocal tasks). In sum, the older adults' performances show a remarkably similar topography of difficulty across experiments with focal and nonfocal cues, yet the age-related differences are reduced when the cues are focal.

In a direct experimental test of the multiprocess view, Rendell, McDaniel, Forbes, and Einstein (in press, Experiment 1) manipulated whether the target event was focal or nonfocal. The ongoing task required subjects to identify the names of a set of famous faces and to write the name of each face on a separate page (which was marked with the appropriate slide number) in a booklet. In the focal-cue condition, younger and older adults were instructed to remember to circle the number of any slide featuring a person with the first name John. In the nonfocal-cue condition, the younger and older adults were instructed to remember to circle the slide number whenever a face wearing glasses appeared. The same faces served as target cues in both conditions. The prospective memory responses are displayed in Figure 7.5, and they mimic the cross-experimental comparisons described above. Age-related differences with the focal "John" cue were slight (though significant) and significantly reduced relative to those with the nonfocal glasses cue.

Resource demands emerge as age-related costs to the ongoing activity. A third explanation for the absence of age-related effects in some event-based prospective memory experiments rests on the observation that older adults might maintain prospective memory by sacrificing performance on the ongoing activity (cf. Smith & Bayen, 2006). In some experiments, older adults perform as well as younger adults on both the prospective memory task (when cues are focal) and the ongoing task, but these patterns may not be conclusive because the ongoing activity was made somewhat easier for the older adults than it was for the younger adults (for example, see Einstein & McDaniel, 1990; Einstein et al., 1995). The rationale for this methodology is that if older adults have declining cognitive resources, these resources would be disproportionately utilized for the ongoing activity, leaving fewer resources for the older adults than for the younger adults for the prospective memory activity. But perhaps the adjustment for the ongoing activity in these experiments more than compensated for older adults' declining resources. Because of these arguments, most existing data do not satisfactorily address this third explanation of the divergent age-related findings.

To more convincingly evaluate this third explanation, McDaniel et al. (in press) measured the baseline performance of the ongoing activity for the younger and older subjects when there were no prospective memory demands. They used a category decision activity that was sensitive to response speed and in which accuracy was high. Of central interest was whether the older adults' response speed would suffer relative to that of the younger adults when the prospective memory task was embedded in the ongoing activity. Performance was examined both when the cue was focal (a particular target word) and when it was nonfocal (a particular syllable contained in the words presented for the category decision). As it turned out, prospective memory performance was equivalent for older adults relative to younger adults in both the focal- and nonfocal-cue conditions. Did older adults sacrifice their speed of performing the ongoing activity to meet the resource demands of the prospective memory task?

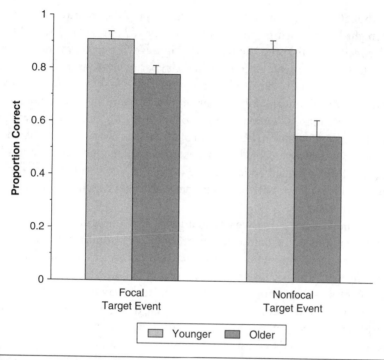

Figure 7.5   Prospective Memory Responses in an Experiment Performed by Rendell, McDaniel, Forbes, and Einstein (in press)

SOURCE: From Rendell, P., McDaniel, M., Forbes, and Einstein (in press). Age-related effects in prospective memory are modulated by ongoing task complexity and relation to target cue. *Aging, Neuropsychology, and Cognition.*

In the focal-cue condition, neither the younger nor the older adults showed significant increases in response times for the category decisions when the prospective memory task was added. On the other hand, in the nonfocal-cue condition, both age groups showed significant slowdowns. Of central importance, the older adults showed more exaggerated slowdown than did the younger adults, suggesting that with nonfocal cues the older adults were disproportionately sacrificing ongoing-task performance to maintain prospective memory at levels equivalent to those achieved by the young adults. Taken in concert, these patterns are entirely in line with the multiprocess analysis. Event-based prospective memory seems to demand minimal resources for retrieval when the target event is focal to the ongoing activity (see also Chapter 4), and accordingly, age-related differences are minimal. In contrast, when the target event is nonfocal, retrieval is relatively resource demanding, and age-related differences emerge either in prospective memory performance or in performance of the ongoing activity, or possibly both.

Although we argue here that the data support the multiprocess theory, you might be troubled by the results summarized earlier in Table 7.4 and the Rendell et al. (in press) finding (see Figure 7.5) that on average there is still at least a modest age difference in the experiments that used a focal cue. If prospective memory retrieval on an event-based task with focal targets is completely the result of spontaneous processes, there should be no age differences. One reasonable explanation of the age differences starts with the view that spontaneous retrieval is a probabilistic process in that when a target item is focally perceived, it will sometimes, but not always, lead to retrieval of the intended action. Therefore, some young-adult subjects may augment this process with a monitoring process, which should improve prospective memory.

A second but not exclusive explanation is that the spontaneous retrieval process may indeed be completely spared in older adults and that the age-related decrement may reflect postretrieval difficulties experienced by older adults. Specifically, because the pacing of the ongoing task is usually fixed and equal for younger and older adults, this task may be functionally more demanding for older adults. Therefore, even though the intended actions may be spontaneously retrieved when the target item is processed, high ongoing-task demands could interfere with selecting and acting upon the intention while it is still active in working memory. Further research is needed to evaluate these possible explanations.

Do It or Lose It: When Responding Is Delayed After Prospective Memory Retrieval

Consider the story that has been circulating on the Internet about the typical day of an older adult:

This is how it goes: I decide to wash the car; I start toward the garage and notice the mail on the table. OK, I'm going to wash the car. But first, I'm going to go through the mail. I lay the keys down on the desk, discard the junk mail, and I notice the trash can is full. OK, I will just put the bills on the desk and take the trash can out, but since I'm going to be near the mailbox anyway, I'll pay the bills first. Now where is my checkbook? Oops, there's only one check left. My extra checks are in my desk. Oh, there is the Coke that I was drinking. I am going to look for those checks. But first I need to put my Coke further away from the computer—oh, maybe I'll pop it into the fridge to keep it cold for a while. I head toward the kitchen and my flowers catch my eye; they need some water. I set the Coke on the counter and uh-oh! There are my glasses. I was looking for them all morning! I better put them away first. End of day: The car isn't washed, the bills aren't paid, the Coke is sitting on the kitchen counter, the flowers are half watered, and the checkbook still only has one check in it.

This humorous story underscores that immediate performance of an intention is not always carried out in everyday situations, perhaps especially for older adults. Yet standard prospective memory laboratory tasks generally allow performance of the intended action immediately upon cue presentation. In other words, subjects are instructed to press the designated response key as soon as the target item occurs. In contrast, in everyday prospective memory situations, performance of a retrieved intended action is often briefly delayed. For example, upon seeing your neighbor, you remember that you need to give that neighbor a message. But the neighbor is in the middle of a conversation with another person, and politeness dictates that you delay delivering the message until there is a pause in the conversation. Or, when you are in your bedroom you retrieve the intention to take your medication, but you must delay taking the medication until you walk to the kitchen to get the medicine bottle.

How does age affect performance in these delayed-execute situations? The above vignette captures the idea that as a person ages, he or she may become more distractible or less able to inhibit irrelevant or competing information (Hasher & Zacks, 1988). Also, there is theoretical and empirical work suggesting that keeping current concerns activated is a core function of working memory (Engle, Tuholski, Laughlin, & Conway, 1999), and working-memory resources have been shown to decline with age (Park et al., 2002; Salthouse, 1991). All of these considerations suggest that brief delays may be very problematic for older adults. On the other hand, the delays are often very brief, a matter of seconds, and such brief delays may not be very challenging for younger or older adults. How do older adults fare when the execution of a retrieved intended action must be briefly delayed?

To answer this question, Einstein, McDaniel, Manzi, Cochran, and Baker (2000) developed a delayed-execute laboratory paradigm that is schematized in Figure 7.6. Subjects read a series of short, three-sentence paragraphs. Following each paragraph were a series of tasks. First, several synonym items were presented, followed by several trivia questions. After the trivia questions, a comprehension question about the paragraph just read was presented. For the prospective memory task, subjects were instructed to press a designated key (the F1 key) whenever they encountered a particular target word in the paragraphs. The target word was always presented in capital letters so that it was a very salient cue. In an immediate-execute condition (in which the action was to be performed immediately upon presentation of the target word), performance was nearly perfect for both young and older adults. Thus, as intended, the salient cue produced virtually perfect retrieval.

The critical conditions were those in which subjects were instructed to delay executing the intended action until they encountered the first trivia question. By manipulation of the number of synonym questions presented, the delay between presentation of the cue and the trivia questions was

---

- Cover Task: Story Comprehension
  - Read three sentences about an event
  - Perform a synonym task
  - Answer two unrelated trivia questions
  - Answer multiple-choice comprehension question

- Prospective Memory Task
  - Immediate: Whenever you see *TECHNIQUE* or *SYSTEM,* press the F1 key
  - Delayed: Whenever you see *TECHNIQUE* or *SYSTEM,* press the F1 key **but not until you begin answering the trivia questions (delay varies from 5 to 40 seconds)**

Figure 7.6   A Delayed-Execute Laboratory Paradigm

SOURCE: From Einstein, McDaniel, Manzi, Cochran, and Baker (2000).

varied. In a series of experiments, Einstein, McDaniel, and their colleagues (Einstein et al., 2000; McDaniel, Einstein, Stout, & Morgan, 2003) showed that older adults display robust and dramatic declines in performance on this task. With delays as brief as 5 seconds (the time it takes to answer one intervening synonym question), older adults remembered to execute the action less than half the time, a substantial drop relative to their immediate-execute performance levels. Younger adults did not show a substantial decline; even with 15-second delays (answering three synonym questions), their performance was correct more than 80% of the time.

Remarkably, the low level of performance for older adults occurred even when the 5-second delay was not filled with any distracter activity (McDaniel et al., 2003) (see Figure 7.7). Again, this low level of performance for older adults was in sharp contrast to younger adults' performance. Younger adults responded nearly 90% of the time after the 5-second unfilled delay. The implication from these findings is that brief delays preceding the opportunity for execution pose serious problems for older adults, apparently causing more difficulty than initial retrieval of the prospective memory intention (especially for focal target events).

At this point, we do not have a clear understanding of why older adults have problems maintaining intentions for 5 to 30 seconds. One possibility is that older adults are less aware of the fleeting nature of passively stored information (a metamemory problem). Consistent with this possibility, the study performed by McDaniel et al. (2003) showed that older adults who were instructed to rehearse the intended activity over the brief delay improved their prospective memory performance (see Figure 7.7). However, these older adults still did not achieve the performance levels displayed by younger adults who had not been so instructed. Perhaps reduction in working-memory resources with age produces difficulty in maintaining the activation of retrieved

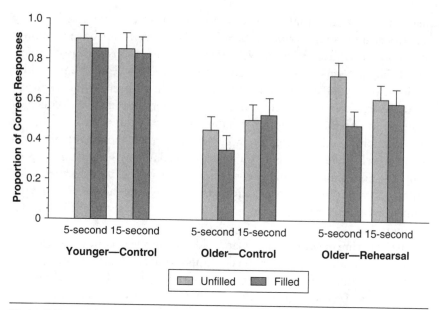

Figure 7.7   Proportion of Correct Responses in an Experiment Performed by McDaniel, Einstein, Stout, and Morgan (2003)

intentions. Compromised working-memory ability could create difficulties in maintaining rehearsal while performing other activities. But this may not be the whole story either, because with unfilled 5-second delays older adults still displayed a dramatic decline in performance relative to younger adults. Perhaps reduced inhibition, even during unfilled delays, allows unrelated thoughts to distract older adults (see Yoon, May, & Hasher, 2005). Still another idea is that in the delayed-execute situations, older adults have difficulty reformulating their plans once the intention cannot be carried out at that moment. For instance, if while in the bathroom a person forms the intention to take his vitamins, but then he is interrupted by a brief phone call that he must answer in the kitchen, he may not be able to reformulate the plan so that once he gets off the phone he will return to the bathroom to take his vitamins. Regardless of the factors responsible for older adults' prospective memory declines, in delayed-execute situations you might advise your grandparent (as well as yourself) to "do it or lose it" upon retrieving an intention.

Habitual Prospective Memory Tasks

A type of task that has received little attention in the experimental literature but seems to be prevalent in daily activity is the habitual prospective memory task. In habitual prospective memory tasks, the intended activity is performed on a regular or systematic basis. Older adults have a number of important habitual prospective memory tasks, perhaps the most prominent being adherence to a medication regimen. On a regular basis, older adults also may have to remember to monitor their physical status (if they are diabetic, for instance) and also remember more mundane tasks such as paying bills. As the task becomes habitual, the possibility of forgetting it may be minimized; however, a new challenge of remembering whether you actually performed the activity on a particular day may become more pronounced. For example, you likely remember that you need to take your multiple vitamin in the morning, but as you leave the house you may be confused about whether you really took it while you were in the bathroom that morning.

One experiment with younger and older adults was conducted using a laboratory paradigm that attempted to approximate a habitual prospective memory situation. In this experiment, participants performed eleven 3-minute tasks. To keep subjects especially busy, there was also a secondary task of detecting odd digits in an ongoing audio stream. The prospective memory action was to press a designated key about 30 seconds into each task (Einstein, McDaniel, Smith, & Shaw, 1998). After each trial (task), to promote more habitual performance of the prospective memory task, subjects were asked whether they had remembered to perform the prospective task. The prospective memory task became more habitual over the course of the experiment, as evidenced by high levels of performance in both younger and older adults after the initial trials. However, as the trials progressed, a new kind of error emerged for older adults. As the prospective memory task became more habitual, older adults demonstrated increasing repetition errors, whereas younger adults demonstrated very low levels of repetition errors (see Figure 7.8). That is, older adults could not remember whether or not they had performed the activity, and consequently often repeated the activity.

It should be noted that older adults' repetition errors were substantially reduced in a condition in which the secondary digit detection task was not included. From this initial experiment, we can provisionally conclude that under very demanding ongoing activity in which older adults' resources are occupied, output monitoring of habitual prospective memory actions may be compromised (see Marsh, Hicks, Cook, & Mayhorn, in press, for additional evidence on older adults' output monitoring in prospective memory). For tasks such as medication taking, it can be critical to avoid repetition (overmedication) or omission (undermedication). Using external cues (for example, pillboxes) to monitor daily execution of these tasks seems to be a prudent step.

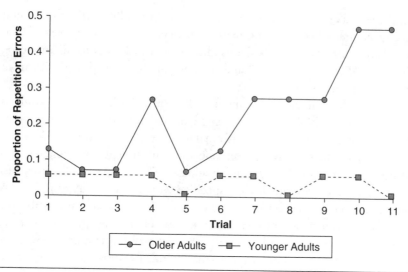

Figure 7.8   Repetition Errors in Prospective Memory Performance When Subjects' Attention to the Ongoing Task Was Divided in an Experiment Performed by Einstein, McDaniel, Smith, and Shaw (1998)

Prospective Memory Performance as a Possible Index of Risk for Dementia

Prospective memory's relationship to dementia is of interest for several reasons. First, prospective memory difficulties may be especially worrisome for adults with Alzheimer's disease, and pose a frustrating challenge for their caretakers (see, for example, Camp, Foss, Stevens, & O'Hanlon, 1996). In Chapter 9, we will discuss some practical techniques for improving prospective memory (see also Chapter 5). Second, prospective memory may be especially sensitive to the mildest forms of dementia, and prospective memory performance may even provide an early warning signal of the onset of Alzheimer's disease in older adults. It is with this second tantalizing possibility that we conclude this chapter.

A variant (allele) of the apolipoprotein E (apo E) gene is associated with Alzheimer's dementia (AD). The presence of just one e4 allele of the apo E gene confers an estimated fourfold risk of developing AD, as well as a risk of developing it at an earlier age (see Small, Rosnick, Fratiglioni, & Bäckman, 2004). One issue of interest in recent years is the extent to which exaggerated memory decline might be evidenced in older apo E e4 carriers who as yet do not display AD. Existing work on memory impairment in nondemented apo E e4 carriers has found mixed results, with general trends suggesting limited e4-related impairments in episodic memory performance (small effect sizes) on standard episodic memory tasks like recall and recognition (Small et al., 2004). Would the pattern change if prospective memory performance were assessed?

Driscoll, McDaniel, and Guynn (2005) tested older adults, some of whom were apo E e4 carriers and some of whom were not, on a standard laboratory event-based prospective memory task. The ongoing task was to rate characteristics of words on one of four dimensions (concreteness, pleasantness, meaningfulness, and vividness). The prospective memory task was to remember to write down a specified word if a particular target word appeared. To minimize retrospective memory demands so that possible retrospective memory impairments would not cloud interpretation of the results, in the critical conditions the response word was highly associated with the target word. For instance, the intended responses for the targets *SPAGHETTI* and *STEEPLE* were *sauce* and *church,* respectively. Postexperimental testing verified that 100% of the e4 carriers (as well as the noncarriers) remembered the intended response for the target word.

Like the normally aging adults in the experiments reviewed earlier in this chapter, the noncarriers displayed good prospective memory performance, correctly responding on 85% of the three trials. In sharp contrast, the apo E e4 carriers remembered to respond on only 25% of the trials. Further, 70% of the carriers failed to respond on any of the prospective memory trials, whereas just 12% of the noncarriers failed to respond on any of the trials.

Were the carriers already in the early stages of Alzheimer's disease? If so, the prospective memory decline was the only behavioral marker that Driscoll et al. (2005) observed that showed a significant difference between the two groups of older adults. The groups did not significantly differ in performance on various cognitive tests that can show decline with AD: the modified mini-mental state exam, recall, Color Trails A and B, and clock drawing. The provocative possibility is that a simple laboratory prospective memory task could become an important diagnostic marker for early detection of AD.

Research by Duchek, Balota, and Cortese (2006) converges with this interpretation. They found a precipitous decline in performance on an event-based prospective memory task (different from the one used by Driscoll et al. [2005]) in older adults diagnosed with early-stage AD relative to normally aging older adults. Moreover, prospective memory performance explained a significant amount of variance in categorizing older adults as either nondiseased or affected by AD, and was a single potent predictor of the disease. Thus, prospective memory could be a unique and valuable cognitive marker fostering earlier detection and treatment of pathological cognitive decline in older adults. Certainly, the results obtained in Driscoll et al.'s and Duchek et al.'s (2006) experiments suggest exciting directions for future research.

Summary and Observations

Some of the earliest theoretical work in prospective memory suggested robust age-related decline in prospective memory based on the assumption that prospective memory retrieval depends heavily on self-initiated retrieval (Craik, 1986). A relatively active research literature on this topic has emerged since the appearance of this important theoretical assertion. Surprisingly, the empirical results are mixed, fueling much debate concerning the inevitability of age-related decline in prospective memory. Some of the mixed findings seem understandable if one notes that prospective memory tasks can vary in their demands. At least in the laboratory, time-based prospective memory tasks appear to rely heavily on self-initiated processes (see Hicks, Marsh, & Cook, 2005, for a different view). Here there are consistent age-related declines. In contrast, some event-based prospective memory tasks appear to support relatively spontaneous retrieval, and age-related differences do not necessarily emerge under these conditions. Much exciting theoretical debate is emerging as researchers attempt to explain these results.

Given the laboratory findings, perhaps more puzzling is the absence or even reversal of age-related deficits in prospective memory in semi-naturalistic studies. Even when experiments are designed to produce close parallels between laboratory and natural settings, the age-related declines found in the laboratory setting are eliminated in natural settings (Rendell & Craik, 2000). We anticipate that richer and more nuanced conceptual frameworks will develop as researchers continue to pursue understanding of prospective memory and aging.

The concerted interest in prospective memory and aging has stimulated consideration of age-related effects on prospective memory processes in addition to retrieval of the intention. New laboratory paradigms have been developed to assess performance of a retrieved intended action when its execution must be very briefly delayed. Age-related declines appear to be substantial when a retrieved intention must be briefly maintained before execution (McDaniel et al., 2003). Additional issues come to the fore in habitual prospective memory tasks, tasks that are centrally important to older adults (for example, medication taking). Habitual prospective memory introduces demands for accurate output monitoring. In the laboratory, under distracting conditions, older adults appear to misremember having performed a habitual task and therefore may repeat the activity (Einstein, Smith, McDaniel, & Shaw, 1997). These initial findings suggest that investigation of older adults' prospective memory in everyday contexts might fruitfully address situations that require delayed execution of retrieved intentions and output monitoring for habitual prospective memory tasks. An experience one of our colleagues had with his older relative illustrates the potentially powerful influence of output monitoring illusions on prospective memory behaviors. The relative strongly claimed she had taken her daily medication even when she was shown the pill remaining in the pillbox. Thus, though external memory aids are available to facilitate adherence to a medication regimen, age-related changes in memory processes may not be entirely neutralized. Also, preliminary work hints that prospective memory declines could serve to signal aspects of pathological aging. Many of these themes are sure to receive increased attention in the next generation of prospective memory and aging work.

We close with two general thoughts. First, as should be clear from the research described in this chapter, the question of whether age (at either the younger or the older end of the spectrum) affects prospective memory is too simplistic. Given that different processes are likely to be more or less important in the wide variety of prospective memory tasks, we believe it is more fruitful to uncover those processes that are and that are not affected by age and then to understand those prospective memory situations that are and that are not especially difficult for very young and older individuals.

Second, we believe it is important to come to grips with the methodological difficulty of studying developmental changes in prospective memory. Given that variables such as the perceived importance of the prospective memory task have been shown to affect prospective memory, it is important to equate these over age groups. What is seen as an interesting and important task for a 5-year-old may not be so for a 7-year-old. Also, in the aging literature, researchers tend to use a fixed presentation rate. Given the well-documented cognitive slowing that occurs with age (see, for example, Salthouse, 1991), the ongoing task may be functionally more demanding for older adults (see Einstein et al., 1997, for a discussion of this issue). In light of these concerns, we recommend getting as much information as possible from subjects about their views of the prospective memory task (for example, the perceived importance of the task). We also recommend that researchers use a self-paced procedure for the ongoing task and measure the speed of performing the ongoing task both with and without the presence of a prospective memory task. This will enable younger and older subjects to proceed at their own pace, and allow the researchers to determine the extent to which either group is trading performance on the ongoing task for higher prospective memory performance (or vice versa). Of course, other factors merit consideration as well, such as the time of day that is optimal for older versus younger adults.

8

Cognitive Neuroscience of Prospective Memory

A s the field of prospective memory has gained wider attention in the memory and cognition literature, researchers in the related area of cognitive neuroscience have started to turn their attention to prospective memory. We will organize our discussion of this emerging work based on the methodologies used to gain insights into the neurological underpinnings of prospective memory. The three general approaches are neuropsychological, functional neuroimaging, and electrophysiological (ERPs).

The Neuropsychology of Prospective Memory

Case Studies

A long-standing neuropsychological method is to examine individual cases who have sustained brain damage from injury, vascular syndromes, disease, or surgical lesions (for example, from tumor excision). In terms of prospective memory, based on the idea presented in previous chapters that prospective memory involves planning, self-initiated retrieval, monitoring, and interruption of ongoing activity, the frontal area of the brain appears to be a good candidate for supporting prospective memory. Accordingly, several studies have examined the performance of individuals with frontal lobe damage (caused by either closed or open head injuries) on tasks involving prospective memory.

In a well-known seminal study, Shallice and Burgess (1991) gave three patients with injury to frontal structures a subgoal scheduling task in which six open-ended tasks (two sets of arithmetic problems, two routes to dictate, and two sets of pictures of objects to name) had to be performed within a time limit. The catch was that the six tasks could not be completed in the 15 minutes allotted. To achieve the highest score, subjects had to work on every one of the six tasks but not complete any task (because there was not enough time). An additional constraint was that similar sets could not be performed consecutively (see Chapter 6 for further description of the six-element task). Subjects could consult a stopwatch to monitor their time. Presumably, effective performance on this task required the formation of intentions regarding the sequence in which the tasks would be performed and how much time would be spent (or how many problems or pictures would be completed) on each subtask. Further, the intentions had to be activated at appropriate moments, and the ongoing subtask had to be interrupted to allow subjects to switch to another subtask. As we have discussed, these are all components of prospective memory.

The patients showed great impairment in their performance of this six-element task compared to a control group without brain injury. Controls attempted 5.7 out of 6 subtasks on average, whereas the patients tended to tackle about 3 subtasks. Also, the longest amount of time spent on any one subtask was greater for the patients (from 6 to 10 minutes) than it was for the controls (5 minutes and 20 seconds on average).

Thus, patients perseverated on a few subtasks and had trouble interrupting a subtask to move on to another task. Based on these results, as well as those from another multiple-subgoal scheduling task performed by the patients and controls, Shallice and Burgess (1991) suggested that the patients could not reactivate previously generated intentions after a delay—in other words, the patients had a fundamental deficit in prospective memory. By implication, then, prospective memory functioning is subserved by frontal structures, and more particularly by a Supervisory System (see Chapter 2) intimately related to frontal function.

However, as pointed out in Chapter 6, this version of the six-element task does not allow separation of several components of prospective memory: intention formation (the actual plans generated by the patient); retrieval (or reactivation) of these intentions during performance of the various subtasks; and the processes required to inhibit and interrupt the ongoing subtask so that another subtask can be initiated. Specifically, it remains unclear from Shallice and Burgess's (1991) data whether frontal systems are specifically involved in reactivation of previously formed intentions or whether they are instead (or additionally) involved in intention formation and planning (which would also produce deficits in performance of the multiple subgoal tasks) and in inhibition of ongoing activity (both of these processes are also thought to be served by frontal systems).

One clue indicating that frontal systems are involved in intention formation comes from an experiment with schizophrenic patients, some of whom had executive-function impairments (perhaps associated with dopamine abnormalities in the frontal system) and some of whom did not (Kondel, 2002). The intention superiority effect (higher activation of encoded intentions—see Chapter 5) was disrupted in those schizophrenics who had executive system impairments but not in those whose executive performance had been spared. To the extent that the intention superiority effect is tied to processes engaged during intention formation (see Freeman & Ellis, 2003), this finding suggests an association between frontally-subserved executive systems and intention formation.

A case study involving three patients with frontal damage from closed head injuries attempted to isolate planning abilities per se from prospective memory performance (Bisiacchi, 1996). Planning abilities were assessed with a standard errand-planning task in which the subjects were given a map of a town and asked to plan to complete as many of 10 assigned errands as possible, using the shortest route. The prospective memory task reflected the typical event-based laboratory task in which the experimenter specifies both the intended activity (write a cross on a list at the end of each experimental task) and the event that signals the moment when the intended activity is to be executed (the experimenter's statement, "Now the task is finished"). Thus, unlike the six-element task used by Shallice and Burgess (1991), this prospective memory task required minimal planning activities (see Chapter 6 for more discussion on this point).

The results suggested that planning components are served by frontal subsystems separable from those that underlie retrieval of an intended action and its subsequent execution (that is, interruption of the ongoing activity and initiation of the intended action). One patient scored within normal ranges on the planning task but failed to perform the prospective memory task on any of the prospective memory trials. It seems unlikely that the problem was a retrospective memory failure (forgetting what action to perform), because the patient performed within normal ranges on a number of short- and long-term retrospective memory tasks. In sharp contrast, another patient performed poorly on the planning task but remembered to perform the prospective memory task on every trial. (The third patient showed a more generalized deficit, performing poorly on the planning, prospective memory, and retrospective memory tasks.) Because the sample was so small, one cannot draw strong conclusions from this study. However, the pattern suggests that different subsystems in the prefrontal structure may each support different components of prospective memory.

This hypothesis was examined in a large-scale study with 60 patients who had circumscribed cerebral lesions and 60 age- and IQ-matched controls. In this study, Burgess, Veitch, de Lacy Costello, and Shallice (2000) used a modified version of the six-element task described above. Important, this version required subjects to plan how they intended to do the six-element task prior to actually performing it. Thus, the researchers gained separate measures of planning and of initiation of the intended actions. Performance on each measure was indeed associated with distinct subsystems in the prefrontal cortex. Planning was impaired in subjects with lesions in the right dorsolateral frontal area, whereas initiation of the intended actions was impaired in subjects with lesions in the left frontal lobe region related to a particular area specified as Brodmann area 10. Brodmann area 10 will surface again when we examine the neuroimaging findings for prospective memory.

An even more complicated neuropsychological framework of prospective memory that involves the hippocampus can be sketched (see, for example, Cohen & O'Reilly, 1996). The hippocampus is strongly implicated in the formation and retrieval of memories. According to one view, the hippocampus supports an associative retrieval process that reflexively delivers information in long-term memory to awareness in the presence of a sufficiently strong cue (Moscovitch, 1994). As described in Chapters 3 and 4, such a reflexive retrieval process could be centrally involved in prospective memory retrieval, in addition to frontal processes that are necessary for inhibiting and interrupting ongoing activity and initiating execution of retrieved intentions.

Initial support for the involvement of temporal lobe structures (for example, the hippocampus and related areas) in prospective memory was reported in a study that tested 13 patients who had surgical lesions in their left temporal lobes from treatment of epilepsy (Palmer & McDonald, 2000). These patients and 12 controls matched on age and education levels were given eight laboratory prospective memory tasks. Performance was evaluated on two components: remembering at the appropriate moment that an action should be performed and remembering the intended action itself. The patients with the temporal lobe lesions showed significant impairments in prospective memory on both components relative to their matched controls. In comparison, another group of 12 patients with stroke-related damage in their prefrontal structures showed less comprehensive prospective memory impairment relative to their own group of matched controls. Clearly, both temporal lobe (probably hippocampal structures) and prefrontal lobe neuropsychological systems play a role in prospective memory. Most readers will likely not find this claim to be particularly controversial, as our consideration of the complexity of prospective memory leads one to expect involvement of processes related to both frontal and hippocampal structures. The more controversial issue is specifying the particular interplay of these structures in supporting prospective memory. To begin to address this issue, we next examine empirical work using another neuropsychological method, then sketch a provisional theoretical framework.

Neuropsychological Assessment of Normal Aging

With normal aging, some cerebral areas decline in functioning, with the degree of decline and the areas of decline varying across individuals. By testing normal older adults on a battery of appropriate neuropsychological tests, researchers can make inferences regarding the particular cerebral areas that are in decline in particular individuals and then evaluate the contribution of such decline to performance on the particular memory/cognitive tasks of interest to the researcher (see Glisky, Polster, & Routhieaux, 1995, for an excellent example of this methodology). McDaniel, Glisky, Rubin, Guynn, and Routhieaux (1999) adopted this methodology to evaluate the contribution of frontal and hippocampal structures to prospective memory. Older adults between the ages of 66 and 85 years were first given several neuropsychological tests selected to assess frontal functioning and several other neuropsychological tests selected to assess hippocampal functioning. Based on these assessments, four groups of older adults were formed: those with high frontal and high hippocampal function, those with high frontal and low hippocampal function, those with low frontal and high hippocampal function, and those with low frontal and low hippocampal function. That is, McDaniel et al. conducted an experiment in which frontal function (high versus low) and hippocampal function (high versus low) were factorially combined. Of interest was whether prospective memory performance would be influenced by frontal function, hippocampal function, or both.

There were eight event-based prospective memory trials. Table 8.1 shows the mean proportion of trials on which subjects remembered to respond. Clearly, frontal function affected prospective memory performance; older adults with low frontal function performed at about half the level of those with high frontal function. One can also see a prospective memory decline for subjects with low hippocampal function relative to those with high hippocampal function, although this decline was not statistically significant (likely due to low power to detect a significant difference). Although we caution that neuropsychological tests do not precisely reflect functioning of the particular brain regions inferred, these results and those from the study described in the last section provide converging evidence for the idea that prospective memory is supported by a combination of frontal and hippocampal processes.

Table 8.1   Prospective Memory Performance as a Function of
              Neuropsychological Condition in an Experiment Performed by
              McDaniel, Glisky, Rubin, Guynn, and Routhieaux (1999)

	High Frontal Function	Low Frontal Function
High Hippocampal Function	81% (N = 11)	45% (N = 10)
Low Hippocampal Function	62% (N = 10)	30% (N = 10)

NOTE: N indicates number of subjects in each condition.

Given the available evidence, the less penetrable issue is specifying the particular components of prospective memory that are served by these different structures. As discussed above, any of several components might be associated with the frontal system. One prominent idea is that the frontal system is involved in monitoring the environment for the target event that signals the appropriateness of performing the intended action (Burgess & Shallice, 1997). To gain leverage on this possibility, McDaniel et al. (1999) manipulated the salience of the prospective memory cue in their experiment. For the low-salience condition, the target word appeared in normal type; for the high-salience condition, the target word was highlighted with boldface type (whereas none of the other words was in boldface).

McDaniel et al. (1999) reasoned that the nonsalient cues would place more demands on monitoring and therefore would be more likely to produce prospective memory deficits if monitoring was compromised. Thus, if the frontal involvement in prospective memory performance shown in Table 8.1 was related to monitoring processes, subjects with high frontal function (who should be able to monitor well) would be expected to show less variation in performance as a function of cue salience than would subjects with low frontal function. For subjects with low frontal function, their presumed impairment in monitoring would be especially damaging to prospective memory when the cues were not salient. Contrary to this prediction, these subjects actually showed somewhat less decline for the nonsalient cues than did subjects with high frontal function. Relative to highly salient cues, nonsalient cues produced a 15% decline in prospective memory for subjects with low frontal function and a 21% decline for those with high frontal function. This result favors the interpretation that frontal processes were not involved in monitoring and reactivation of the intention and instead were involved in other components of the prospective memory task.

A Provisional Neuropsychological Theory

We suggest that the interrelationship of frontal and hippocampal systems in prospective memory may be as follows: Frontally-mediated processes are instrumental in constructing a plan of how one will accomplish an intended action in the future. The planning activates representations of the anticipated events, landmarks (or people), and activities that will be present when the action is intended to be executed. Hippocampal processes are involved in creating the distinct episodic associations that represent the specific intended action bound with particular anticipated events (Cohen & O'Reilly, 1996). When these events, landmarks, or activities are encountered at a later point, the intended action is activated (or retrieved) by hippocampal processes. Finally, after the intention is retrieved, the frontal processes must again be involved to maintain the ongoing goals in working memory (goals associated with the ongoing activity and the intended action) (Kimberg & Farah, 1993), organize the sequence in which the responses will be executed (Petrides & Milner, 1982), and interrupt the ongoing activity (Shallice & Burgess, 1991). Figure 8.1 provides a schematic of this framework.

As an illustration, consider having breakfast and finding there is no orange juice in the refrigerator. To remedy this situation, your frontal processes

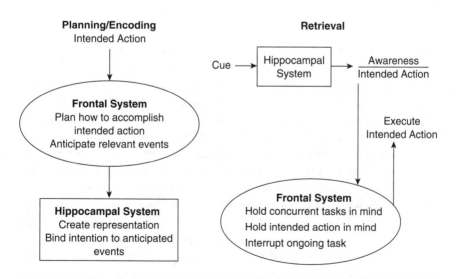

Figure 8.1   A Provisional Scheme of Frontal and Hippocampal Involvement in Prospective Memory

become engaged to plan a stop at the grocery store for orange juice on your way home from work that evening. This plan may activate representations of the grocery store as well as environmental landmarks near the grocery store, such as the gas station across the street and the stone wall you come to just before you reach the grocery store. Perhaps even global contextual aspects of the environment are anticipated and activated, such as the dull light of dusk at the end of the workday. Because you are thirsty at the moment, features of thirst may also be active. Because these representations are all activated coincidentally with the intention to buy orange juice, hippocampal processes bind these activated representations together into an associative-episodic trace.

Upon your return home from work at the end of the day, any one of these cues (representations) associated with the intention to buy orange juice might elicit memory of the intention through associative retrieval processes mediated by hippocampal systems. Certainly, seeing the grocery store seems the most likely event to elicit retrieval of the intention (see the discussion of McDaniel, Guynn, Einstein, and Breneiser's work [2004] in Chapter 3), but other features bound to the intention may stimulate retrieval of the intention as well. Noticing that it is dusk, passing the stone wall, seeing the gas station, or even noting that you are thirsty may prompt remembering of the intention to buy orange juice. Finally, frontal systems mediate the assembly of actions required to suppress the usual go-home actions (such as turning right at the gas station rather than turning left toward the grocery store). In instances when the retrieved action cannot be executed immediately, frontal systems are needed to maintain the intended action for a brief period of time (see Chapter 7 for further discussion of these instances). For example, before you pass the grocery store you may notice the dusk, perhaps because you have to turn on your headlights, and this may prompt remembering of the intention to buy orange juice. Because you cannot execute the intention immediately, frontal processes are engaged to keep that goal in mind until you arrive at the grocery store.

Based on considerations outlined in Chapters 3 and 4, we believe that in many everyday prospective memory situations the posited interplay of frontal and hippocampal processes is prevalent, with frontal processes being involved in planning and execution and hippocampal processes primarily mediating retrieval of the intended activity based on encounters with external events or internal events (for example, thirst). However, it is clear that under some conditions, as detailed in Chapter 4, a more active monitoring process can be engaged to support prospective remembering. Under these conditions, we would expect more intensive involvement of frontal processes during prospective memory tasks. We turn to neuroimaging investigations to inform this possibility.

Neuroimaging and Prospective Memory

Positron Emissions Tomography (PET)

The PET technique monitors regional cerebral blood flow by scanning emissions of a radioactive substance injected into subjects' bloodstreams. The idea is that blood flow to brain areas actively engaged in the experimental task increases, and PET measures these changes in blood flow across the brain. A few pioneering researchers have begun to use PET to explore the neuroscience of prospective memory (Burgess, Quayle, & Frith, 2001; Burgess, Scott, & Frith, 2003; Okuda et al., 1998). These studies reported that a number of brain areas were active during prospective memory tasks, but did not completely converge on an identical set of brain areas. However, there is good agreement that frontal brain areas were activated during prospective memory tasks. This result adds weight to the neuropsychological findings discussed earlier implicating frontal involvement in prospective memory. It is also consistent with the cognitive and neurocognitive theories discussed.

Yet the frontal activation reported by the PET studies might not be associated with prospective memory per se. Adding a prospective memory task to an ongoing task may increase the difficulty of the experimental task in general, or it may increase stimulus-processing demands. For instance, perhaps the additional prospective memory instructions prompt subjects to concentrate more completely on the experimental task or produce extra demands to process the stimuli more completely. Difficulty or increased stimulus processing, rather than prospective memory processes per se, could produce increased frontal activation (Burgess et al., 2003). Even particular stimulus characteristics chosen for the ongoing and prospective memory tasks might contribute to particular activation patterns. To circumvent these alternative interpretations, the experimental design must be able to gauge brain activation patterns due to attentional difficulty and then note the additional activation patterns produced by prospective memory. Using several different ongoing tasks is also desirable.

Burgess et al. (2003) implemented just such an experimental design in their PET study. Different domains of tasks were used to ensure that the neuroimaging results were not particular to any one kind of ongoing task. For each domain (numbers, letters, or pictures), a baseline and an attention-demanding version were constructed, as follows: In all of the baseline conditions, subjects pressed one of two response buttons as soon as a stimulus pair appeared on the screen. Subjects were to alternate their responses between a left-hand and a right-hand key. The attention-demanding conditions were designed to increase concentration and to prompt more involved stimulus processing. For instance, in the number condition, subjects had to decide whether the higher number was on the left or the right and then respond with the appropriate key, and in the letter condition, subjects had to decide which of two letters came first in the alphabet and press the corresponding left or right key.

In the prospective memory conditions, subjects performed the attention-demanding task and in addition were instructed to try to remember to press both keys together whenever a particular stimulus configuration occurred. For instance, for the number task, subjects were to make the prospective memory response if two even numbers appeared on the trial; in the letter task, the prospective memory response was cued by two vowels appearing on the trial. Thus, from the baseline conditions to the attention-demanding ongoing-task conditions, and then from the attention-demanding ongoing-task conditions to the prospective memory conditions, we can assume that the tasks become more difficult. This setup allowed the researchers to use an elegant logical process to interpret the brain activation patterns. Activation in a particular area that increased incrementally across the conditions would likely be a marker of brain activity attributable to general task difficulty.

Alternatively, brain regions in which changes in activation from baseline were different for the prospective memory conditions relative to the attention-demanding ongoing-task conditions would be implicated in prospective memory processes per se. Figure 8.2 shows that two frontal regions clearly displayed a pattern of activation suggesting involvement in processes tied to prospective memory. (Activations for the prospective memory trial were divided into two blocks, "PM1" indicating the first block and "PM2" indicating the second.) First, note that panel A indicates that the medial anterior (rostromedial) regions of the prefrontal cortex showed a *decrease* in activation during the prospective memory blocks, whereas they showed a slight increase over baseline during the attention-demanding ongoing tasks. Second, panels B and C indicate that the lateral anterior (rostrolateral) regions of the prefrontal cortex showed an *increase* in activity during the prospective memory blocks but a decrease during the attention-demanding ongoing tasks. (For readers with some background, both of these regions were Brodmann area 10.)

These findings are important because they converge with the neuropsychological findings discussed previously in this chapter and with the other PET findings (Burgess et al., 2001; Okuda et al., 1998) implicating frontal processes in prospective memory, and they do so with a method that rules out the possibility that the frontal involvement is due to general task difficulty. Further, the role of these frontal regions in prospective memory can be delineated by considering the nature of the prospective memory tasks in this experiment. In all conditions, the prospective memory task required processing of features that were not extracted as part of the ongoing activity, such as the parity of numbers (even numbers) or letters (vowels). From the

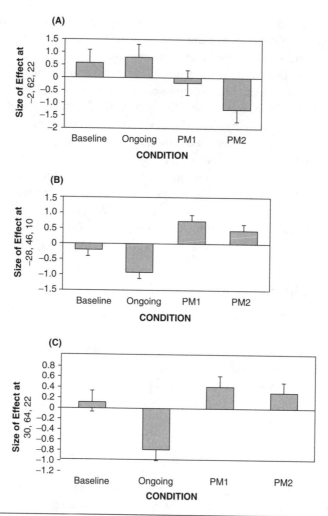

Figure 8.2   Relative Blood Flow in the Rostromedial Prefrontal Cortex (A) and Rostrolateral Regions (B and C) by Condition in an Experiment Performed by Burgess, Scott, and Frith (2003)

SOURCE: From Burgess, P., Scott, S. K., Frith, C. D., The role of the rostral frontal cortex (area 10) in prospective memory: A lateral versus medial dissociation., in *Neuropsychologia, 41,* 906–918, copyright © 2003. Reprinted with permission from Elsevier.

viewpoint of the multiprocess framework (described in Chapter 4), all of the prospective memory conditions involved nonfocal cues, and therefore likely required monitoring. Moreover, the importance of the prospective memory task was emphasized by monetary rewards for every successful prospective memory response, which also stimulates monitoring (Einstein et al., 2005; Kliegel, Martin, McDaniel, & Einstein, 2004). Finally, the response latencies for nontarget trials were slower when the prospective memory task was added to the ongoing activity than they were when there was only the ongoing activity, and this also implicates monitoring.

Therefore, it is likely that the frontal regions have something to do with monitoring or maintenance of the prospective memory intention during the ongoing activity. More particularly, Burgess et al. (2003) suggest that maintenance of the intention involves attentional focus upon internally generated cognitions, a role played by the rostrolateral frontal areas (which showed increased activation during the prospective memory blocks in both Burgess et al. [2001, 2003] studies). Such internal focus is assumed to withdraw processing from the external stimuli (ongoing task), processing that is presumably supported by the rostromedial areas (which showed decreased activation during the prospective memory blocks). (See Burgess, Simons, Dumontheil, & Gilbert, 2005, for a more detailed discussion of this "gateway" hypothesis.)

Functional Magnetic Resonance Imaging (fMRI)

The fMRI technique assesses blood oxygen levels in the brain. The idea is that more active brain areas recruit oxygen, so that increased signaling of oxygen usage implicates more brain activity in a particular area. Using fMRI to investigate the neuroscience of prospective memory is a very recent development. Simons, Scholvinck, Gilbert, Frith, and Burgess (2006) reported a study that implemented different prospective memory conditions and compared fMRI activation during those conditions to activation during a control condition with the same ongoing activities but no prospective memory task. The results dovetailed nicely with those of the Burgess et al. (2003) PET study. Specifically, the rostrolateral frontal regions bilaterally showed increased activation during blocks of trials in which the prospective memory task was included. In contrast, the rostromedial frontal region showed deactivation. Consistent with the Burgess et al. view described above, this deactivation was accompanied by reduced performance (slowing) on the ongoing activity (relative to performance on the ongoing activity in the control condition). The convergence of these specific frontal-activation dynamics across PET and fMRI is impressive, given that different ongoing activities and prospective memory tasks were used across the studies.

Though not as pronounced, one other effect emerged that is consistent with the idea that rostromedial and rostrolateral areas reflect trade-offs in processing of external stimuli and internally derived representations during a prospective memory task. In the Simons et al. (2006) study, one prospective memory condition involved nonsalient target events, whereas another involved perceptually salient target events. For instance, one ongoing activity involved presentation of word pairs: one lowercase word and one uppercase word. In the nonsalient prospective memory condition, the target words continued in this vein, whereas in the salient condition, the target words were both uppercase. In the nonsalient condition, in which there were more demands involved in cue detection (maintaining attention toward external stimuli), prospective memory–related rostrolateral activation was dampened and rostromedial area deactivation was lessened (relative to activation/deactivation in the salient condition).

In sum, the PET and fMRI work provide the initial suggestion that two primary frontal regions show complementary interaction in prospective memory when monitoring processes are recruited by the subject. The rostrolateral areas support activation of the representation of the intention during the retention interval, and the rostromedial area is somewhat deactivated as attention is withdrawn from the ongoing stimuli. With more sophisticated work in the future, a more complete picture of brain activity associated with prospective memory in paradigms that do not recruit monitoring will hopefully illuminate the neurocognitive bases of other processes in prospective memory, such as intention superiority and spontaneous retrieval of intentions.

Event-Related Brain Potentials (ERPs)

The ERP technique uses electrodes placed on the scalp to record electrophysiological signals associated with cognitive activities. The electrophysiological signal has high temporal resolution, meaning that modulation of neuronal events occurring over durations of milliseconds can be distinguished. Accordingly, ERP allows fine-grained analysis of neuronal activity both within the entire envelope of a particular type of trial and across trials of different types. In the PET and fMRI studies of prospective memory, to acquire a signal, activity had to be sampled over entire trial blocks of ongoing activity and compared to activity sampled over an entire block of the prospective memory phase. Though excellent for localization of the signal, these PET and fMRI neuroimaging data reveal little about how neuronal activity is associated with particular component processes of prospective memory retrieval (at the moment a target event is encountered, for instance) or the time-course of these processes. While ERPs do not allow precise localization of the neuronal activity, the ERP technique does afford great potential for (a) examining the neural activity correlated with the presumably rapid component processes assumed to be involved in prospective memory retrieval and (b) contrasting activity involved on target and on nontarget trials during the presence of the prospective memory task. A programmatic series of ERP experiments conducted by West and his students (see West, in press) has produced important initial information on both of these issues.

West and his colleagues report two consistent patterns of neural activity associated with prospective memory, patterns that are obtained across a variety of ongoing activities and a variety of prospective memory targets (West & Krompinger, 2005) (for instance, the prospective memory cue can be a particular word, a particular letter case, or a particular color of type font). The consistency of the findings inspires confidence that the ERP signals are not related to some stimulus-specific feature of any one experiment. The first pattern (termed the N300) relates to the negative phase of the signal over the occipital-parietal region that occurs between 300 and 500 ms after the onset of a stimulus. On prospective memory trials during which subjects make the intended response, the N300 is amplified relative to its signal on nontarget trials and on prospective memory trials during which subjects fail to perform the intended response. A schematic of this signal and its amplification during prospective memory response is shown in Figure 8.3.

The second distinctive pattern is a sustained positivity over the parietal region occurring between 500 and 1000 ms after the onset of the prospective memory cue on successful trials. As the bottom panel of Figure 8.3 shows, this sustained positivity is quite pronounced for prospective memory trials relative to non–prospective memory trials. For this reason, this component has been termed *prospective positivity*. There are likely a number of processes that contribute to the prospective positivity over its temporal duration. For example, the earlier components (the first 500 to 600 ms) of the prospective positivity respond to the salience of the prospective memory cue (West, Wymbs, Jakubek, & Herndon, 2003). In contrast, the later portion of the prospective positivity (the last 600 to 800 ms) shows greater amplitude when the prospective memory task involves multiple cue-intention associations compared to when the task involves only a single target cue (West et al., 2003). This finding may suggest that the later portion of the prospective positivity is reflective of neural activity associated with retrieval of the intention from memory (but see West & Krompinger, 2005, Experiment 2, for a diverging finding).

The temporal dynamics of these two distinct ERP patterns in prospective memory provide another clue regarding the possible function associated with the neural activity reflected by the ERP results. Clearly, the N300 precedes the prospective positivity. Presuming that prospective positivity is associated with retrieval of an intention, it makes sense to suppose that the N300 is associated with noticing or detection of the prospective memory target cue. The astute reader may realize that these neural dynamics accord well with the noticing-plus-retrieval model of prospective memory discussed in Chapter 3 (Einstein & McDaniel, 1996), in which particular processes (for example, familiarity or discrepancy detection) support noticing of the prospective memory cue (perhaps associated with the N300),

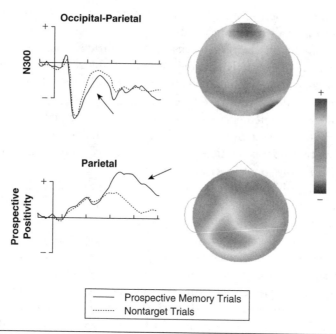

Figure 8.3   Grand Average ERPs and Scalp Topography Maps (as Viewed From Above) Demonstrating the Time-Course and Topography of the N300 and Prospective Positivity From an Experiment Performed by West and His Colleagues (2001)

SOURCE: From West, R., Herndon, R. W., & Crewdson, S. J., "Neural Activity Associated with the Realization of Delayed Intention" in *Cognitive Brain Research, 12*(1), p. 1–9, copyright © 2001. Reprinted with permission of Elsevier.

which is then followed by further consideration of the event and retrieval of the intended action (perhaps associated with the earlier and later portions of the prospective positivity).

Do we know that the N300 response is associated with detection of prospective memory cues per se, or is it more generally associated with detection of any stimulus that reflects features not ordinarily seen in the ongoing activity? West, Herndon, and Crewdson (2001, Experiment 2) addressed this question within one of their usual ERP prospective memory paradigms. The ongoing activity required subjects to determine whether two words presented in lowercase letters were semantically similar or different. The prospective memory task required subjects to remember to press a particular key on the keyboard when both words appeared in uppercase letters. The critical feature in this experiment was that for the first 20 blocks of trials, subjects were instructed to perform the semantic judgment task on every trial, regardless of the case of the letters. A second set of 20 trial blocks that included the prospective memory task followed. Figure 8.4 shows the ERP results for the trials involving words in uppercase letters (these were ongoing-task trials for the first 20 blocks—the "Prospective Ignore" trials, and prospective memory trials for the second 20 blocks—the "Prospective Attend" trials). There was an increased N300 response for the trials involving uppercase letters relative to the normal ongoing trials, but this response was significantly muted compared to the response observed on prospective memory trials (at least over the right hemisphere). This experiment establishes that the more amplified N300 is associated with neural processes related specifically to prospective memory.

So West and his colleagues' initial work has established plausible links between certain components of prospective remembering and signature neural activation patterns. With these foundational patterns in hand, the stage is set to exploit ERP imaging for even more penetrating analyses of the neurocognitive processes supporting prospective memory. Two new exciting studies have taken steps in this direction. One study tackled a recurring issue in the science of prospective memory—the extent to which extra attentional processes are required to detect an environmental event or appreciate that it signals the opportunity for performing an intended action.

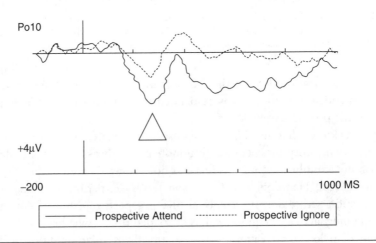

Figure 8.4   Difference Waves in the Prospective Ignore and Prospective Attend Conditions in an Experiment Performed by West, Herndon, and Crewdson (2001)

SOURCE: From West, R., Herndon, R. W, and Ross-Monroe. "Event-related Neural Activity Associated with Prospective Remembering," In *Applied Cognitive Psychology, 14*. Copyright © 2000, John Wiley & Sons Limited. Reproduced with permission.

The experimental approach was to manipulate the capacity demands of a working-memory task that served as the ongoing activity (West, Bowry, & Krompinger, 2006). The working task was the N-back task, in which subjects had to say whether the letter appearing on the present trial matched the letter presented N trials back. The low-demand condition was a one-back task, in which subjects simply indicated whether the letter in the current trial matched the last letter presented. The high-demand condition was a three-back task; here subjects had to continuously update which letter had been presented three trials back and decide if the present letter matched the three-back item. In both conditions, subjects also had a prospective memory task. The letters were printed in a variety of colors, and the prospective memory task was to press the V key whenever a letter was printed in a specified color (for example, red). This specified color appeared on 10% of the trials.

One finding is that the trials requiring an N-back response (the working-memory trials) elicited a different pattern of ERPs from the one elicited by the prospective memory trials. This pattern suggests that prospective memory is not mediated by the same neural processes that support working memory. Of primary interest is the effect of the variation in working-memory load on the N300 signal associated with detection of the prospective memory cue. The idea is that if detection of the cue requires attentional resources (see Chapter 2), the working-memory load of the N-back task should affect the N300 response, with N300 decreasing for the high-load three-back task. Alternatively, if detection is fairly spontaneous (see Chapter 3), the N300 should be invariant to N-back load.

Using a sophisticated analysis technique to partition the causes of variance in the ERP responses into underlying (latent) factors, the researchers found that the ERPs associated with prospective memory could be explained by two latent factors. One factor was expressed in the N300 primarily, and this factor was sensitive to the N-back load. The other factor showed a strikingly different pattern: a tight coupling between the N300 and the prospective positivity, and no influence of N-back load. This last result maps nicely onto the idea that prospective memory retrieval may involve the conjoint processes of noticing (of the cue) plus retrieval (of the intention), and further, that the noticing process is relatively spontaneous (does not require extra attentional resources). More generally, the entire pattern provides support for the multiprocess model (Chapter 4), which suggests that either attentional processes (for example, monitoring) or relatively spontaneous processes can support prospective remembering. According to the multiprocess view, on any one trial one process or the other may predominate; therefore, collapsing data across many trials, as is done in ERP analyses, produces evidence for both processes.

The second exciting development in the ERP investigations has been examination of the overlap between the neural processes underlying recognition and those underlying prospective memory. Cognition theories of recognition assume that both relatively spontaneous familiarity processes and recollective retrieval processes support recognition performance (Jacoby, 1991; Jacoby, Toth, & Yonelinas, 1993; Mandler, 1980; Yonelinas, 1999). Further, ERP modulations that appear to be uniquely associated with familiarity processes on the one hand and recollection processes on the other hand have been reported during recognition tasks (Curran, 2000; Rugg et al., 1998). The crucial point for present purposes is that these ERP modulations can be used to gauge the kinds of retrieval processes involved in prospective remembering. Specifically, one can examine the extent to which recognition processes generally activated in retrospective tasks are also involved in prospective memory. More interesting, the ERPs associated with prospective memory can be further analyzed in terms of neural signatures for familiarity and for recollection.

To informatively conduct the comparisons across recognition tasks and prospective memory tasks, care must be taken to equate the tasks on all other dimensions. For example, one clear difference is that recognition tasks involve relatively long lists of target items, whereas prospective memory tasks involve very short lists of targets. West and Krompinger (2005) implemented the needed experiment. The recognition and prospective memory tasks were presented in the context of the same ongoing activity: Subjects were shown a pair of words, and they had to make a semantic-relatedness judgment for each pair. Prior to each block of semantic judgment trials, subjects were given a prospective memory target item and a recognition target item. For the prospective memory task, when the target appeared, the subjects had to indicate the position on the screen in which the word appeared (upper or lower). For the recognition task, a single trial followed the last judgment trial in a block. This trial involved a pair of words just as the judgment trials had, but followed a signal to prepare for the recognition test. The output demands of the recognition task paralleled those of the prospective memory task in that subjects had to indicate the position of the recognition target item (upper or lower).

The first important finding was that the ERP responses that had been associated with recognition in the past literature were replicated in this experiment. Thus, the novel aspects of the recognition trials that made them compatible with the prospective memory trials (for example, a word list of one item) did not alter the usual ERP patterns for recognition. What about the ERPs for the prospective memory trials? One key ERP pattern (termed the FN400) was a positivity over the frontal region of the scalp between 300 and

500 ms after the stimulus was presented that was significantly more pronounced for recognition hits and for prospective memory hits than it was during nontarget ongoing-task trials. Because the FN400 has been regarded as an index of familiarity (Curran, 2000; Curran & Dien, 2003), the implication is that familiarity processes may be involved in prospective memory. Such a finding is consistent with the above-mentioned cognitive theory that familiarity may be involved in prospective memory, perhaps in the service of noticing the prospective memory cue (Einstein & McDaniel, 1996) (see Chapter 3).

The two components of the ERPs associated with recollective processes in recognition (*recognition positivity* and *frontal slow wave*) showed a less conclusive pattern. On recognition trials but not on prospective memory trials, these components were significantly more activated than they were on ongoing-task trials. However, in a factor analysis of the ERP components, one latent factor reflecting these recollection-like components (in addition to the familiarity component) showed more enhancement for prospective memory trials (as well as recognition trials) than it showed for ongoing-activity trials.

Summary and Future Directions

To sum up, ERP research has developed increasingly sophisticated experiments and analyses that show great potential for informing and linking to cognitive theories of prospective memory. From the most recent results, we can find patterns that are consistent with several different views. The idea that spontaneous familiarity processes support detection of the prospective memory target links well to the finding that some ERP modulations associated with prospective memory are insensitive to attentional load and are reflective of neural signals associated with familiarity-like processes in recognition. The idea that attentional resources monitor the environment and stimulate recognition checks for the prospective memory target event is compatible with the findings that (a) other ERP components associated with prospective memory are impacted by attentional load and (b) prospective memory appears to activate ERP components presumably associated with recollective processes in explicit recognition.

These patterns clearly merit further investigation, but as they stand now they implicate a multiprocess view that assumes that several types of processes as just outlined are exploited by the cognitive system to support prospective memory. To gain leverage on this view, future work could implement experiments with conditions in which one type of process will predominantly emerge. In this way, researchers can directly link particular neural responses to the cognitive processes stimulated in particular prospective memory conditions. Heuristics for such conditions are suggested by the multiprocess theory (as detailed in Chapter 4) and are starting to appear in experiments designed to legislate among the posited cognitive processes (Einstein et al., 2005; Loft & Yeo, in press; McDaniel, Guynn, et al., 2004). The trick is to find ways to preserve the integrity of these manipulations in the context of the relatively large numbers of prospective memory trials required by neuroimaging techniques.

Existing neuroimaging and ERP paradigms using large numbers of prospective memory trials and sometimes nonfocal target events (as in some PET studies) likely encourage subjects to adopt a monitoring strategy. Thus, conclusions about the neural responses and brain areas recruited for prospective memory are probably most pertinent to prospective memory tasks for which monitoring is prominent. For instance, for prospective tasks in which monitoring is not prominent, which likely include many real-world prospective situations (see the next chapters for more discussion), the role of frontal areas may be somewhat different from what current findings imply. For these prospective memory situations, we have developed in this chapter a provisional neuropsychological theory that awaits investigation.

A more general challenge for the next generation of cognitive neuroscience work is to integrate the functional neuropsychological systems associated with prospective memory (as illuminated by neuropsychological and functional imaging techniques) with the temporally bounded neural responses stimulated by prospective memory (as illuminated by electrophysiological techniques). The available neuropsychological and neuroimaging evidence converge on the conclusion that the prefrontal structure, particularly Brodmann area 10, is intimately involved in prospective memory. As well, there is less extensive but equally plausible evidence that the medial-temporal structure, probably the hippocampal system, is involved in prospective memory. The particular processes supported by these systems and the models that develop will hinge on linking the particular topography and temporal dynamics of the neural activity as evidenced by ERPs to these particular systems. One neuroimaging technique that may prove fruitful in this regard is magnetoencephalography (MEG), which has the temporal resolution of ERPs and potentially the spatial resolution of PET and fMRI. One new experiment applying MEG to prospective memory has been completed (Martin et al., in press). We believe that the combination of spatial and temporal sensitivity afforded by MEG will be highly useful for legislating among the various fine-grained cognitive processes posited to be involved in prospective memory (as detailed in Chapters 2 through 4).

9

Prospective Memory as It Applies to Work and Naturalistic Settings

Although the pilot had set the flaps on his plane to takeoff position thousands of times as part of a well-scripted routine, following a series of interruptions, he forgot to do so. Tragically, the warning system also failed on this occasion, and the plane crashed, killing all but one person.

Eight months after hernia surgery, the patient complained of abdominal pain and nausea. A scan of his abdominal area revealed that a 16-cm clamp had been left from his surgery. Despite the best intentions of a conscientious surgical team of doctors and nurses, they had forgotten to remove the clamp.

The errors above represent true to life failures of prospective remembering (Holbrook, Dismukes, & Nowinski, 2005; Gawande, Studdert, Orav, Brennan, & Zinner, 2003). Although these errors highlight the possible dire

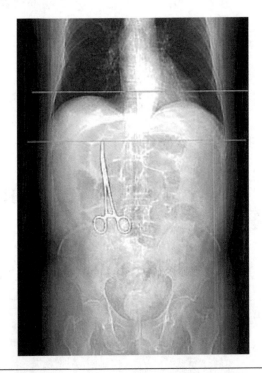

Figure 9.1   Scan of a 16-cm Clamp Left in the Abdominal Area of a Patient

SOURCE: From Dembitzer, A., & Lai, E. J. "Retained Surgical Instrument," in *The New England Journal of Medicine, 348*, p. 228. Copyright © 2003 Massachusetts Medical Society. All rights reserved.

consequences of prospective memory errors in work contexts, it is important to realize that our everyday lives are also filled and sometimes overflowing with prospective memory demands. From managing our work activities (for example, remembering to attend committee meetings) to coordinating our social relations (remembering dinner engagements) to handling our health-related needs (remembering to monitor blood pressure or take medication), good prospective memory is essential for normal functioning.

To get a sense of the pervasiveness of prospective memory demands relative to retrospective memory demands, we have over the years asked our students on the first day of class to list the last thing they remember forgetting. We then categorize their memory failures as either prospective or retrospective in nature. For example, renting a video and then discovering that you have already seen it would be classified as a retrospective memory failure, whereas forgetting to give a friend a message would be classified as a prospective memory failure. Interestingly, with groups of both younger and older adults, we consistently find that over 50% of the reported failures were prospective memory lapses.

Prospective memory failures, such as forgetting to take your lecture notes with you when you drive to work in the morning, can cause problems in effectiveness and efficiency. They can also lead to a great deal of embarrassment, as one of the authors painfully realized after he forgot to attend his first department meeting as chair of the department. (He had been called to the lab by one of his research students and then gotten absorbed in discussions there.) The other author was equally embarrassed when he forgot his first faculty meeting after arriving at his new institution, despite reminders on both his wall calendar and his desk calendar.

As noted in the introductory vignettes, consequences of prospective memory lapses can be devastating. Reason (1990), in his classic book on human error, argues that human frailty is the cause of many catastrophic work accidents. Moreover, he proposes that "failures of prospective memory . . . are among the most common form of human fallibility" (p. 107). Consistent with this impression, Nowinski, Holbrook, and Dismukes's (2003) analysis of the database of self-reported errors by airline pilots revealed that 74 of the 75 errors involving memory failures were prospective in nature. Thus, it seems that insight into the prospective memory conditions that are especially sensitive to failure can have important implications for improving safety conditions in work settings.

Consider also adherence to prescribed medication schedules. The majority of medications are taken by older adults (Park & Morrell, 1991), many of whom take three or more medications on a daily basis (Morrell, Park, Kidder, & Martin, 1997). Adherence to medication regimens is often problematic, with some estimates of nonadherence being as high as 50% (Dunbar-Jacob et al., 2000; Haynes, McDonald, Garg, & Montague, 2003; Stilley, Sereika, Muldoon, Ryan, & Dunbar-Jacob, 2004). Nonadherence may be particularly problematic for patients with asymptomatic conditions like hypertension. In one study, Insel and Cole (2005) found 65% adherence with an antihypertensive medication over an 8-week period in the absence of any intervention. Although there are probably many causes of nonadherence to medication regimens, it seems likely that at least part of the problem is prospective memory failure (Insel & Cole).

In this chapter, based on existing laboratory research, we develop general recommendations for improving prospective memory in work and everyday situations, and in doing so we also highlight those conditions that are particularly prone to prospective forgetting. Some aspects of complex real-world prospective memory demands may be difficult to capture in the laboratory, and we explore limitations of current paradigms. Finally, in an effort to stimulate thinking about profitable new directions for future research on prospective memory in work and naturalistic contexts, we describe nonlaboratory paradigms.

We agree with Loukopoulos, Dismukes, and Barshi (2003a, 2003b; see also Dismukes, in press; Reason, 1990) that most of the prospective memory errors that occur in work contexts are not the result of negligence on the part of uninterested, careless, or "bad" people. Instead, most errors arise from conscientious people who are in contexts that place challenges on the human cognitive system. Thus, an understanding of the underlying cognitive demands is essential for improving safety conditions in critical work contexts. Loukopoulos et al. (2003a) say it this way:

> The question of why errors happen to well-trained, experienced, and conscientious pilots may seem quite perplexing to anyone who is not a cognitive psychologist. Countless examples of "carelessness" or "complacency" errors during routine operations are reported by pilots who, surprised to have made errors in tasks at which they are quite skillful, cite fatigue, distractions, high workload, or schedule pressures. In incident reports, pilots often resolve "to be more careful" when encountering similar situations in the future. We argue that labels such as "carelessness" and "complacency" do little to help understand and prevent these errors and that merely resolving to be more careful will not improve safety. Rather, these errors can be understood by analyzing task characteristics in detail, identifying associated forms of error, and relating these task characteristics and error forms to underlying cognitive processes. This approach can provide a meaningful foundation for developing countermeasures to prevent errors and to catch them before they lead to accidents.

General Recommendations for Improving Prospective Memory

As we explained when we first attempted a definition of prospective memory in Chapter 1, the unique challenge in remembering delayed intentions (relative to remembering in retrospective tasks like free recall and recognition) is that there is no external request to remember. For example, after planning to pick up milk on the way home, at a later time we somehow have to switch from focusing on driving home to thinking about stopping at the grocery store to get milk. As we indicated earlier (Chapter 4), our belief is that prospective memory is more difficult in situations in which there are few cues that can serve to trigger spontaneous retrieval. In these situations, successful prospective memory is more dependent on developing and maintaining a monitoring strategy—something that is difficult for the human cognitive system to sustain over extended periods of time (see Bargh & Chartrand, 1999; Einstein et al., 2005). Our recommendations therefore focus on identifying those prospective memory situations that are likely to be especially problematic and also on how to make it more likely that cues can serve to produce spontaneous retrieval of the intended action.

Remove the Delay in Delayed Intentions: Do It or Lose It

One factor that contributes to real-world memory lapses is that we sometimes create unnecessary delays in prospective memory situations. For example, in casual conversation with a patient's relatives, a nurse may learn some important information that needs to be communicated to the attending physician. Instead of finding the patient's chart and writing this immediately, the nurse may decide to complete a couple of chores along the way—and then forget to update the chart. Or, we may form the intention to send an e-mail attachment to a friend. However, upon opening the e-mail, we may become absorbed in writing a clever cover note and fail to remember to include the attachment, which was the main point of sending the e-mail in the first place. Incidentally, failing to include the attachment occurs more often than we two prospective memory researchers care to admit!

Laboratory studies with younger adults (Einstein, McDaniel, Williford, Pagan, & Dismukes, 2003) and especially with older adults (Einstein, McDaniel, Manzi, Cochran, & Baker, 2000; McDaniel, Einstein, Stout, & Morgan, 2003) have shown that retrieved intentions can be forgotten over surprisingly brief delays. In one study with younger adults under very demanding divided-attention conditions, there was approximately 25% forgetting after just 5-second delays (Einstein et al., 2003). In another study, when older adults had to delay their intended action by 5 seconds, they forgot to perform the intended action about 50% of the time (McDaniel et al., 2003). These results indicate that maintaining an intention over a brief delay before executing the intended action is not a trivial task for the human cognitive system.

Our suspicion is that people in general do not realize that retrieved intentions that cannot be realized immediately are quite fragile. Often, retrieved intentions are so salient at the moment that they create the misimpression that they are indelible, at least over very brief delays. We suspect that most people are unaware of the research of Muter (1980) and Schweickert and Boruff (1986), showing that thoughts, without refreshing or rehearsal, fade from focal awareness (consciousness) in about 2 seconds. To test our impression that people do not appreciate the ephemeral nature of currently activated intentions, we recently gave 34 participants the following assignment:

Imagine that you are working on an easy essay question and get the thought to add an argument to a previous question. Before adding that argument, however, you first want to finish answering the question. Based on what you know about how your own memory works, rate how likely (from 0% to 100%) you will be to remember to add the argument to the earlier question when it takes you 5, 15, or 40 seconds to finish the current question.

Participants were asked to make their ratings for both "normal exam conditions" and "very hurried exam conditions." The results indicated that participants viewed the 5-second delay as minimally problematic and expected to remember 98.3% and 90.4% of the time under normal and hurried conditions, respectively. Participants had lower estimates of 91.2% and 79.1% at the 15-second delay and still lower estimates of 81% and 62.9 % at the 40-second delay. Interestingly, our research (Einstein et al., 2000) showed that forgetting occurs quickly, and there was no difference between prospective memory performance after a 5-second delay and performance after a 40-second delay. Thus, people do not seem to realize that brief 5-second delays are just as problematic as 40-second delays.

In light of this research, we believe that whenever possible it is important to perform an intended action as soon as we think about it and not take the chance of forgetting it over a delay. For example, when you are in the bedroom and get the thought to take your medication, which is in the kitchen, you ordinarily might decide to complete a few chores in the bedroom before going to the kitchen to take your medication. The current research suggests that it is important to interrupt your current activities and act on the intention right away. In a similar vein, both of the authors have gotten in the habit of attaching documents to their e-mail messages before writing the cover note.

There are many situations, however, in which we are not able to perform the action immediately. The time may simply not be appropriate, or interruptions or delays over which we have no control may be introduced. For instance, an air traffic controller who gets the thought to reroute an airplane may first have to finish her current conversation with the pilot of another airplane before she can act on her intention. For those situations, the recommendations listed below are likely to be effective.

Use Good External Cues

The research is clear in showing that good cues for prospective memory retrieval are salient or distinctive ones that attract focal processing and are meaningfully connected to the intended action. Under these conditions, prospective memory retrieval has been shown to be very high and to be insensitive to the effects of divided attention (McDaniel & Einstein, 1993;

McDaniel, Guynn, Einstein, & Breneiser, 2004). In one experiment, for example, when the prospective memory target was a common word that occurred among other common words in the ongoing task, subjects remembered to perform the prospective memory task 31% of the time. However, when the prospective memory target was an uncommon word in the context of common items in the ongoing task, subjects remembered the prospective memory task 100% of the time (McDaniel & Einstein, 1993).

It is important to consider all three of these factors in designing a maximally effective cue. A cue that is meaningfully related to the intended action but goes unnoticed will not be effective. For example, if you want to remember to buy milk in the morning, adding one more sticky note to a refrigerator cluttered with sticky notes is unlikely to work because the note is not distinctive and therefore unlikely to be attended to. A better cue would be an empty milk carton (a cue that is related to the action of buying milk) placed in the middle of the kitchen floor or on the driver's seat of your car. The milk carton will be distinctive in both of these locations and is likely to be focally processed, assuming that you walk through your kitchen or get in your car in the morning, and thus is very likely to get noticed. Figure 9.2 lists the characteristics and some examples of effective prospective memory cues.

Anticipate the Triggering Cues: Use Implementation Intentions

We believe that good external cuing is critical for successful prospective remembering. If you are not in a position to create distinctive external cues,

---

Characteristics of Good Prospective Memory Cues

Salience or distinctiveness

Ability to attract focal processing

Meaningful association with the intended action

Examples of Good Prospective Memory Cues

To remember to take out the trash when you get home in the evening, lean a small indoor trash bucket against your bedroom door.

To remember to take your lunch to work, tape a sticky note with "lunch" written on it to the front of your briefcase.

Figure 9.2   Characteristics and Examples of Effective Prospective Memory Cues

we recommend anticipating the triggering cues that are likely to be present in the retrieval context (cf. Mantyla, 1993). In Chapters 3 and 5, we described several processes by which cues can stimulate spontaneous retrieval of prospective memory intentions, and it is important during planning to associate the intended action with the possible cues. This recommendation emanates also from the perspective that we often fail to remember to perform actions because we tend to formulate only general intentions (Gollwitzer, 1999). Gollwitzer and others (Cohen & Gollwitzer, in press; Sheeran & Orbell, 1999) believe that the reason we sometimes do not follow through on our intentions in the real world is that we often form broad intentions that tend to focus on the action and not on the triggering events (see Chapter 6 for an extensive discussion). Thus, we might form the intentions to "send an e-mail to a colleague," "buy stamps," "exercise more often," and "take vitamins." The problem here is that we do not clearly specify the triggering conditions for these actions, and thus we are more dependent on controlled processes for actively maintaining our goal intentions or on fortuitous reflection on our future plans and unfulfilled activities at appropriate times.

By using implementation intentions, which take the form of, "When situation x arises, I will perform response y" (Gollwitzer, 1999, p. 494), we specify in advance the cues that signal the occasion to perform the intended action (where and when the intended action will occur) and directly associate the cues to the action. In this way, we make it possible that later processing of the cue will spontaneously lead to retrieval of the intended action. For example, by thinking through, "When I get back to my office and sit in my chair and look at my monitor, I will send an e-mail to my colleague," I increase the probability that the seeing of my office, chair, and monitor will trigger remembering of the intended action. As described in Chapter 6, there is compelling evidence that implementation intentions are effective in improving prospective memory.

Further evidence for the value of anticipating cue conditions comes from the research of Kvavilashvili and Fisher (2007), who have recently shown that spontaneous cuing of intentions occurs frequently in the real world. They gave subjects (on a Monday) the task of remembering to give a telephone call to the experimenter 1 week later (on a Sunday). They also gave them a diary and asked them to make an entry in the diary whenever they thought of the intention to make the phone call over the 1-week delay period. In the diary, subjects were asked to give their impression of what led to the recollection of an intention. Specifically, they were asked to indicate whether they thought there was a triggering cue, and if so, to indicate, among other things, whether it was an incidental external cue (for example, seeing a telephone pole), an incidental internally stimulated cue (for example, thinking about making a phone call to a friend), or self-initiated thoughts related to reviewing of future plans (for example, pausing to reflect on and review the activities for the day ahead). Across three studies, Kvavilashvili and Fisher found that a substantial proportion of prospective memory recollection (about 54% when averaged across studies) was triggered by incidental external or internal cues associated with the intended action. Although these data rely on subjective interpretations of the cuing conditions, they indicate that cues do stimulate retrieval of prospective memory intentions and suggest that anticipating the triggering cues in advance and associating them with the intended action should lead to frequent reminders of the prospective memory intention later.

One other feature of implementation intentions that enhances their usefulness is their effectiveness with a variety of populations, including drug addicts going through withdrawal (Brandstatter, Lengfelder, & Gollwitzer, 2001), people with schizophrenia (Brandstatter et al.), frontal lobe patients (Lengfelder & Gollwitzer, 2001), and older adults (Chasteen, Park, & Schwarz, 2001; Liu & Park, 2004). Interestingly, all of these populations have been characterized as having problems with controlled attention and with keeping current concerns activated. According to Gollwitzer, the benefits of implementation intentions extend to these populations because anticipating the cues in advance leads to relatively automatic retrieval of the intention (a process assumed to be preserved in these populations) when the cues are later encountered.

In closing this section, we note that it generally takes time and mental effort to form implementation intentions, and thus this strategy may not be useful in all situations. For example, in the midst of a very demanding and unrelenting work schedule, it may be difficult for an air traffic controller to take the time to form an implementation intention for every intended action (cf. Einstein et al., 2003).

Beware of Busy and Demanding Conditions

A classic finding in the prospective memory literature is that demanding situations interfere with prospective memory. Marsh and Hicks (1998) found that adding a concurrent task that engages central executive resources to the ongoing task significantly lowers prospective remembering. Although the effects of dividing attention seem to be larger on prospective memory tasks that are more dependent on monitoring than they are on those that are more likely to be remembered through spontaneous retrieval (see Chapter 4), dividing attention seems to compromise prospective memory performance in most situations. Thus, it is important to realize that prospective remembering is likely to suffer under busy and demanding conditions (as both of us demonstrated when we forgot important departmental meetings) and to take appropriate steps, such as using reliable external cues (highly salient ones, such as alarms) under these conditions.

Beware of Interruptions

Recent research has shown that brief interruptions can dramatically interfere with prospective remembering (Einstein et al., 2003; McDaniel, Einstein, Graham, & Rall, 2004). Interruptions are prevalent in everyday life. For example, while in the kitchen, I may form the intention to cull clothes I no longer wear from my closet. Just then, however, the phone may ring, and my brief conversation may interfere with my remembering to clean out my closet. Interruptions are also frequent in demanding work contexts like aviation settings and can be a significant source of forgetting (Loukopoulos et al., 2003b). In one example, an air traffic controller was in the process of giving instructions to a light aircraft on a course for a final approach. At the point at which the controller would normally give the pilot clearance to make the final approach, he was interrupted by an emergency involving another aircraft. In responding to the emergency, the controller forgot to return to the pilot to change the path and issue the final clearance, thus leaving the aircraft flying in the direction of mountainous terrain (R. K. Dismukes, personal communication, February 20, 2003).

To examine the effects of interruptions on prospective memory, Einstein et al. (2003) involved participants in a demanding and dynamic series of 1-minute tasks lasting a total of 32 minutes. Subjects were given the prospective memory task of pressing a designated key whenever they saw a red screen, but they were instructed not to press the key until they completed the current task and started a new task (that is, until they encountered a task change). All of the delays were 40 seconds long, but some included a 15-second interruption during which participants had to perform a new task. Interestingly, despite the fact that both conditions had 40-second delays, the results revealed that including a 15-second interruption during the delay lowered prospective memory by 25% (relative to not including an interruption). This disruptive effect of interruptions has been found repeatedly (Cook, 2005; McDaniel, Einstein, et al., 2004), and although there is no generally agreed upon explanation for this effect, one interpretation is that task switching requires resources (see, for example, Monsell, Sumner, & Waters, 2003). The idea here is that the extra resources required to apprehend the new task could interfere with active maintenance of the intention.

A recent experiment conducted in our laboratory strongly suggests that external cues can be highly effective in overcoming interruption-related forgetting of intentions (McDaniel, Einstein, et al., 2004). In a follow-up of the experiment described in the above paragraph, the onset of the prospective memory intention was associated with turning on a noticeable blue light in the corner of the computer monitor, and this remained on throughout the retention interval. The presence of this cue completely eliminated the negative effects of an interruption. One potential application of this finding is that people might be trained to alter some aspect of their environment when they form an intention and believe that they are likely to encounter an interruption. For example, when I am in the kitchen and form the intention to clean the closet, as I encounter the interruption of the telephone call, I could put a book in the middle of the kitchen floor as a reminder that I have an unfulfilled intention. To leave an even better cue, one that is related to the intended action, I could take off my shirt or a sock and put it on the kitchen floor. In aviation contexts, perhaps the display monitor in front of an air traffic controller or pilot could include a "prospective memory light" that can be turned on whenever something interrupts an active intention.

In a recent set of experiments, Cook (2005) showed that the negative effects of an interruption were dramatically more pronounced (causing forgetting on an additional 25% of the trials) when the interruption served to change the context at retrieval so that it no longer matched the one at encoding. The idea here is that forming an intention in a particular task context causes the context to become associated with that intention, and thus the presence of that task context periodically prompts retrieval of the intention. Thus, if the interruption in some way changes the context at retrieval so that it no longer matches the one during which the intention was formed or in which it is typically retrieved, prospective remembering is especially likely to suffer. For example, if I form the intention to clean out my closet when I am in the kitchen but then go to the den to answer a phone call, while I am in the den I am more likely to forget to remember the intention to clean out my closet. For another example, imagine a pilot who forms the intention to perform the pre-takeoff checklist at a typical point in the taxiing process. Imagine also that the pilot receives a call from the ground controller and continues to taxi to the runway during the conversation. After the call, the context has changed, and to the extent that it is different from the context that normally triggers performance of the pre-takeoff checklist, remembering is likely to be more vulnerable.

Address the Special Problems of Habitual Prospective Memory Tasks

In this section, prior to describing methods for improving habitual prospective memory, we first describe some special problems associated with it. Habitual prospective memory tasks are those in which the action is performed repeatedly and in a routine manner (Meacham & Lieman, 1982). Taking vitamins or medication on a regular basis, turning off the oven, closing the fireplace flue, shampooing your hair in the shower in the morning, and, if you are an experienced pilot, setting the flaps on an airplane to takeoff position are all examples of habitual prospective memory tasks. A common habitual prospective memory task with important health implications is taking medication. As mentioned earlier in this chapter, adhering to a prescribed medication regimen is a significant problem in health care (Park & Kidder, 1996), as estimates for chronic illnesses suggest that adherence is only 50% (see Vedhara et al., 2004). Although some of the nonadherence is likely to be due to disinterest in complying with medical prescriptions, some of it is due to cognitive failures (Okuno, Yanagi, & Tomura, 2001). This is especially likely for older adults, who are the largest consumers of prescription medication and who also tend to experience cognitive decline. One problem is that a person may fail to think of taking the medication at the proper time, and the suggestions listed in the previous sections should be useful for developing effective measures to counter this.

At least two other factors conspire to produce problems on habitual prospective memory tasks—problems that could lead either to performing the action again or to mistakenly not performing the action. One factor is that when we perform an action on a frequent basis, we are also likely to often think about the action. According to Johnson and Raye's (1981) work on reality monitoring, this is a situation that creates confusion regarding the source of a memory, especially for older adults (Hashtroudi, Johnson, & Chrosniak, 1990; Johnson, Hashtroudi, & Lindsay, 1993; see also McDaniel, Butler, & Dornburg, 2006). For example, a person might confuse a thought about a dose of medication with the act of taking it or vice versa, and thus may end up missing a dose or repeating it. Another potential problem is that actions performed on a routine basis may be carried out automatically and during execution of other activities, and this may interfere with your ability to consciously recollect whether or not you have performed the action. Because output-monitoring problems have generally been shown to be exacerbated with age (Koriat, Ben-Zur, & Sheffer, 1988), these kinds of problems would be expected to be more pronounced in older adults.

To examine prospective memory problems that can arise in habitual prospective memory tasks, Einstein, McDaniel, Smith, and Shaw (1998) developed a laboratory paradigm in which participants were given a series of 11 tasks to perform, with each task lasting 3 minutes. In addition, subjects were asked to perform the prospective memory task of pressing a key on the keyboard once and only once during each task. In order not to strictly tie the prospective memory response to the start of each task, subjects were told to press the key some time during the task but not within the first 30 seconds of each task. Subjects were also told that if they were unsure whether or not they had already made the prospective memory response for a given task, it was better to press the key a second time than it was to omit it (see Chapter 7 for a detailed presentation of this experiment). Our main interest was in seeing if some confusions concerning whether or not the response had already been made would arise by the later trials (that is, after the task had become habitual). We tested both younger and older adults. For younger adults, there were relatively few (5%) repetition errors on both the early and later trials—although, depending on the situation, even a 5% error rate could be problematic in real life. For older adults, there were modest levels of repetition errors on the early tasks (11%) but high rates on the later tasks (18%), particularly in the divided-attention condition (28%). Indeed, on the final task, in the divided-attention condition, over 40% of the older adults made a repetition error. A similar pattern of repetition effects was found by Ramuschkat, McDaniel, Kliegel, and Einstein (2006). A related finding was that older subjects were more likely than younger subjects to omit a response during a task but then to mistakenly indicate at the end of the task that they had performed the response during that task. Taken together, these results suggest that source-monitoring and/or output-monitoring errors can develop in habitual prospective memory tasks and that older adults are more susceptible to these kinds of confusions.

Use external aids. Research has shown that external organizers (pill organizers into which one is able to load a supply of medication for a given period of time) are effective in improving adherence to medication regimens (e.g., Park, Morrell, Frieske, & Kincaid, 1992). Although it is unclear which of the above-mentioned cognitive processes benefit from these devices, external organizers can potentially facilitate cuing and can eliminate source-monitoring errors (that is, if your pill is there, you have not yet taken it, and if it is not there, you have taken it). In a laboratory analogue of a medication adherence task, subjects had to make the same response on each of 20 blocks of trials (Vedhara et al., 2004). External cues (an auditory cue signaling when the response should be performed along with a visual cue on the appropriate response key) dramatically reduced omission errors (from 52% in the control condition to 6% in the condition with both cues). Although most of this improvement was probably due to the auditory and visual cues serving as a reminder to perform the prospective memory action, it is likely that the external cues served also to reduce source- and output-monitoring confusions (for example, if subjects tied the performance of the action to the occurrence of the auditory cue, thoughts about performing the action at other times would not lead to an additional response). Supporting this interpretation, repetition errors were reduced by over half in the conditions with an auditory cue.

Increase the complexity of the action. Ramuschkat et al. (2006), using a paradigm very similar to that of Einstein et al. (1998), conducted a laboratory experiment in which subjects were asked to press a response key sometime during each of twelve 3-minute tasks. A novel aspect of this experiment was that it included a complex motor action condition in which each subject was required to put one hand on top of his or her head while pressing the key with the other hand. Making the action more complex (relative to requiring subjects to simply press the key with one hand) significantly reduced repetition errors for older adults (from 17% to 6%). The more elaborate response could have reduced repetition errors by improving output monitoring (that is, by making subjects pay more attention to performing the response) and/or by improving source monitoring (by making the response more distinctive so that it could be more easily distinguished from a thought about performing the action). These initial results suggest that training people to perform a complex and distinctive action when they execute a habitual prospective memory task (for example, to swirl the pill around in their mouth when they take medication) might, in the absence of external cues, be an effective way to reduce repetition errors.

Use the Spaced-Retrieval Technique

Spaced retrieval is a technique that has been successfully used in prospective memory situations by people who are experiencing mild to moderate deficits from Alzheimer's disease (Camp, Foss, Stevens, & O'Hanlon, 1996). The basic idea is to get people to practice retrieving the intended action, with each retrieval occurring after a delay longer than the previous one. Let's say, for example, that you want to train your uncle to take his medication with dinner. Initially you tell him, "You need to take your medication with dinner"; you then wait 20 seconds and ask, "What is it that you are supposed to do?" Given that the delay has been so short, he should be able to remember. Then you gradually increase the length of the delay by 20-second intervals (first you wait 20 seconds, then 40 seconds, then 60 seconds, and so on), asking your uncle at the end of each interval what it is that he is supposed to do. If he ever forgets, you remind him, then decrease the length of the delay by 20 seconds. Eventually, your uncle should be able to remember on his own.

Camp and his colleagues (Camp, Foss, Stevens, & O'Hanlon, 1996) have used this exact technique to help people with mild to moderate dementia remember to check a calendar in the morning to determine their chores for the day. The participants were given 30- to 45-minute training sessions each day over a 2-week period, at the end of which 61% of them were able to remember what it was they were supposed to do. With additional training and practice, 75% of the patients were eventually able to effectively check the calendar to determine their chores (see Chapter 5 for a more detailed description of this work).

The story in Figure 9.3 illustrates the nature and usefulness of this technique. As you can see, its effectiveness is not limited to prospective memory situations.

An Analysis of a Prospective Memory Failure and Possible Interventions

We believe that the basic principles described above are useful for discovering those situations that are especially susceptible to prospective memory failure and also for designing effective countermeasures in those situations. To provide one illustration, we analyze below a particularly shattering prospective memory failure.

In 2003, Mark, a university professor and a loving father, carefully and securely strapped his 10-month-old son in the car seat in the back of his car. His son, Mikey, who had been conceived only after heroic efforts with in

---

I drive my mother to the Alzheimer's center each weekday. Since we live on the north shore (of Lake Pontchartrain) and the center is on the south shore, this is a long drive (about 35 miles one way). All the way to the center my mom would keep asking, "Where are we going?" I'd tell her, "We're going to the school" (that is the name the family uses to refer to the center). Then she'd ask again, and again, and again. It used to drive me crazy. Well, after your talk I decided to try the thing you were talking about. So, the next day when we got into the car, I said, "Mom, we're going to the school now." Then I waited a few seconds and asked her, "Where are we going?" and she answered, "You said we were going to the school." Then I waited a couple of minutes and asked her, "Where are we going?" She looked at me like I was a little crazy and said, "We're going to school!" Then I waited a few more minutes and asked, "Where are we going?" Mom seemed a little mad, but said, "We're going to school, like you said." That was the last I brought up the subject, but you know, she never asked me that question the whole trip. Now I ask her when we get in the car, she answers, and that's that. I just thought you'd like to know that it actually works.

Figure 9.3   A True Story Illustrating the Effectiveness of the Spaced-Retrieval Technique

SOURCE: From Camp, Foss, and O'Hanlon (1996, p. 193).

vitro fertilization, was the joy of his life. Mark was preparing to drive to work, but on this particular morning he was also planning to drop his 10-month-old son off at day care on the way in. Although his usual routine was to drive to work alone, over the previous several months he had occasionally taken his son to the day care center on the way to work. The drive to the day care center and the drive to his office were very similar except for a different turn at the last intersection. On this day, Mikey fell asleep in the backseat. Mark "lost his concentration" and probably got absorbed in thinking about other things (such as the demands awaiting him at work). Instead of making the turn to the day care center, he drove straight to work, parked his car, and got out and walked to his office. It was 80 degrees outside that day, and Mikey died of heat stroke several hours later (see www.4rkidssake.org/mikeysstory.htm for more information about this tragic event).

How could this happen? How could a man described by his wife as "the most adoring, doting, and devoted father in the world" forget that his child was in the backseat? Rather than thinking of this as a failure of conscientiousness on the part of the father, we see this error as a memory lapse, albeit a heartbreaking one, that is an inherent consequence of normal cognitive functioning. We see it as an error that all of us are capable of making under the same circumstances. Although he was sleep deprived that morning, Mark was initially very aware of the intention to take Mikey to day care, and in the early stages of the ride, while Mikey was still awake, there were external cues that kept this intention activated. After Mikey fell asleep, however, there were no longer external cues that triggered the intention, and therefore it was up to Mark to maintain this goal or intention in memory. As we have indicated, this can be difficult to do, and the intention can be lost surprisingly quickly, especially if pressing work demands start to occupy one's mind. It is also important to realize that Mark did not normally drive Mikey to the day care center on his way to work. Thus, the habitual set of actions involved in driving to work was carried out. At work, there again were no cues, and Mark followed the normal set of actions—getting out of his car and walking to work (see "An atypical action is required instead of a habitual action" below).

What can be done to avoid tragic accidents like this? In our view, given that it is generally difficult to continuously use capacity-consuming resources to maintain intentions in mind (Bargh & Chartrand, 1999; Einstein et al., 2005), it is important to create good external cues that can serve to trigger remembering of the intention. As Mark states on his Web site (www.4rkidssake.org/mikeysstory.htm), "Put a diaper bag in the front seat every time your baby is in the car. Or put your purse, briefcase, wallet, or cell phone in the back seat where you will have to retrieve it before leaving the car." It may also be possible to develop alarms in car seats. Given the vicissitudes of our mental thoughts, it's important to have these kinds of external cues in place so that they can support prospective memory retrieval.

As stated at the beginning of this section, it is clear that current laboratory research is useful in identifying those conditions that are particularly vulnerable to prospective memory failure and for designing procedures for reducing failures. Nonetheless, it is also clear that existing laboratory paradigms do not fully capture all real-world and work-related prospective memory demands. We examine some of these limitations now.

Limitations of Existing Laboratory Experiments

Good prospective memory is critical to many work settings. For example, a mechanic who is performing maintenance on a complicated system must remember to perform a complex set of actions in the proper sequence (Reason, 1990). A nurse who has recently learned that a patient has an allergy not listed in the chart must remember to tell this information to the anesthesiologist. And, after a grueling 5-hour operation, the surgical team must remember to search for instruments and sponges that may have been left in the body—an error that occurs about once in 13,000 operations (Gawande et al., 2003).

In aviation settings, prospective memory failures can be similarly catastrophic. Although airline accidents that result in death or hull loss are extremely rare (1 in 1.4 million flights), especially in developed countries (1 in 5 million flights) (Dismukes, in press), accidents often have severe consequences. Thus, the cognitive demands of airline crews in safely launching, flying, and landing aircraft have been extensively analyzed (see, for example, Dismukes, in press, and Loukopoulos et al., 2003b). One approach used by scientists to understand these demands has been to carefully analyze reports from accidents as well as the more frequent voluntary reports from pilots about crew errors. In examining these data, Dismukes has identified several prospective memory demands that pilot crews encounter and that have not been examined in typical laboratory experiments (see also Loukopoulos et al., 2003b). In the sections below, which are based mainly on Dismukes's analysis, we describe prospective memory demands that are rarely captured in laboratory prospective memory experiments. The intention here is not to denigrate existing research but rather to inspire further thinking about the adequacy and limitations of current paradigms for investigating prospective memory as well as to stimulate creative development of new paradigms for capturing important processes.

Real-World Prospective Memory Demands Are Embedded in Meaningful Events

Imagine that an air traffic controller requests that the crew of an airplane, while making a descent from an altitude of 15,000 feet, report when the plane passes through 10,000 feet of altitude. Although the prospective memory demand ostensibly resembles prospective memory demands present in nonfocal event-based prospective memory tasks studied in the laboratory (see, for example, Park, Hertzog, Kidder, Morrell, & Mayhorn, 1997), the fact that an experienced pilot performs this in the richer context of a familiar sequence of actions may change the nature of the task. For example, the crew can anticipate that they will descend through 10,000 feet in about 5 minutes, and knowing their upcoming tasks and the duration of them (something that is rare in the laboratory), they can associate the altimeter reading with tasks that are likely to occur in 4 to 5 minutes. One indication that strategies change in well-known contexts comes from the work of Ceci and Bronfenbrenner (1985), who found that children's monitoring strategies were more efficient when a time-based prospective memory task was performed in the more familiar home context than they were when the same task was performed in the laboratory.

Real-World Habitual Prospective Memory Tasks Are Deeply Cued

Dismukes (in press) points out that pilots perform a complex set of procedures very often, usually in the same sequence, and that the execution of these actions eventually becomes automatic. Each individual action in the sequence is cued by the previous action and/or the perceptual context. For example, a pilot's normal sequence may be to set the flaps to takeoff position after performing a given checklist and prior to taxiing to the runway. Thus, completion of the checklist as well as the perceptual environment prior to taxiing are powerful cues for setting the flaps, and these serve the pilot well under normal conditions. Occasionally, however, because of weather conditions, the pilot may be asked to defer setting the flaps until after taxiing. At the runway, the normal kinesthetic and perceptual cues for setting the flaps to takeoff position are no longer available, and the pilot may be highly vulnerable to omitting this step. Dismukes convincingly argues, and we would agree, that the deeply cued nature of habitual prospective memory tasks has not been captured in laboratory prospective memory tasks—even in those studies examining habitual prospective memory (see, for example, Einstein et al., 1998)—which thereby underestimate the potential challenges and pitfalls of habitual tasks in the real world. In theory, by giving subjects extensive training with a sequence of tasks, it would be possible to mimic these characteristics in the laboratory. Another approach would be to develop laboratory paradigms that capitalize on already well-learned complex action sequences (for example, preparing a meal) (see Craik & Bialystok, 2006).

Interruptions can interfere with habitual actions. Another consequence of working in a highly proceduralized and sequential environment is that interruptions can disrupt the conditions that normally serve to trigger an action. According to Loukopoulos et al. (2003b), interruptions from flight attendants, ground personnel, and others are common in cockpit settings. Often these are in the form of requests that must be attended to. Also, interruptions remove the crew from the normal sequential and perceptual cuing conditions. During the interruption, the perceptual environment continues to move forward, so that the normal and routine cues for triggering the interrupted action may no longer be present. As Dismukes (in press) points out, these conditions are different from those in typical laboratory experiments examining the effects of interruptions on prospective memory. In these laboratory studies, subjects are given an action to perform (for example, "Press a key at the next task change") and then receive an interruption during the delay. Here, the interruption does not remove the subject from the typical cuing conditions for performing the action. That is, after the interruption, the cue which triggers performing of the action still occurs (although see Cook, 2005, for a paradigm in which the cue occurs during the interruption).

An atypical action is sometimes required instead of a habitual action. Another problem in real-world habitual prospective memory tasks is that a person may occasionally be asked to perform a novel action in a complex sequence of actions but because of habit will instead perform the old action. For example, you may decide that you will no longer put sugar on your breakfast cereal to reduce caloric intake, and then, out of habit, sprinkle sugar on your cereal the next morning (Reason, 1990). Or, after a long day at work, you may have the goal of getting home as quickly as possible. This goal is antagonistic to the intention to stop at the store to purchase bread on the way home. Still another example is the situation described earlier, in which a father who was taking his child to day care instead drove his usual route to work. Given that prospective memory researchers have tended not to examine well-ingrained sequences of actions in the laboratory, existing laboratory research has done little to help us understand these intrusions upon habit.

Monitoring for Low-Frequency Events May Be Required Over Extended Periods of Time

Dismukes (in press) points out that pilots often have to monitor for low-probability events while busily engaged in other tasks. For example, under certain weather conditions, pilots need to visually monitor the airspace for planes that are on a conflicting path. Although most of the laboratory research on prospective memory has not directly examined the ability of people to monitor for very low probability events, this prospective memory ability seems likely to be quite amenable to laboratory study.

Complex Sets of Actions Need to Be Planned and Initiated

A characteristic of many real-world prospective memory demands (although not necessarily in cockpit situations) is that we may have several actions to perform within a period of time without there being an inherent order to performing these tasks. Instead, we must plan to perform the actions within the parameters of our life space and later activate the plan and execute it. Complex planning and initiation are rarely captured in laboratory studies of prospective memory. Typically, the prospective memory demand is fairly simple and the experimenter makes the plans for the subjects by asking them to perform an action whenever they see a presented stimulus (event-based prospective memory task) or at a particular point in time (time-based prospective memory task). The one exception is the six-element task developed by Shallice and Burgess (1991) and modified by Kliegel, McDaniel, and Einstein (2000) to examine performance on the planning, initiation, and execution processes. For this task, subjects were given instructions regarding six subtasks as well as rules for sequencing the subtasks and maximizing performance. Maximum points could be earned by performing the tasks correctly and by performing the early items on a subtask and then moving on. Also, some subtasks could follow a given subtask and others could not (see Chapter 6 for more details about this research). Although rarely used in experimental research, this laboratory task is an initial attempt to capture planning and initiation strategies that occur in the real world when we are faced with carrying out multiple intentions within the constraints of our life space.

Real-World Retention Intervals Are Often Long

A characteristic of most laboratory prospective memory tasks is that the delay between the presentation of the prospective memory demand and the occurrence of the target item is fairly brief (typically on the order of 5 to 20 minutes). In the real world, the delays are often several hours (for example, the delay involved in planning to go to the gym later in the day), several days (planning to shop for a camera next weekend), or several weeks (planning to attend a friend's soccer game next month). Theoretically, we would expect prospective memory retrieval to be less reliant on monitoring and more dependant on spontaneous retrieval processes with longer delays. Although there have been several studies that have examined long-term prospective memory by asking subjects to mail cards to the experimenter on designated days (see, for example, Dobbs & Rule, 1987; Kvavilashvili & Fisher, 2007; Meacham & Leiman, 1982), there has been little research examining prospective memory after long delays under tightly controlled laboratory situations. Thus, delays extending beyond an hour or so, which occur frequently in the real world, have rarely been captured in laboratory experiments.

Nonlaboratory Methods for Investigating Prospective Memory

Our firm belief is that laboratory research on prospective memory is extremely useful not only for testing theoretical positions but also for predicting the real-world prospective memory situations that are especially susceptible to failure and for designing interventions that improve prospective memory in these situations. We believe the laboratory is a simplified reality that captures important aspects of real-world prospective memory demands. For example, extrapolating findings from the laboratory to real-world and work contexts, it is very reasonable to assume (based on the principles presented at the beginning of this chapter) that prospective memory is more likely to fail when a delay is introduced between the initial retrieval of an intention and the opportunity to perform the intended action, when interruptions are presented during the retention interval, when the work environment is stressful (for example, when attention is divided), and when prospective memory cues are not salient, distinctive, and related to the action. And existing research shows that removing delays and using better external cues improves prospective memory.

Even so, there may be important aspects of real-world prospective memory tasks that are difficult to capture in the typical laboratory paradigms that have thus far been used in prospective memory research. To increase awareness of less frequently used methods as well as to stimulate thinking about novel uses of these paradigms, below we briefly describe general classes of methods that have been used to study prospective memory in the real world. It is important to consider both ecological validity and the ability to control extraneous variables in evaluating the usefulness of these paradigms.

Incident Reports

As noted in an earlier section, Dismukes and his colleagues (Nowinski et al., 2003) have effectively analyzed airline accident reports as well as pilot reports of errors in order to document prospective memory errors and to assess the conditions that contribute to them. This technique was also used by Gawande et al. (2003) to examine the conditions in surgical cases that lead to failure to remove foreign objects (for example, sponges or clamps) from a patient's body. They compared problem surgeries (obtained from incident reports over a 6-year period) to control surgeries (surgeries in which the same procedures were performed but no foreign objects were left in the body) and found that leaving a foreign object in the body was nine times more likely when operations were performed on an emergency basis, four times more likely when there was an unexpected change in procedure, and also more likely with patients who had larger body mass indexes.

Clinical Assessment Techniques

Given that memory researchers have until recently tended to ignore prospective memory research, it is not surprising that traditional memory batteries (Wechsler, 1997) have not measured prospective memory. The earliest inclusion of a prospective memory task in a clinical assessment test was in the Rivermead Behavioral Test (Wilson, Cockburn, & Baddeley, 1985). This test contained two items measuring prospective memory, and both appeared in the context of performing retrospective memory tasks. Each prospective memory item required the respondent to remember to perform a simple action some time later in the experiment (one action was to be performed at the end of the session and the other when an alarm was heard). One problem with these test items is that they have not been shown to predict performance on real-world prospective tasks (Mills et al., 1997). A more recent test, called the Cambridge Test of Prospective Memory (Wilson et al., 2005), assesses both time-based prospective memory (three items) and event-based prospective memory (three items). Early indicators suggest that this may be a reliable and valid instrument for clinical assessment (Thöne-Otto & Walther, in press; Wilson et al., 2005).

In principle, the development of a valid and reliable clinical assessment of prospective memory ability could serve several important purposes. For instance, such a test would be useful in diagnosing patients with extensive prospective memory problems, who are thus at risk if they live independently. Given some initial indication that those with genetic liabilities for Alzheimer's disease are especially susceptible to prospective memory failures (Driscoll, McDaniel, & Guynn, 2005), such a test could also potentially serve as an early detector of dementia. In addition, this type of test could be useful in individual-difference research (for example, to see if prospective memory ability is independent of retrospective memory ability, as suggested by Salthouse, Berish, & Siedlecki, 2004).

Existing efforts to develop a clinical assessment technique for measuring prospective memory performance have assumed that prospective memory ability can be captured as one or possibly two constructs defined by the nature of the prospective memory task (for example, the event- and time-based items in the Cambridge Test of Prospective Memory). In light of the analyses presented throughout this book suggesting that different processes become prominent in different prospective situations (for example, different processes are recruited for focal and for nonfocal event-based tasks [see Chapter 4]), we suspect that the next generation of clinical assessment tools will benefit from additional analysis of the kinds of processes involved in different prospective memory tasks (for example, making a distinction between spontaneous retrieval and monitoring processes involved in focal and nonfocal event-based tasks, respectively). In addition to suggesting the kinds of prospective memory tasks that are most risky for a particular individual, this deeper analysis could suggest different pathologies.

Observational Studies

In an effort to understand the prospective memory demands that occur in cockpit situations, Loukopoulos et al. (2003b) have conducted observations from the jump seat of Boeing 737 airplanes. Sitting in the jump seat allowed clear observation of the cockpit controls, the cockpit displays, and the actions and interactions of both pilots. Although in the ideal situation pilots follow well-scripted routines in a serial fashion during flights, Loukopoulos et al.'s observations of 60 flights revealed that the pilots often handled several tasks simultaneously and that there were frequent disruptions to normal operating procedures. Thus, they discovered that interruptions, delays, and changes in the normal sequence of actions, all of which increase the probability of prospective memory errors, were common during the flights.

Simulations

Dieckmann, Reddersen, Wehener, and Rall (2003) conducted a study in which they asked fourth- and fifth-year medical students to perform action sequences typical of those involved in operations. They performed these on simulator manikins, which allowed authentic procedures (for example, blood pressure monitoring) to be performed, in a room that realistically simulated an operating theater. The scenarios lasted about 15 minutes each, and each contained between one and five prospective memory intentions. Working with realistic procedures in a simulation situation allows an ecologically valid method for assessing prospective memory under conditions that are highly controlled and amenable to the manipulation of variables (for example, stress levels). Simulations also allow people to bring well-learned skills into highly realistic prospective memory contexts, and thus hold great promise for identifying real-world prospective memory demands that are especially vulnerable to prospective memory failure.

Naturalistic Studies

Some of the earliest research on prospective memory was conducted using semi-naturalistic approaches in which the prospective memory demands were embedded into the person's ongoing life activities. For example, Meacham and Singer (1977) asked participants to mail in postcards on designated days and found that incentives were associated with greater use of external cues (for example, calendars) and better prospective memory.

Another approach to examining prospective memory in natural contexts is to examine the participants' success in carrying out their own intentions. Marsh, Hicks, and Landau (1998) conducted a classic set of studies of this type in which they asked participants to list their upcoming activities for the next week and rate the importance of each. Then, 1 week later, they asked the participants to indicate which actions had and had not been completed and to explain why the uncompleted intentions had not been performed. They also assessed the participants' memory and attentional capacities as well as their beliefs about these capacities. In addition, they manipulated variables, such as the presence of a "reminder" wristband over the delay interval. As Marsh, Hicks, and Landau point out, this method, although dependent on subjects' self-reports, enables researchers to examine how people handle multiple prospective memory demands that they themselves have established over an extended period of time. It also enables researchers to examine planning and reprioritizing processes that have been difficult to study in the laboratory.

As noted earlier, naturalistic studies often produce different results from those of laboratory studies (Ceci & Bronfenbrenner, 1985). For example, in performing a meta-analysis of the prospective memory and aging literature, Henry, MacLeod, Phillips, and Crawford (2004) found that younger adults generally outperform older adults on laboratory tests of prospective memory (although see Chapter 7 for variables that affect the presence and magnitude of age differences), yet older adults outperform younger adults in naturalistic studies. It is not clear why this is. It may be that older adults in naturalistic settings have greater control over the pacing of the ongoing activities (that is, they can perform their ongoing activities at their own pace, whereas in the laboratory, the pacing is usually equivalent for younger and older adults), use better external devices, or place greater emphasis on the prospective memory task than do younger adults. Also, it may be that the processes we rely on for remembering in naturalistic settings are different from those we rely on in laboratory settings. Though we do not know which of these factors explains the discrepancy between laboratory and naturalistic studies, at least some of these possible explanations are amenable to empirical investigation.

Naturalistic studies with a diary. One limitation of naturalistic studies is that it is very difficult to control and assess the strategies that participants use in their natural environment as well as the rehearsals that occur over the delay period. Kvavilashvili and Fisher (2007) have developed an interesting technique in which they ask participants to record information relevant to the prospective memory intention in a diary over the retention interval. As described earlier in this chapter, participants were asked to make a phone call to the experimenter 1 week later and to record in the diary any thoughts about the intention (the time of rehearsal, the participant's current location, the activity in which he or she was engaged, impressions of what triggered the thought, etc.) during the 1-week delay period. Although there are important questions regarding subjects' abilities to accurately identify intention-related thoughts as well as to identify the triggering stimuli, this technique holds promise for enhancing our understanding of how and when intentions come to mind over a retention interval.

Naturalistic studies with recording devices. One potential problem with naturalistic studies is that the researcher is often dependent on subjects' reports for assessing the accurate fulfillment of prospective memory intentions. In Marsh, Hicks, and Landau's (1998) research, for example, it was the participants who reported whether or not they had accomplished their prospective memory intentions in a satisfactory manner. Current technology allows us more objective and detailed recording of the accuracy of responding. For example, Park and Kidder (1996) describe the Medication Event Monitoring System, which is an electronic bottle cap system that records the date and time a medication bottle is opened over a period as long as 6 months. Thus, one could use this system to evaluate the extent to which a patient has complied with a medication regimen (see also Insel, Morrow, Brewer, & Figueredo, 2006).

An effective use of this type of technology was recently reported by Liu and Park (2004). They trained participants to use glucometers to monitor blood glucose levels on a regular basis (four times per day) over a 3-week period. Use of the glucometers was electronically recorded, and when they were turned in, the researchers could download how often and when the glucometers had been used. The results showed that implementation intentions (described earlier in this chapter) improved adherence to the glucose-monitoring regimen.

Sellen, Louie, Harris, & Wilkins (1997) developed a particularly clever use of technology to begin to investigate how and when thoughts about intentions come to mind (Chapter 5 elaborates on this work). Participants in the study were employees in a company who agreed to wear special badges, and there were sensors in their building that could identify the location of the badges and when the button on the badges had been clicked. For the time-based prospective memory task, participants were asked to triple-click their badge at designated times for each of 5 days. For the event-based prospective memory task, they were asked to triple-click their badge whenever they happened to be in a certain room over a 5–day period. Also, they were asked to single-click their badge whenever the prospective memory intention came to mind. The researchers found that participants were more likely to think about the prospective memory task when they were in transition (for example, in a stairwell walking from one room to another) than they were when they were settled in a particular location (for example, their office). These results suggest that we are more likely to review our plans and think about intentions when we are not busily engaged in an ongoing task and instead are having a "down" time, such as when we are taking a break or pausing after completing a task. As wireless computer technology advances and becomes more prevalent, this technique appears to hold great promise for monitoring of peoples' thoughts and actions and therefore for informing theories of prospective memory.

External Reminding Devices

Before closing this chapter, we briefly consider creative attempts to develop external aids that take advantage of current technology for improving prospective remembering. From setting the timer on the oven to using calendars, all of us have used external devices to help us remember to perform actions in the future. These have the potential to help us initiate retrieval of the intention at the appropriate time, remember the retrospective memory component of the intended action (that is, what it is that has to be done), and/or monitor performance of the action so that it is not repeated later on.

In recent years, there has been considerable interest in developing electronic memory aids for improving prospective remembering in individuals with memory impairments. Problems in living independently tend to be correlated with the severity of memory impairment, and the idea is that external memory aids can help give autonomy to people with these kinds of problems. Palm organizers, pager systems, and mobile phones with an agenda mode have been shown to be effective for patients with brain injuries (see, for example, Wilson, Evans, Emslie, & Malinek, 1997). For example, Thöne-Otto and Walther (2003) tested the utility of palm organizers and mobile phone systems for helping subjects remember to perform 20 experimental tasks over a 2-week period. These devices sounded an alarm at the appropriate times and also displayed the intended action. Although these devices generally improved prospective memory (see also Oriani et al., 2003, for evidence that this type of external aid is helpful with mildly to moderately impaired Alzheimer's patients), one limitation is that programming of these devices is not simple, and Thöne-Otto and Walther found that this was too difficult for some of the patients. Another limitation is that these devices mainly facilitate the initial retrieval of the intended action along with recollection of the specific action. They do not guide the person through the actual execution of the intended action or protect the person against untimely distractions or interruptions that could interfere with the execution of the intended action.

One memory aid that seems to be easier for patients to use and that also appears to facilitate execution in addition to retrieval is the Mobile Extensible Memory Aid System (MEMOS) (Schulze, Hoffmann, Voinikonis, & Irmscher, 2003; Thöne-Otto, Schulze, Irmscher, & von Cramon, 2001). MEMOS allows caregivers or patients to enter appointments on a central server. Patients can set up an appointment simply by speaking into their personal memory assistant (PMA), which is similar to a mobile phone. The central server then sends an alarm, as well as the steps for the appropriate execution of the action, to the PMA at the proper time. Additionally, because the communication between the central server and the PMA can be bidirectional, the system can be programmed so that the patient has to confirm performance of each step of the action protocol. Thus, there can be feedback about whether or not the action has been executed. In light of continuing technological advancements, it seems that external reminding devices have tremendous potential for improving prospective memory in a variety of work and everyday settings.

Summary

As noted in the first part of this chapter, the past two decades of prospective memory research have advanced our understanding to the point where the field has much to offer in terms of identifying conditions that are especially prone to prospective memory failure and designing effective interventions. We have reviewed a number of potentially valid interventions in this chapter. Nevertheless, given the variety of prospective memory tasks that exist in the real world and the complexity of the processes involved in prospective memory (including planning, memory, and attention), we agree with Dismukes (in press) and others that the prevalent laboratory paradigms do not fully capture all flavors of prospective memory tasks as they exist in naturalistic and work settings.

Often, when reducing a phenomenon into something that can be experimentally studied in the laboratory, we strip it, at least initially, of some important processes. One approach to closing this gap is to analyze critical aspects of real-world prospective memory tasks that are not represented in laboratory paradigms and to creatively develop new laboratory tasks. Another is to continue to develop and refine nonlaboratory approaches for studying prospective memory. We have offered examples of different kinds of tasks that may help us understand at least some components of prospective memory. In general, we believe that there is a healthy interplay between the laboratory and nonlaboratory approaches. Naturalistic studies can often suggest interesting processes and results, which can then be examined under more controlled conditions in the laboratory. Also, conducting laboratory and nonlaboratory studies has the potential for providing converging evidence which can be used to more convincingly support theoretical and empirical positions. This chapter illustrates the value of both laboratory and naturalistic research in developing useful applications of prospective memory research.

10

Final Thoughts

When we first approached the task of writing this book, we were optimistic but yet a bit concerned about the availability of enough quality research on prospective memory to support a full-length text on the topic. After all, there were only a trickle of papers on prospective memory prior to 1990. Indeed, in the early years of prospective memory research, Harris (1984) stated, "Until recently psychological research on memory, from Ebbinghaus to Bartlett, has dealt, almost exclusively, with remembering information rather than remembering to do things" (p. 71).

Since that time, research on the topic has progressed at a geometric rate, but even so we were worried that it would be highly scattered, perhaps not address common themes, and in general be difficult to organize. This was certainly the state of affairs in the mid-1980s, when Harris (1984) concluded his paper by writing

> In this chapter I have argued that remembering to do things is an important aspect of memory, I have given an account of the studies that have been performed, and I have discussed some embryonic theoretical notions. If the account seems to be like a list, it is because the studies have been performed in the absence of any encompassing theory and the researchers have performed their investigations for various, sometimes applied reasons, with little knowledge of each other's work. (p. 90)

As we delved into each topic, we became increasingly stimulated, if not outright excited, by the depth and breadth of the empirical findings, the creative development of new methods, the insightful applications of prospective memory research to new domains, and the richness of the theorizing on cognitive and neurocognitive processes. We believe that we now know a lot about prospective memory and, more important, that we have a firm foundation of data, methods, and theories from which to move forward into even more prosperous decades of research. And, although there has been heartening progress on a number of issues, the research has also naturally opened up a host of issues and questions that penetrate to a deeper analysis of prospective memory and will likely guide future research. In this final chapter, we offer some thoughts (many of which are suggestions) for shaping some of this future research. In making these observations, we admittedly occasionally step back from the data and take some latitude in offering our opinions on profitable future directions. We offer these not as divinely inspired prescriptions for how to conduct research but as starting points for critical discussion of fruitful avenues for future research.

General Observations

Beware of Unitary Interpretations

In examining the literature, it is tempting at times to overgeneralize and to ignore or minimize opposing findings. For example, upon seeing that a majority of experiments demonstrate age differences on laboratory event-based prospective memory tasks (see Table 7.4), we believe that it is important not to easily dismiss the discrepant findings and quickly conclude that aging generally disrupts prospective memory. Instead, we see this as an opportunity to examine the details of the different prospective memory tasks and unpack the different processes involved in them in an effort to identify the processes that are more and less disrupted by normal aging. Moreover, in looking at these processes, it's important to realize that the preponderance of the evidence from laboratory tasks may not reflect the state of affairs in the real world. It is possible, for example, that laboratory tasks emphasize one process (for example, monitoring), whereas real-world tasks emphasize a different process (for example, spontaneous retrieval).

Keep in Mind Real-World Prospective Memory Tasks When Designing Laboratory Prospective Memory Tasks

As described in Chapter 1, we have developed a broad definition of prospective memory—one that can potentially encompass a wide variety of prospective memory tasks, including episodic and habitual tasks, tasks with very brief delays, tasks with very long delays, tasks with few targets, and tasks with many different target events. Moreover, the targets can be focal or non-focal, common or distinctive, simple (for example, the word *red*) or complex in terms of having to satisfy multiple criteria (for example, a word that is in capital letters and in red), presented every so often or presented frequently, and so on. In designing a prospective memory task, it is critical to keep in mind that decisions about these characteristics have implications regarding the cognitive processes that are recruited for a particular prospective memory task.

Thus, researchers need to have a good idea of the cognitive processes and prospective memory situations they wish to measure and to make their choices accordingly. This is sometimes difficult to do, because the measurement challenges in prospective memory research can suggest a different direction. To maximize the number of observations and hence the reliability of one's measurement, researchers might be tempted to include many target events in a particular task. At one extreme, for example, a researcher might decide to use 10 different target events and present each one five times among a list of 200 ongoing-task items. Researchers should be aware that this decision in all likelihood fundamentally alters the nature of the cognitive processes involved so that they differ from those underlying many real-world prospective memory tasks, such as those with one target event (for example, a colleague) and a single execution of the intended action (for example, give a message). With so many different targets occurring so often, this design amplifies the importance of monitoring processes for successful retrieval.

So, how do we decide on which processes to examine? Well, as noted above, researchers must consider the theoretical issues that they are examining. In selecting processes for study, we believe it is also important to keep in mind the real-world prospective memory tasks we are trying to understand. Although we have touted the usefulness of nonexperimental methods throughout this book, we remain firm experimentalists who believe that tightly controlled laboratory research will be the ultimate arbiter of theoretical disagreements. Nonetheless, our general impression is that laboratory tasks have sometimes sacrificed ecological validity in the spirit of overcoming measurement problems. Specifically, we believe that the majority of laboratory experiments on prospective memory have tended to emphasize monitoring processes. As such, the data from these studies are useful for generalizing to real-world prospective memory situations that require fairly constant monitoring processes. But, as Kvavilashvili and Fisher's (2007) and Sellen, Louie, Harris, and Wilkins's (1997) studies suggest (see Chapters 5 and 9), people tend not to engage in fairly constant monitoring processes in many real-world settings. From the perspective of understanding prospective memory as it occurs in these kinds of settings, it would make sense to construct experimental paradigms in such a way as to specifically discourage monitoring.

In general, we (and we include ourselves here) need to be ever mindful of the real-world prospective memory processes that we are trying to explain.

Continuing with this theme of ecological validity, we urge researchers to consider other aspects of real-world prospective memory tasks that have been underrepresented in experimental paradigms. For example, as discussed in Chapter 6, laboratory research typically preempts planning and encoding processes, and as discussed in Chapter 9, laboratory research has tended to use a limited range of retention intervals. Also, laboratory paradigms have tended to remove the richly textured and meaningful sequences within which real-world prospective memory tasks are typically embedded (Dismukes, in press) as well as events that are potentially related to prospective memory targets, thereby precluding important reminding processes (Kvavilashvili & Fisher, 2007).

Investigate How Individual Differences on Cognitive, Neurocognitive, and Personality Dimensions Affect Prospective Memory

As we develop increasingly more sophisticated methods for analyzing the processes involved in prospective remembering, we believe that including individual-difference variables will be helpful for testing theoretical positions as well as for understanding those prospective memory situations that are most risky for particular individuals. For example, individuals with low working-memory capacity might be expected to perform especially poorly on prospective memory tasks in which extensive planning is needed. They would also be expected to perform poorly on tasks in which monitoring processes are needed for prospective memory retrieval but well on those in which spontaneous retrieval processes are likely to accomplish retrieval.

Explore People's Metacognitive Knowledge About Prospective Memory

In a related vein, based on the multiprocess view that different processes come to the fore in different prospective memory tasks, it is important to study people's metacognitive awareness of the demands of different prospective memory situations. With the exception of research by Meeks, Hicks, and Marsh (2006), there has been little research exploring the extent to which people are sensitive to the presence of important features of prospective memory tasks (for example, the presence of environmental support) and to their ability to develop effective internal or external strategies in these situations.

Continue to Conduct Finer-Grained Analysis of the Processes Involved in Prospective Remembering

In examining prospective memory retrieval, for example, Marsh, Hicks, and Watson (2002) articulated three microprocesses, each of which is interesting in its own right. Specifically, they argued that prospective memory responding involves noticing the cue, retrieving the intended action, and coordinating the inhibition of ongoing activity with the initiation of the intended action. Further, they developed experimental procedures for inferring the effects of different variables on the different components. By the same token, monitoring may also involve multiple processes (for example, see Guynn, 2003, and Chapter 2 of this book for a discussion of retrieval mode and checking processes).

Continue to Develop and Accept New Methodological Approaches, Including Naturalistic Ones, for Studying Prospective Remembering

It is very difficult to bring key features of real-world prospective memory into the laboratory, and as should be evident from the research described in this book, our current understanding of prospective memory has benefited from a variety of laboratory and nonlaboratory methods. We believe that a key to furthering our understanding of prospective memory will be the creative development of new methodological techniques—both experimental and naturalistic. It is important to keep in mind the advantages of multiple approaches as well as the useful interplay between laboratory and nonlaboratory methods (while also being mindful of the limitations of each method). Kvavilashvili and Fisher (2007), for example, have recently developed an interesting naturalistic paradigm (in which people were asked to record the thoughts that triggered their memories of an intention over a 1-week period) for illuminating the cognitive processes that occur between the formation of the intention and the execution of the intention.

Methodological Recommendations for Encouraging Consistency Across Experiments and for Understanding Existing Inconsistencies

First, it is becoming increasingly clear that subjects monitor in some experiments and not in others. Moreover, even within the same experiment, some subjects monitor and some do not (Einstein et al., 2005, Experiment 4). Given that it is usually, if not always, important to know the underlying processes that subjects are recruiting to remember, following Smith's (2003) important work, we recommend that researchers routinely measure costs or interference on the ongoing task. Thus, in the ideal experiment, researchers would measure the speed and accuracy of performing the ongoing task in both the presence and the absence of a prospective memory task.

Second, when making comparisons across different populations (for example, different age groups), we believe it is critical to keep in mind that prospective memory intentions are embedded within an ongoing task, which, if held constant, could be differentially demanding for the different groups. If this is the case, any differences in prospective memory performance could be due to differences in ongoing-task demands and not to prospective memory per se. Consequently, researchers should consider functionally equating the difficulty and pacing of the ongoing tasks across the populations. One way of handling this is to use a self-paced task and, as noted above, measure the accuracy and speed of performing the ongoing task both with and without a prospective task.

Third, we recommend making other suitable adjustments when making comparisons across populations. For example, the retrospective memory literature is clear in showing that time of day is a relevant variable in comparing younger and older adults (May & Hasher, 1998). There is good evidence that morning is the optimal time of day for most older adults and that afternoon/evening is the optimal time of day for younger adults. At the 2005 International Conference on Prospective Memory, it was clear that some researchers adjusted their testing times for younger and older adults to suit their optimal time of day whereas other researchers did not. Thus, our recommendation is to make adjustments to equate populations on relevant dimensions (that is, to test younger and older adults at their optimal times).

Fourth, recent research has shown that the instructional emphasis on either the ongoing task or the prospective memory task clearly affects the strategic approach that subjects use in a prospective memory task. Thus, minor differences in instructions could lead to very different experimental outcomes. In this light, we encourage researchers to clearly define the relative importance of these tasks to their subjects and to include a verbatim description of the instructions in their publications.

Fifth, poor prospective memory could be the result of prospective memory or retrospective memory problems. For example, failing to press a key during an experiment whenever the target item *star* occurs could be due to failing to remember the target item or the target action (a retrospective memory problem) or failing to remember to perform the action despite good retrospective memory for the task demands (a prospective problem). To distinguish between these possibilities, it is important for researchers to probe subjects' retrospective memory for the task demands at the end of the experiment.

Understanding the Nature of the Task Interference, or Costs, Involved in Prospective Memory

As noted above, laboratory research in recent years has shown that subjects often slow down on the ongoing task when they are also performing the prospective memory task. Although this slowing is typically interpreted to reflect preparatory attentional or monitoring processes, the nature of this task interference is not well understood. It is possible, for example, that it reflects attentional monitoring for the target item, and this could be a relatively quick, perhaps unconscious, and constant process, or this slowing could reflect an average level of interference resulting from occasional periods of conscious monitoring. Still other possibilities are that the slowing reflects rehearsals of the target items, reflections on whether any target items have been missed, and/or ruminations about the frequency of occurrence of target items. The point here is that we do not yet have a good understanding of what is producing the slowing when subjects "monitor."

Expanding Theories and Investigations of Prospective Memory to Arenas Not Typically Termed Prospective Memory

We are in our infancy in terms of exploring applications of prospective memory research in real-world settings. For the most part, applied researchers have focused on understanding prospective memory demands in aviation and medication adherence contexts and more recently during medical operations. Given that the topic of prospective memory broadly encompasses remembering to perform actions in the future, it is integrally involved in our daily lives. For example, consider psychotherapeutic contexts. Psychotherapists often give their clients actions to perform and other actions to inhibit in response to certain events (Arbuthnott & Arbuthnott, 1999). Successful completion of these prescribed activities likely involves prospective memory, at least in part. Psychotherapists themselves undergo training to incorporate new clinical methods into their practice, and adherence to the new methods can be difficult (Rogers, 1995), possibly due to prospective memory challenges in overcoming long-standing clinical practice habits (for reasons described in our analysis of intrusions upon habits in Chapter 9). Thus, successful use of retraining techniques may benefit from consideration of prospective memory principles.

For another example, an important goal of our educational system is to impart knowledge and problem-solving skills to students so that they can later effectively apply them in relevant situations. Educators tend to think of these situations as those in which it is important for the students to have good retrospective memory for the new knowledge. However, this is only part of the solution, and we also need to understand the conditions that allow people to remember to apply this information in the appropriate contexts. Prospective memory research, both basic and applied in nature, may be helpful in our discovering how to improve spontaneous retrieval or transfer in educational settings.

Capitalizing on the Prospective Memory Paradigm for Studying the Broader Issue of Spontaneous Retrieval

Finally, in the bigger picture, prospective memory research may allow leverage on the more general issue of understanding spontaneous retrieval. Over 100 years ago, Ebbinghaus (1885/1964) drew a distinction between three kinds of fundamental processes. Two of these can be characterized as explicit recollection and implicit remembering, and these have been studied extensively in the scientific memory literature. The third process was described as the spontaneous appearance of a mental state, "without any act of will" (p. 2), that is recognized as having been previously experienced. Though such spontaneous retrieval is arguably prominent in everyday memory functioning, it is not easily isolated or studied in laboratory paradigms. Retrospective memory paradigms intertwine explicit recollection and spontaneous retrieval (see Ste-Marie & Jacoby, 1993, for an attempt to reveal spontaneous retrieval in the laboratory). Because of difficulties of this sort, some have adopted a naturalistic self-report approach to exploring spontaneous retrieval (Kvavilashvili & Mandler, 2004). We envision that prospective memory paradigms (precisely because they do not include direct requests to remember) could provide foundational techniques for understanding the intriguing topic of spontaneous retrieval.

Epilogue

We are struck with the enormous progress that has been made in understanding prospective memory since Harris (1984) published his important review paper in the mid-1980s. At that time, he pleaded for additional research on this "forgotten topic" (p. 71), and he characterized the research as sparse, "embryonic" (p. 89), and lacking in "encompassing theory" (p. 90). Furthermore, the few prospective memory researchers were largely working independently.

What a difference two decades have made! They have confirmed Harris's belief that "prospective memory is an interesting topic, worthy of study, and accessible to experimentation" (p. 90). Today, the research is more thematic, highly accessible, and appearing in varied journals, including the best journals. As a result, there is now an impressive theoretical and empirical basis for understanding the cognitive processes involved in prospective memory, how they change across the life span, and the neuroscience underlying these processes. We are also making progress in understanding important applied issues, such as which conditions are most susceptible to forgetting and how to improve prospective remembering. We are confident that this richly textured empirical, methodological, and theoretical basis will stimulate even more research and interest in prospective memory in the coming decades.

References

Aarts, H., & Dijksterjuis, A. (1999). How often did I do it? Experienced ease of retrieval and frequency estimates of past behavior. *Acta Psychologica, 103,* 77–99.

Anderson, J. R. (1983). *The architecture of cognition.* Cambridge, MA: Harvard University Press.

Arbuthnott, K., & Arbuthnott, D. (1999). The best intentions: Prospective remembering in psychotherapy. *Psychotherapy: Theory, Research, Practice, Training, 36,* 247–256.

Baddeley, A. (1986). *Working memory.* New York: Oxford University Press.

Baddeley, A. D., & Hitch, G. J. (1994). Developments in the concept of working memory. *Neuropsychology, 8,* 485–493.

Banaji, M. R., & Hardin, C. D. (1996). Automatic stereotyping. *Psychological Science, 7,* 136–141.

Bargh, J. A. (1994). The Four Horsemen of automaticity: Awareness, intention, efficiency, and control in social cognition. In R. S. Wyer & T. K. Srull (Eds.), *Handbook of social cognition* (2nd ed., pp. 1–40). Hillsdale, NJ: Erlbaum.

Bargh, J. A. (1997). The automaticity of everyday life. In R. S. Wyer (Ed.), *The automaticity of everyday life: Advances in social cognition* (Vol. 10, pp. 1–61). Mahwah, NJ: Erlbaum.

Bargh, J. A., & Chartrand, T. L. (1999). The unbearable automaticity of being. *American Psychologist, 54,* 462–479.

Bargh, J. A., Chen, M., & Burrows, L. (1996). Automaticity of social behavior: Direct effects of trait construct and stereotype activation on action. *Journal of Personality and Social Psychology, 71,* 230–244.

Battig, W. F. (1978). An unremembered principal serial-position feature. *American Journal of Psychology, 91,* 587–605.

Baumeister, R. F., Bratslavsky, E., Muraven, M., & Tice, D. M. (1998). Ego depletion: Is the active self a limited resource? *Journal of Personality and Social Psychology, 74,* 1252–1265.

Bisiacchi, P. S. (1996). The neuropsychological approach in the study of prospective memory. In M. Brandimonte, G. Einstein, & M. McDaniel (Eds.), *Prospective memory: Theory and applications* (pp. 199–225). Mahwah, NJ: Erlbaum.

Bjork, E. L., & Bjork, R. A. (2003). Intentional forgetting can increase, not decrease, residual influences of to-be-forgotten information. *Journal of Experimental Psychology: Learning, Memory, and Cognition, 29,* 524–531.

Bjork, E. L., Bjork, R. A., & Anderson, M. C. (1998). Varieties of goal-directed for-getting. In J. M. Golding & C. M. MacLeod (Eds.), *Intentional forgetting: Interdisciplinary approaches* (pp. 103–137). Mahwah, NJ: Erlbaum.

Bjork, R. A., & Whitten, W. B. (1974). Recency-sensitive retrieval processes in long-term free recall. *Cognitive Psychology, 6,* 173–189.

Brandimonte, M. A., & Passolunghi, M. C. (1994). The effect of cue-familiarity, cue-distinctiveness, and retention interval on prospective remembering. *Quarterly Journal of Experimental Psychology: Human Experimental Psychology, 47*(A), 565–588.

Brandstatter, V., Lengfelder, A., & Gollwitzer, P. M. (2001). Implementation inten-tions and efficient action initiation. *Journal of Personality and Social Psychology, 81,* 946–960.

Breneiser, J. E. (2004). *Prospective memory retrieval: Associativity, discrepancy, and individual differences.* Unpublished master's thesis, University of New Mexico, Albuquerque.

Breneiser, J. E., & McDaniel, M. A. (2006). Prospective memory retrieval and discrepancy plus search: Further evidence. *Psychonomic Bulletin & Review, 13,* 837–841.

Buckner, R. L., Snyder, A. Z., Shannon, B. J., LaRossa, G., Sachs, R., Fotenos, A. F., et al. (2005). Molecular, structural, and functional characterization of Alzheimer's disease: Evidence for a relationship between default activity, amyloid, and mem-ory. *Journal of Neuroscience, 24,* 7709–7717.

Burgess, P. W., Quayle, A., & Frith, C. D. (2001). Brain regions involved in prospec-tive memory as determined by positron emission tomography. *Neuropsychologia, 39,* 545–555.

Burgess, P. W., Scott, S. K., & Frith, C. D. (2003). The role of the rostral frontal cortex (area 10) in prospective memory: A lateral versus medial dissociation. *Neuropsychologia, 41,* 906–918.

Burgess, P. W., & Shallice, T. (1997). The relationship between prospective and retrospective memory: Neuropsychological evidence. In M. A. Conway (Ed.), *Cognitive models of memory* (pp. 247–272). Cambridge: MIT Press.

Burgess, P. W., Simons, J. S., Dumontheil, I., & Gilbert, S. J. (2005) The gateway hypothesis of rostral PFC function. In J. Duncan, L. Phillips, & P. McLeod (Eds.), *Measuring the mind: Speed, control, and age* (pp. 215–246). Oxford, UK: Oxford University Press.

Burgess, P. W., Veitch, E., de Lacy Costello, A., & Shallice, T. (2000). The cognitive and neuroanatomical correlates of multitasking. *Neuropsychologia, 38,* 848–863.

Camp, C. J, Foss, J. W., & O'Hanlon, A. M. (1996). Memory interventions for persons with dementia. *Applied Cognitive Psychology, 10,* 193–210.

Camp, C. J., Foss, J. W., Stevens, A. B., & O'Hanlon, A. M. (1996). Improving prospective memory task performance in persons with Alzheimer's disease. In M. Brandimonte, G. Einstein, & M. McDaniel (Eds.), *Prospective memory: Theory and applications* (pp. 351–367). Mahwah, NJ: Erlbaum.

Ceci, S. J., & Bronfenbrenner, U. (1985). "Don't forget to take the cupcakes out of the oven": Prospective memory, strategic time-monitoring, and context. *Child Development, 56,* 152–164.

Chasteen, A. L., Park, D. C., & Schwarz, N. (2001). Implementation intentions and facilitation of prospective memory. *Psychological Science, 12,* 457–461.

Cherry, K. E., & LeCompte, D. C. (1999). Age and individual differences influence prospective memory. *Psychology and Aging, 14,* 60–76.

Cherry, K. E., Martin, R. C., Simmons-D'Gerolamo, S. S., Pinkston, J. B., Griffing, A. & Gouvier, W. D. (2001). Prospective remembering in younger and older adults: Role of the prospective cue. *Memory, 9,* 177–193.

Cohen, A. L., & Gollwitzer, P. M. (in press). The cost of remembering to remember: Cognitive load and implementation intentions influence ongoing task performance. In M. Kliegel, M. A. McDaniel, & G. O. Einstein (Eds.), *Prospective memory: Cognitive, neuroscience, developmental, and applied perspectives.* Mahwah, NJ: Erlbaum.

Cohen, A. L., West, R., & Craik, F. I. M. (2001). Modulation of prospective and retrospective components of memory for intentions in younger and older adults. *Aging, Neuropsychology, and Cognition, 8,* 1–13.

Cohen, J. D., & O'Reilly, R. C. (1996). A preliminary theory of the interactions between prefrontal cortex and hippocampus that contribute to planning and prospective memory. In M. Brandimonte, G. Einstein, & M. McDaniel (Eds.), *Prospective memory: Theory and applications* (pp. 199–225). Mahwah, NJ: Erlbaum.

Colegrove, F. W. (1899). Individual memories. *American Journal of Psychology, 10,* 228–255.

Cook, G. I. (2005). Investigating task interruptions in the delay-execute prospective memory task. Unpublished doctoral dissertation, University of Georgia, Athens.

Cook, G. I., Marsh, R. L., & Hicks, J. L. (2005). Associating a time-based prospective memory task with an expected context can improve or impair intention completion. *Applied Cognitive Psychology, 19,* 345–360.

Coren, S., & Ward, L. M. (1989). *Sensation and perception* (3rd ed.). Orlando, FL: Academic Press.

Cowan, N. (1999). The differential maturation of two processing rates related to digit span. *Journal of Experimental Child Psychology, 72,* 193–209.

Craik, F. I. M. (1986). A functional account of age differences in memory. In F. Clix & H. Hangendorf (Eds.), *Human memory and cognitive capabilities: Mechanisms and performances* (pp. 409–422). Amsterdam: Elsevier.

Craik, F. I. M. (2003). Aging and memory in humans. In J. H. Byrne, H. Eichenbaum, H. L. Roediger, & R. F. Thompson (Eds.), *Learning and memory* (pp. 11–14). New York: Macmillan.

Craik, F. I. M., & Bialystok, E. (2006). Planning and task management in older adults: Cooking breakfast. *Memory & Cognition, 34,* 1236–1249.

Craik, F. I. M., Govoni, R., Naveh-Benjamin, M., & Anderson, N. D. (1996). The effects of divided attention on encoding and retrieval processes in human memory. *Journal of Experimental Psychology: General, 125,* 159–180.

Curran, T. (2000). Brain potentials of recollection and familiarity. *Memory & Cognition, 28,* 923–938.

Curran, T., & Dien, J. (2003). Differentiating amodal familiarity from modality-specific memory processes: An ERP study. *Psychophysiology, 40,* 979–988.

Dembitzer, A., & Lai, E. J. (2003). Retained surgical instrument. *New England Journal of Medicine, 348*, 228.

Devolder, P. A., Brigham, M. C., & Pressley, M. (1990). Memory performance awareness in younger and older adults. *Psychology and Aging, 5*, 291–303.

Dieckmann, P., Reddersen, S., Wehener, T., & Rall, M. (in press). Prospective memory failures as an unexplored threat to patient's safety: Results from a pilot study using patient simulators to investigate the missed execution of intentions. *Ergonomics.*

Dismukes, R. K. (in press). Prospective memory in aviation and everyday settings. In M. Kliegel, M. A. McDaniel, & G. O. Einstein (Eds.), *Prospective memory: Cognitive, neuroscience, developmental, and applied perspectives.* Mahwah, NJ: Erlbaum.

Dobbs, A. R., & Reeves, M. B. (1996). Prospective memory: More than memory. In M. Brandimonte, G. Einstein, & M. McDaniel (Eds.), *Prospective memory: Theory and applications* (pp. 199–225). Mahwah, NJ: Erlbaum.

Dobbs, A. R., & Rule, B. G. (1987). Prospective memory and self-reports of memory abilities in older adults. *Canadian Journal of Psychology, 41*, 209–222.

Driscoll, I., McDaniel, M. A., & Guynn, M. J. (2005). Apolipoprotein E and prospective memory in normally aging adults. *Neuropsychology, 19*, 28–34.

Duchek, J. M., Balota, D. A., & Cortese, M. (2006). Prospective memory and apolipoprotein E in healthy aging and early stage Alzheimer's disease. *Neuropsychology, 20*, 633–644.

Dunbar-Jacob, J., Erlen, J. A., Schlenk, E. A., Ryan, C. M., Sereika, S. M., & Doswell, W. M. (2000). Adherence in chronic disease. *Annual Review of Nursing Research, 18*, 48–90.

d'Ydewalle, G., Luwel, K., & Brunfaut, E. (1999). The importance of on-going concurrent activities as a function of age in time- and event-based prospective memory. *European Journal of Cognitive Psychology, 11*, 219–237.

Ebbinghaus, H. (1964). *Memory: A contribution to experimental psychology.* New York: Dover. (Original work published 1885; translated 1913)

Einstein, G. O., Holland, L. J., McDaniel, M. A., & Guynn, M. J. (1992). Age-related deficits in prospective memory: The influence of task complexity. *Psychology and Aging, 7*, 471–478.

Einstein, G. O., & McDaniel, M. A. (1990). Normal aging and prospective memory. *Journal of Experimental Psychology: Learning, Memory, and Cognition, 16*, 717–726.

Einstein, G. O., & McDaniel, M. A. (1996). Retrieval processes in prospective memory: Theoretical approaches and some new empirical findings. In M. Brandimonte, G. Einstein, & M. McDaniel (Eds.), *Prospective memory: Theory and applications* (pp. 115–142). Hillsdale, NJ: Erlbaum.

Einstein, G. O., & McDaniel, M. A. (2005). Prospective memory: Multiple retrieval processes. *Current Directions in Psychological Science, 14*, 286–290.

Einstein, G. O., McDaniel, M. A., Manzi, M., Cochran, B., & Baker, M. (2000). Prospective memory and aging: Forgetting intentions over short delays. *Psychology and Aging, 15*, 671–683.

Einstein, G. O., McDaniel, M. A., Richardson, S. L., Guynn, M. J., & Cunfer, A. R. (1995). Aging and prospective memory: Examining the influences of self-initiated retrieval processes. *Journal of Experimental Psychology: Learning, Memory, and Cognition, 21,* 996–1007.

Einstein, G. O., McDaniel, M. A., Shank, H., & Mayfield, S. (2002, November). The costs of performing a prospective memory task on cover activities: Support for the multiprocess view. Poster presented at the meeting of the Psychonomic Society, Kansas City, MO.

Einstein, G. O., McDaniel, M. A., Smith, R. E., & Shaw, P. (1998). Habitual prospective memory and aging: Remembering intentions and forgetting actions. *Psychological Science, 9,* 284–288.

Einstein, G. O., McDaniel, M. A., Thomas, R., Mayfield, S., Shank, H., Morrisette, N., et al. (2005). Multiple processes in prospective memory retrieval: Factors determining monitoring versus spontaneous retrieval. *Journal of Experimental Psychology: General, 134,* 327–342.

Einstein, G. O., McDaniel, M. A., Williford, C. L., Pagan, J. L., & Dismukes, R. K. (2003). Forgetting of intentions in demanding situations is rapid. *Journal of Experimental Psychology: Applied, 9,* 147–162.

Einstein, G. O., Smith, R. E., McDaniel, M. A., & Shaw, P. (1997). Aging and prospective memory: The influence of increased task demands at encoding and retrieval. *Psychology and Aging, 12,* 479–488.

Ellis, J. (1988a). Memory for future intentions: Investigating pulses and steps. In M. M. Gruneberg, P. E. Morris, & R. N. Sykes (Eds.), *Practical aspects of memory: Current research and issues* (Vol. 1, pp. 371–376). Chichester, UK: Wiley.

Ellis, J. (1988b). *Memory for naturally occurring intentions.* Unpublished doctoral dissertation, Cambridge University.

Ellis, J. (1996). Prospective memory or the realization of delayed intentions: A conceptual framework for research. In M. Brandimonte, G. Einstein, & M. McDaniel (Eds.), *Prospective memory: Theory and applications* (pp. 1–51). Hillsdale, NJ: Erlbaum.

Ellis, J. (1998). Prospective memory and medicine-taking. In L. B. Myers & K. Midence (Eds.), *Adherence to treatment in medical conditions* (pp. 113–131). Amsterdam: Harwood Academic Publishers.

Engle, R. W., Tuholski, S. W., Laughlin, J. E., & Conway, A. R. A. (1999). Working memory, short-term memory, and general fluid intelligence: A latent-variable approach. *Journal of Experimental Psychology: General, 128,* 309–331.

Engelkamp, J. (1997). Memory for to-be-performed tasks versus memory for performed tasks. *Memory & Cognition, 25,* 117–124.

Engelkamp, J. (1998). *Memory for actions.* Hove, UK: Taylor and Francis.

Engelkamp, J., & Zimmer, H. D. (1997). Sensory factors in memory for subject-performed tasks. *Acta Psychologica, 96,* 43–60.

Finstad, K., Bink, M., McDaniel, M. A., & Einstein, G. O. (2006). Breaks and task switches in prospective memory. *Applied Cognitive Psychology, 20,* 705–712.

Freeman, J. E., & Ellis, J. (2003). The representation of delayed intentions: A prospective subject-performed task? *Journal of Experimental Psychology: Learning, Memory, and Cognition, 29,* 976–992.

Freud, S. (1952). *Psychopathology of everyday life*. New York: Mentor. (Original work published 1909)

Gao, J., & Graf, P. (2005, July). *Retrieval processes for event cued prospective memory tasks*. Poster presented at the 2nd International Prospective Memory Conference, Zurich, Switzerland.

Gardiner, J. M. (1988). Functional aspects of recollective experience. *Memory & Cognition, 16*, 309–313.

Gawande, A. A., Studdert, D. M., Orav, E. J., Brennan, T. A., & Zinner, M. J. (2003). Risk factors for retained instruments and sponges after surgery. *New England Journal of Medicine, 348*, 228–235.

Glisky, E., Polster, M. R., & Routhieaux, B. C. (1995). Double dissociation between item and source memory. *Neuropsychology, 9*, 229–235.

Gollwitzer, P. M. (1996). The volitional benefits of planning. In P. M. Gollwitzer & J. A. Bargh (Eds.), *The psychology of action: Linking cognition and motivation to behavior* (pp. 287–312). New York: Guilford Press.

Gollwitzer, P. M. (1999). Implementation intentions: Strong effects of simple plans. *American Psychologist, 54*, 493–503.

Gollwitzer, P. M., & Brandstatter, V. (1997). Implementation intentions and effective goal pursuit. *Journal of Personality & Social Psychology, 73*, 186–199.

Goschke, T., & Kuhl, J. (1993). Representation of intentions: Persisting activation in memory. *Journal of Experimental Psychology: Learning, Memory, and Cognition, 19*, 1211–1226.

Goschke, T., & Kuhl, J. (1996). Remembering what to do: Explicit and implicit memory for intentions. In M. Brandimonte, G. Einstein, & M. McDaniel (Eds.), *Prospective memory: Theory and applications* (pp. 53–91). Hillsdale, NJ: Erlbaum.

Graf, P., & Uttl, B. (2001). Prospective memory: A new focus for research. *Consciousness and Cognition: An International Journal, 10*, 437–450.

Guynn, M. J. (2003). A two-process model of strategic monitoring in event-based prospective memory: Activation/retrieval mode and checking. *International Journal of Psychology, 38*, 245–256.

Guynn, M. J., & McDaniel, M. A. (in press). Target pre-exposure eliminates the effect of distraction in event-based prospective memory. *Psychonomic Bulletin & Review*.

Guynn, M. J., McDaniel, M. A., & Einstein, G. O. (1998). Prospective memory: When reminders fail. *Memory & Cognition, 26*, 287–298.

Guynn, M. J., McDaniel, M. A., & Einstein, G. O. (2001). Remembering to perform actions: A different type of memory? In H. D. Zimmer, R L. Cohen, M. J. Guynn, J. Engelkamp, R. Kormi-Nouri, & M. A. Foley (Eds.), *Memory for action: A distinct form of episodic memory?* (pp. 25–48). New York: Oxford University Press.

Guynn, M. J., McDaniel, M. A., Strosser, G. L., Ramirez, J. M., Hinrichs, E. L., & Hayes, K. H. (2005). Relational and item-specific influences on generate-recognize processes in recall. Unpublished manuscript.

Harris, J. E. (1984). Remembering to do things: A forgotten topic. In J. E. Harris & P. E. Morris (Eds.), *Everyday memory, actions, and absent-mindedness* (pp. 71–92). London: Academic Press.

Harris, J. E., & Wilkins, A. J. (1982). Remember to do things: A theoretical framework and an illustrative experiment. *Human Learning, 1*, 123–136.

Hasher, L., & Zacks, R. T. (1988). Working memory, comprehension, and aging: A review and a new view. In G. H. Bower (Ed.), *The psychology of learning and motivation: Advances in research and theory* (Vol. 22, pp. 193–225). San Diego, CA: Academic Press.

Hashtroudi, S., Johnson, M. K., & Chrosniak, L. D. (1990). Aging and qualitative characteristics of memories for perceived and imagined complex events. *Psychology and Aging, 5*, 119–126.

Haynes, R. B., McDonald, H., Garg, A. X., & Montague, P. (2003). Interventions for helping patients to follow prescriptions for medications. *Cochrane Database of Systematic Reviews, 3*, 3.

Henry, J. D., MacLeod, M. S., Phillips, H., & Crawford, J. R. (2004). A meta-analytic review of prospective memory and aging. *Psychology and Aging, 19*, 27–39.

Hertel, P. T., & Rude, S. S. (1991). Depressive deficits in memory: Focusing attention improves subsequent recall. *Journal of Experimental Psychology: General, 120*, 301–309.

Hicks, J. L., Marsh, R. L., & Cook, G. I. (2005). Task interference in time-based, event-based, and dual intention prospective memory conditions. *Journal of Memory and Language, 53*, 430–444.

Hicks, J. L., Marsh, R. L., & Russell, E. J. (2000). The properties of retention intervals and their affect [sic] on retaining prospective memories. *Journal of Experimental Psychology: Learning, Memory, and Cognition, 26*, 1160–1169.

Holbrook, J. B. (2005, July). Do intentions linger after a prospective memory task has been performed? Paper presented at the 2nd International Prospective Memory Conference, Zurich, Switzerland.

Holbrook, J. B., Dismukes, R. K., & Nowinski, J. L. (2005, January). *Identifying sources of variance in everyday prospective memory performance.* Presentation at the biennial meeting of the Society for Applied Research in Memory and Cognition, Wellington, New Zealand.

Insel, K., & Cole, L. (2005). Individualizing memory strategies to improve medication adherence. *Applied Nursing Research, 18*, 199–204.

Insel, K., Morrow, D., Brewer, B., & Figueredo, A. (2006). Executive function, working memory, and medication adherence among older adults. *Journal of Gerontology: Psychological Sciences, 61*, 102–107.

Intons-Peterson, M. J., Rocchi, P., West, T., McLellan, K., & Hackney, A. (1998). Aging, optimal testing times, and negative priming. *Journal of Experimental Psychology: Learning, Memory, and Cognition, 24*, 362–376.

Jacoby, L. L. (1991). A process dissociation framework: Separating automatic from intentional uses of memory. *Journal of Memory and Language, 30*, 513–541.

Jacoby, L. L., & Dallas, M. (1981). On the relationship between autobiographical memory and perceptual learning. *Journal of Experimental Psychology: General, 110*, 306–340.

Jacoby, L. L., & Hollingshead, A. (1990). Toward a generate/recognize model of performance on direct and indirect tests of memory. *Journal of Memory and Language, 29*, 433–454.

Jacoby, L. L., Jennings, J. M., & Hay, J. F. (1996). Dissociating automatic and consciously-controlled processes: Implications for diagnosis and rehabilitation of memory deficits. In D. J. Herrmann, C. L. McEvoy, C. Hertzog, P. Hertel, & M. K. Johnson (Eds.), *Basic and applied memory research: Theory in context* (Vol. 1, pp. 161–193). Hillsdale, NJ: Erlbaum.

Jacoby, L. L., Kelley, C. M., & Dywan, J. (1989). Memory attributions. In H. L. Roediger & F. I. M. Craik (Eds.), *Varieties of memory and consciousness: Essays in honor of Endel Tulving* (pp. 391–422). Hillsdale, NJ: Erlbaum.

Jacoby, L. L., Toth, J. P., & Yonelinas, A. P. (1993). Separating conscious and unconscious influences of memory: Measuring recollection. *Journal of Experimental Psychology: General, 122,* 139–154.

Jamison, J. P., Cook, G. I., Amir, N., Marsh, R. L., & Hicks, J. L. (2006). How obsessive compulsive disorder affects event-based prospective memory. Manuscript submitted for publication.

Jenkins, J. J. (1979). Four points to remember: A tetrahedral model of memory. In L. S. Cermak & F. I. M. Craik (Eds.), *Levels of processing in human memory* (pp. 429–446), Hillsdale, NJ: Erlbaum.

Johnson, M. K., Hashtroudi, S., & Lindsay, D. S. (1993). Source monitoring. *Psychological Bulletin, 114,* 3–28.

Johnson, M. K., & Raye, C. L. (1981). Reality monitoring. *Psychological Review, 88,* 67–85.

Kail, R. (1984). *The development of memory in children.* New York: Freeman.

Kane, M. J., Bleckley, M. K., Conway, A. R. A., & Engle, R. W. (2001). A controlled-attention view of working-memory capacity. *Journal of Experimental Psychology: General, 130,* 169–183.

Keefe, D. E., & McDaniel, M. A. (1993). The time course and durability of predictive inferences. *Journal of Memory and Language, 32,* 446–463.

Kelemen, W. L., Weinberg, W. B., Oh, H. S. Y., Mulvey, E. K., & Kaeochinda, K. F. (in press). Improving the reliability of event–based laboratory tests of prospective memory. *Psychonomic Bulletin & Review.*

Kerns, K. (2000). The CyberCruiser: An investigation of development of prospective memory in children. *Journal of the International Neuropsychological Society, 6,* 62–70.

Kidder, D. P., Park, D. C., Hertzog, C., & Morrell, R. W. (1997). Prospective memory and aging: The effects of working memory and prospective memory task load. *Aging, Neuropsychology, and Cognition, 4,* 93–112.

Kimberg, D. Y., & Farah, M. J. (1993). A unified account of cognitive impairments following frontal lobe damage: The role of working memory in complex, organized behavior. *Journal of Experimental Psychology: General, 122,* 411–428.

Kliegel, M., Martin, M., McDaniel, M. A., & Einstein, G. O. (2001). Varying the importance of a prospective memory task: Differential effects across time- and event-based prospective memory. *Memory, 9,* 1–11.

Kliegel, M., Martin, M., McDaniel, M. A., & Einstein, G. O. (2002). Complex prospective memory and executive control of working memory: A process model. *Psychologische Beitrage, 44,* 303–318.

Kliegel, M., Martin, M., McDaniel, M. A., & Einstein, G. O. (2004). Importance effects in event-based prospective memory tasks. *Memory, 12, 553–561*.

Kliegel, M., Martin, M., McDaniel, M. A., Einstein, G. O., & Moor, C. (2005). The delayed realization of intended actions: How intention planning affects performance. Manuscript submitted for publication.

Kliegel, M., Martin, M., McDaniel, M. A., & Phillips, L. H. (in press). Adult age differences in errand planning: The role of task familiarity and cognitive resources. *Experimental Aging Research*.

Kliegel, M., McDaniel, M. A., & Einstein, G. O. (2000). Plan formation, retention, and execution in prospective memory: A new approach and age-related effects. *Memory & Cognition, 28, 1041–1049*.

Kondel, T. K. (2002). Prospective memory and executive function in schizophrenia. *Brain and Cognition, 48, 405–410*.

Koriat, A., Ben-Zur, H., & Nussbaum, A. (1990). Encoding information for future action: Memory for to-be-performed tasks versus memory for to-be-recalled tasks. *Memory & Cognition, 18, 568–578*.

Koriat, A., Ben-Zur, H., & Sheffer, D. (1988). Telling the same story twice: Output monitoring and age. *Journal of Memory and Language, 27, 23–39*.

Kreutzer, M. A., Leonard, C., & Flavell, J. H. (1975). An interview study of children's knowledge about memory. *Monographs of the Society for Research in Child Development, 40, 1–60*.

Kvavilashvili, L. (1987). Remembering intention as a distinct form of memory. *British Journal of Psychology, 78, 507–518*.

Kvavilashvili, L. (2005, July) *Automatic or controlled? Rehearsal and event-based prospective memory tasks*. Paper presented at the 2nd International Prospective Memory Conference, Zurich, Switzerland.

Kvavilashvili, L., & Ellis, J. (1996). Varieties of intention: Some distinctions and classifications. In M. Brandimonte, G. Einstein, & M. McDaniel (Eds.), *Prospective memory: Theory and applications* (pp. 23–51). Mahwah, NJ: Erlbaum.

Kvavilashvili, L., & Fisher, L. (2007). Is time-based prospective remembering mediated by self-initiated rehearsals? Effects of incidental cues, ongoing activity, age, and motivation. *Journal of Experimental Psychology: General, 136*, pp. 112–132.

Kvavilashvili, L., Kyle, F., & Messer, D. J. (in press). The development of prospective memory in children: Methodological issues, empirical findings, and future directions. In M. Kliegel, M. A. McDaniel, & G. O. Einstein (Eds.), *Prospective memory: Cognitive, neuroscience, developmental, and applied perspectives*. Mahwah, NJ: Erlbaum.

Kvavilashvili, L., & Mandler, G. (2004). Out of one's mind: A study of involuntary semantic memories. *Cognitive Psychology, 48, 47–94*.

Kvavilashvili, L., Messer D. J., & Ebdon, P. (2001). Prospective memory in children: The effects of age and task interruption. *Developmental Psychology, 37, 418–430*.

Lebiere, C., & Lee, F. J. (2001). Prospective memory: A computational account. In *Proceedings of the Fourth International Conference on Cognitive Modeling* (pp. 139–144). Mahwah, NJ: Erlbaum.

Leirer,V. O., Tanke, E. D., & Morrow, D. G. (1994). Time of day and naturalistic prospective memory. *Experimental Aging Research, 20,* 127–134.

Lengfelder, A., & Gollwitzer, P. M. (2001). Reflective and reflexive action control in patients with frontal brain lesions. *Neuropsychology, 15,* 80–100.

Lewin, K. (1961). Intention, will, and need (D. Rapaport, Trans.). In T. Shipley (Ed.), *Classics in psychology* (pp. 1234–1289). New York: Philosophical Library. (Original work published 1926)

Lieberman, H. R., Balthalon, G. P., Falco, C. M., Kramer, F. M., Morgan, C. A., & Niro, P. (2005). Severe decrements in cognitive function and mood induced sleep loss, heat, dehydration, and undernutrition during simulated combat. *Biological Psychiatry, 57,* 422–429.

Liu, L. L., & Park, D. C. (2004). Aging and medical adherence: The use of automatic processes to achieve effortful things. *Psychology and Aging, 19,* 318–325.

Loft, S., & Yeo, G. (in press). Automatic and non-automatic processes in event-based prospective memory. *Memory & Cognition.*

Loftus, E. F. (1971). Memory for intentions: The effect of presence of a cue and inter-polated activity. *Psychonomic Science, 23,* 315–316.

Loukopoulos, L. D., Dismukes, R. K., & Barshi, I. (2003a, June). The challenge of routine flight operations. *Proceedings of the 22nd European Annual Conference on Human Decision Making and Control.* Linköping, Sweden: Linköping University. Retrieved October 20, 2006, from http://human-factors.arc.nasa.gov/ihs/flightcognition/publications.html

Loukopoulos, L. D., Dismukes, R. K., & Barshi, I. (2003b). Concurrent task demands in the cockpit: Challenges and vulnerabilities in routine flight operations. *Proceedings of the 12th International Symposium on Aviation Psychology* (pp. 737–742). Dayton, OH: The Wright State University. Retrieved October 20, 2006, from http://human-factors.arc.nasa.gov/ihs/flightcognition/publications.html

Mandler, G. (1980). Recognizing: The judgment of prior occurrence. *Psychological Review, 87,* 252–271.

Mantyla, T. (1993). Priming effects in prospective memory. *Memory, 1,* 203–218.

Mantyla, T. (1994). Remembering to remember: Adult age differences in prospective memory. *Journal of Gerontology, 49,* 276–282.

Mantyla, T. (1996). Activating actions and interrupting intentions: Mechanisms of retrieval sensitization in prospective memory. In M. Brandimonte, G. Einstein, & M. McDaniel (Eds.), *Prospective memory: Theory and applications* (pp. 93–113). Mahwah, NJ: Erlbaum.

Mantyla, T., & Carelli, M. G. (2005, July). *Time monitoring and executive functions in children and adults.* Paper presented at the 2nd International Prospective Memory Conference, Zurich, Switzerland.

Marsh, R. L., Cook, G. I., & Hicks, J. L. (2006). An analysis of prospective memory. In D. L. Medin (Ed.), *The psychology of learning and motivation* (Vol. 46, pp. 115–153). San Diego, CA: Academic Press.

Marsh, R. L., Hancock, T. W., & Hicks, J. L. (2002). The demands of an ongoing activity influence the success of event-based prospective memory. *Psychonomic Bulletin & Review, 9,* 604–610.

Marsh, R. L., & Hicks, J. L. (1998). Event-based prospective memory and executive control of working memory. *Journal of Experimental Psychology: Learning, Memory, and Cognition, 24*, 336–349.

Marsh, R. L., Hicks, J. L., & Bink, M. L. (1998). Activation of completed, uncompleted, and partially completed intentions. *Journal of Experimental Psychology: Learning, Memory, and Cognition, 24*, 350–361.

Marsh, R. L., Hicks, J. L., & Cook, G. I. (2005). On the relationship between effort toward an ongoing task and cue detection in event-based prospective memory. *Journal of Experimental Psychology: Learning, Memory, and Cognition, 29*, 861–870.

Marsh, R. L., Hicks, J. L., & Cook, G. I. (2006). Task interference from prospective memories covaries with contextual associations of fulfilling them. *Memory & Cognition, 34*, 1037–1045.

Marsh, R. L., Hicks, J. L., Cook, G. I., Hansen, J. S., & Pallos, A. L. (2003). Interference to ongoing activities covaries with the characteristics of an event-based intention. *Journal of Experimental Psychology: Learning, Memory, and Cognition, 29*, 861–870.

Marsh, R. L., Hicks, J. L., Cook, G. I., & Mayhorn, C. B. (1999). Stereotype reliance in source monitoring: Age differences and neuropsychological test correlates. *Cognitive Neuropsychology, 16*, 437–458.

Marsh, R. L., Hicks, J. L., Cook, G. I., & Mayhorn, C. B. (in press). Comparing older and younger adults in an event-based prospective memory paradigm containing an output monitoring component. *Aging, Neuropsychology, and Cognition.*

Marsh, R. L., Hicks, J. L., & Landau, J. D. (1998). An investigation of everyday prospective memory. *Memory & Cognition, 26*, 633–643.

Marsh, R. L., Hicks, J. L., & Watson, V. (2002). The dynamics of intention retrieval and coordination of action in event-based prospective memory. *Journal of Experimental Psychology: Learning, Memory, and Cognition, 28*, 652–660.

Martin, M. (1986). Aging patterns of change in everyday memory and cognition. *Human Learning, 5*, 63–74.

Martin, M., & Schumann-Hengsteler, R. (2001). How task demands influence time-based prospective memory performance in young and older adults. *International Journal of Behavioral Development, 25*, 386–391.

Martin, T., McDaniel, M. A., Guynn, M., Houck, J., Woodruff, C., Pearson-Bish, J., et al. (in press). Brain regions and their dynamics in prospective memory retrieval: A MEG study. *International Journal of Psychophysiology.*

May, C. P. (1999). Synchrony effects in cognition: The costs and a benefit. *Psychonomic Bulletin & Review, 6*, 142–147.

May, C. P., & Hasher, L. (1998). Synchrony effects in inhibitory control over thought and action. *Journal of Experimental Psychology: Human Perception and Performance, 24*, 363–379.

May, C. P., Hasher, L., & Stoltzfus, E. R. (1993). Optimal time of day and the magnitude of age differences in memory. *Psychological Science, 4*, 326–330.

Maylor, E. A. (1993). Aging and forgetting in prospective and retrospective memory tasks. *Psychology and Aging, 8*, 420–428.

Maylor, E. A. (1996). Age-related impairment in an event-based prospective memory task. *Psychology and Aging, 11,* 74–78.

Maylor, E. A. (1998). Changes in event-based prospective memory across adulthood. *Aging, Neuropsychology, and Cognition, 5,* 107–128.

Maylor, E. A. (2005, July). *Final comments.* Presentation at the 2nd International Prospective Memory Conference, Zurich, Switzerland.

Maylor, E. A., Smith, G., Della Sala, S., & Logie, R. H. (2002). Prospective and retrospective memory in normal aging and dementia: An experimental study. *Memory & Cognition, 30,* 871–884.

Maylor, E. A., Darby, R. J., Logie, R., Della Sala, S., & Smith, G. (2002). Prospective memory across the lifespan. In P. Graf & N. Ohta (Eds.), *Lifespan development of human memory* (pp. 235–256). Cambridge: MIT Press.

McDaniel, M. A. (1995). Prospective memory: Progress and processes. In D. L. Medin (Ed.), *The psychology of learning and motivation* (Vol. 33, pp. 191–222). San Diego, CA: Academic Press.

McDaniel, M. A., Butler, K. M., & Dornburg, C. (2006). Binding of source and content: New directions revealed by neuropsychological and age-related effects. In H. D. Zimmer, A. Mecklinger, & U. Lindenberger (Eds.), *Binding in human memory: A neurocognitive approach* (pp. 657–675). New York: Oxford University Press.

McDaniel, M. A., & Einstein, G. O. (1993). The importance of cue familiarity and cue distinctiveness in prospective memory. *Memory, 1,* 23–41.

McDaniel, M. A., & Einstein, G. O. (2000). Strategic and automatic processes in prospective memory retrieval: A multiprocess framework. *Applied Cognitive Psychology, 14,* S127–S144.

McDaniel, M. A., & Einstein, G. O. (2007). Spontaneous retrieval in prospective memory. In J. S. Nairne (Ed.), *The foundations of remembering: Essays in honor of Henry L. Roediger III* (pp. 227–242). New York: Psychology Press.

McDaniel, M. A., Einstein, G. O., Graham, T., & Rall, E. (2004). Delaying execution of intentions: Overcoming the costs of interruptions. *Applied Cognitive Psychology, 18,* 533–547.

McDaniel, M. A., Einstein, G. O., & Rendell, P. G. (in press). The puzzle of inconsistent age-related declines in prospective memory: A multiprocess explanation. In M. Kliegel, M. A. McDaniel, and G. O. Einstein (Eds.), *Prospective memory: Cognitive, neuroscience, developmental, and applied perspectives.* Mahwah, NJ: Erlbaum.

McDaniel, M. A., Einstein, G. O., Stout, A. C., & Morgan, Z. (2003). Aging and maintaining intentions over delays: Do it or lose it. *Psychology and Aging, 18,* 807–822.

McDaniel, M. A., Friedman, A., & Bourne, L. E. (1978). Remembering the levels of information in words. *Memory & Cognition, 6,* 156–164.

McDaniel, M. A., Glisky, E. L., Rubin, S. R., Guynn, M. J., Routhieaux, B. C. (1999). Prospective memory: A neuropsychological study. *Neuropsychology, 13,* 103–110.

McDaniel, M. A., Guynn, M. J., Einstein, G. O., & Breneiser, J. E. (2004). Cue focused and automatic-associative processes in prospective memory. *Journal of Experimental Psychology: Learning, Memory, and Cognition, 30,* 605–614.

McDaniel, M. A., & Masson, M. E. (1985). Altering memory representations through retrieval. *Journal of Experimental Psychology: Learning, Memory, and Cognition, 11,* 371–385.

McDaniel, M. A., Robinson-Riegler, B., & Einstein, G. O. (1998). Prospective remembering: Perceptually driven or conceptually driven processes? *Memory & Cognition, 26,* 121–134.

McGann, D., Defeyter, M. A., Ellis, J. A., & Reid, C. (2005, July). *Prospective memory in children: The effects of age and target salience.* Paper presented at the 2nd International Prospective Memory Conference, Zurich, Switzerland.

McNerney, M. W., & West, R. (in press). An imperfect relationship between prospective memory and the prospective interference effect. *Memory & Cognition.*

Meacham, J. A. (1982). A note on remembering to execute planned actions. *Journal of Applied Developmental Psychology, 3,* 121–133.

Meacham, J. A. (1988). Interpersonal relations and prospective remembering. In M. M. Gruneberg, P. E. Morris, & R. N. Sykes (Eds.), *Practical aspects of memory: Current research and issues: Vol. 1. Memory in everyday life* (pp. 354–359). Oxford, UK: Wiley.

Meacham, J. A., & Leiman, B. (1982). Remembering to perform future actions. In U. Neisser (Ed.), *Memory observed: Remembering in natural contexts* (pp. 327–336). San Francisco: Freeman.

Meacham, J. A., & Singer, J. (1977). Incentive effects in prospective remembering. *Journal of Psychology: Interdisciplinary and Applied, 97,* 191–197.

Meeks, J. T., Hicks, J. L., & Marsh, R. L. (2006). Metacognitive awareness of event-based prospective memory. *Consciousness and Cognition.*

Miller, G. A., Galanter, E., & Pribram, K. H. (1960). *Plans and the structure of behavior.* New York: Holt, Rinehart & Winston.

Mills, V., Kixmiller, J. S., Gillespie, A., Allard, J., Flynn, E., Bowman, A., et al. (1997). The correspondence between the Rivermead Behavioral Memory Test and ecological prospective memory. *Brain and Cognition, 35,* 322–325.

Milne, S., Orbell, S., & Sheeran, P. (2002). Combining motivational and volitional interventions to promote exercise participation: Protection motivation theory and implementation intentions. *British Journal of Health Psychology, 7,* 163–184.

Monsell, S., Sumner, P. & Waters, H. (2003). Task-set reconfiguration with predictable and unpredictable task switches. *Memory & Cognition, 31,* 327–342.

Morrell, R. W., Park, D. C., Kidder, D. P., & Martin, M. (1997). Adherence to antihypertensive medications across the life span. *Gerontologist, 37,* 609–619.

Morris, C. D., Bransford, J. D., & Franks, J. J. (1977). Levels of processing versus transfer appropriate processing. *Journal of Verbal Learning and Verbal Behavior, 16,* 519–533.

Morris, P. E. (1992). Prospective memory: Remembering to do things. In M. Gruneberg & P. Morris (Eds.), *Aspects of memory: The practical aspects* (Vol. 1, pp. 196–222). London: Routledge.

Moscovitch, M. (1982). A neuropsychological approach to memory and perception in normal and pathological aging. In F. I. M. Craik & S. Trehub (Eds.), *Aging and cognitive processes* (pp. 55–78). New York: Plenum.

Moscovitch, M. (1994). Memory and working with memory: Evaluation of a component process model and comparisons with other models. In D. L. Schacter and E. Tulving (Eds.), *Memory systems* (pp. 269–310). Cambridge: MIT Press.

Muter, P. (1980). Very rapid forgetting. *Memory & Cognition, 8,* 174–179.

Niro, P. (2005). Severe decrements in cognitive function and mood induced by sleep loss, heat, dehydration, and under nutrition during simulated combat. *Biological Psychiatry, 57,* 422–429.

Nowinski, J. L., Holbrook, J. B., & Dismukes, R. K. (2003). Human memory and cockpit operations: An ASRS study. *Proceedings of the 12th International Symposium on Aviation Psychology* (pp. 888–893). Dayton, OH: The Wright State University. Retrieved October 20, 2006, from http://human-factors.arc.nasa .gov/ihs/flightcognition/Publications/Nowinski_etal_ISAP03.pdf

Okuda, J. T., Fujii, T., Yamadori, A., Kawashima, R., Tsukiura, T., Ohtake, H., et al. (1998). Retention of words in long-term memory: A functional neuroanatomical study with PET. *Neuroreport: For Rapid Communication of Neuroscience Research, 11,* 323–328.

Okuno, J., Yanagi, H., & Tomura, S. (2001). Is cognitive impairment a risk factor for poor compliance among Japanese elderly in the community? *European Journal of Clinical Pharmacology, 57,* 589–594.

Orbell, S., Hodgkins, S., & Sheeran, P. (1997). Implementation intentions and the theory of planned behavior. *Personality and Social Psychology Bulletin, 23,* 945–954.

Oriani, M., Moniz-Cook, E., Binetti, G., Zanieri, G., Frisoni, G. B., Geroldi, C., et al. (2003). An electronic memory aid to support prospective memory in patients in the early stages of Alzheimer's disease: A pilot study. *Aging and Mental Health, 7,* 22–27.

Otani, H., Landau, J. D., Libkuman, T. M., St. Louis, J. P., Kazen, J. K., & Throne, G. W. (1997). Prospective memory and divided attention. *Memory, 5,* 343–360.

Palmer, H. M., & McDonald, S. (2000). The role of frontal and temporal lobe processes in prospective remembering. *Brain and Cognition, 44,* 103–107.

Park, D. C., Hertzog, C., Kidder, D. P., Morrell, R. W., & Mayhorn, C. B. (1997). Effect of age on event-based and time-based prospective memory. *Psychology and Aging, 12,* 314–327.

Park, D. C., & Kidder, D. P. (1996). Prospective memory and medication adherence. In M. Brandimonte, G. Einstein, & M. McDaniel (Eds.), *Prospective memory: Theory and applications* (pp. 1–22). Mahwah, NJ: Erlbaum.

Park, D. C., Lautenschlager, G., Hedden, T., Davidson, N. S., Smith, A. D., & Smith, P. K. (2002). Models of visuospatial and verbal memory across the adult life span. *Psychology and Aging, 17,* 299–320.

Park, D. C., & Morrell, R. W. (1991). Improving correct medication usage in older adults. *Experimental Aging Research, 17,* 87–88.

Park, D. C., Morrell, R. W., Frieske, D., & Kincaid, D. (1992). Medication adherence behaviors in older adults: Effects of external cognitive supports. *Psychology and Aging, 7,* 252–256.

Passolunghi, M. C., Brandimonte, M. A., & Cornoldi, C. (1995). Encoding modality and prospective memory in children. *International Journal of Behavioral Development, 18,* 631–648.

Patton, G. W., & Meit, M. (1993). Effect of aging on prospective and incidental memory. *Experimental Aging Research, 19,* 165–176.

Petrides, M., & Milner, B. (1982). Deficits of subject-ordered tasks after frontal-and temporal-lobe lesions in man. *Neuropsychologia, 20,* 249–262.

Potts, G. R., Keenan, J. M., & Golding, J. M. (1988). Assessing the occurrence of elaborative inferences: Lexical decision versus naming. *Journal of Memory and Language, 27,* 399–415.

Rabbitt, P. (1996). Commentary: Why are studies of "prospective memory" planless? In M. Brandimonte, G. Einstein, & M. McDaniel (Eds.), *Prospective memory: Theory and applications* (pp. 239–248). Mahwah, NJ: Erlbaum.

Ramuschkat, G., McDaniel, M. A., Kliegel, M., & Einstein (2006). *Habitual prospective memory and aging: Benefits of a complex motor action.* Unpublished manuscript.

Ratcliff, R., Gomez, P., & McKoon, G. (2004). A diffusion model account of the lexical decision task. *Psychological Review, 111,* 159–182.

Reason, J. T. (1990). *Human error.* Cambridge, NY: Cambridge University Press.

Reese, C. M., & Cherry, K. E. (2002). The effects of age, ability, and memory monitoring on prospective memory task performance. *Aging, Neuropsychology, and Cognition, 9,* 98–113.

Reitman, J. S. (1974). Without surreptitious rehearsal, information in short-term memory decays. *Journal of Verbal Learning and Verbal Behavior, 13,* 365–377.

Rendell, P. G., & Craik, F. I. M. (2000). Virtual week and actual week: Age-related differences in prospective memory. *Applied Cognitive Psychology, 14,* S43–S62.

Rendell, P. G., McDaniel, M. A., Forbes, R. D., & Einstein, G. O. (in press). Age-related effects in prospective memory are modulated by ongoing task complexity and relation to target cue. *Aging, Neuropsychology, and Cognition.*

Rendell, P. G., Ozgis, S., & Wallis, A. (2004, April). *Age-related effects in prospective remembering: The role of delaying execution of retrieved intentions.* Paper presented at the 10th Cognitive Aging Conference, Atlanta, GA.

Rendell, P. G., & Thompson, D. M. (1993). The effect of aging on remembering to remember: An investigation of simulated medical regimens. *Australian Journal of Ageing, 12,* 11–18.

Rendell, P. G., & Thompson, D. M. (1999). Aging and prospective memory: Differences between naturalistic and laboratory tasks. *Journal of Gerontology: Psychological Sciences, 54,* P256–P269.

Roediger, H. L. (1996). Commentary: Prospective memory and episodic memory. In M. Brandimonte, G. Einstein, & M. McDaniel (Eds.), *Prospective memory: Theory and applications* (pp. 149–155). Mahwah, NJ: Erlbaum.

Roediger, H. L., & Karpicke, J. D. (2006). Test-enhanced learning: Taking memory tests improves long-term retention. *Psychological Science, 17,* 249–255.

Roediger, H. L., Weldon, M. S., & Challis, B. H. (1989). Explaining dissociations between implicit and explicit measures of retention: A processing account. In H. L. Roediger & F. I. M. Craik (Eds.), *Varieties of memory and consciousness: Essays in honour of Endel Tulving* (pp. 3–41). Hillsdale, NJ: Erlbaum.

Rogers, E. M. (1995). *Diffusion of innovations* (4th ed.). New York: Free Press.

Rude, S. S., Hertel, P. T., Jarrold, W., Covitch, J., & Hedlund, S. (1999). Depression-related impairments in prospective memory. *Cognition and Emotion, 13,* 267–276.

Rugg, M. D., Mark, R. E., Walla, P., Schloerscheidt, A. M., Birch, C. S., & Allan, K. (1998). Dissociation of the neural correlates of implicit and explicit memory. *Nature, 392,* 595–598.

Rusted, J. (2005, July). *Examining the pharmacology of prospective memory: Implications for psychological models.* Paper presented at the 2nd International Prospective Memory Conference, Zurich, Switzerland.

Salthouse, T. A. (1991). *Theoretical perspectives on cognitive aging.* Hillsdale, NJ: Erlbaum.

Salthouse, T., Berish, D., & Siedlecki, K. (2004). Construct validity and age sensitivity of prospective memory. *Memory & Cognition, 32,* 1133–1148.

Schmidt, I. W., Berg, I. J., & Deelman, B. G. (2001). Prospective memory training in older adults. *Educational Gerontology, 27,* 455–478.

Schulze, H., Hoffmann, T., Voinikonis, A., & Irmscher, K. (2003). Modeling a mobile memory aid system. In K. Irmscher & K. Fähnrich (Eds.), *Kommunikation in Verteilten Systemen* (KiVS) [Communication in Shared Systems] (pp. 143–153). New York: Springer.

Schweickert, R., & Boruff, B. (1986). Short-term memory capacity: Magic number or magic spell? *Journal of Experimental Psychology: Learning, Memory, and Cognition, 12,* 419–425.

Searleman, A. (1996). Personality variables and prospective memory. In D. Herrmann, C. McEvoy, C. Hertzog, P. Hertel, & M. K. Johnson (Eds.), *Basic and applied memory research* (Vol. 2, pp. 111–119). Mahwah, NJ: Erlbaum.

Sellen, A. J., Louie, G., Harris, J. E., & Wilkins, A. J. (1997). What brings intentions to mind? An *in situ* study of prospective memory. *Memory, 5,* 483–507.

Sgaramella, T. M., Zettin, M., Bisiacchi, P. S., Verne, D., & Rago, R. (1993, June). *Retrospective memory and planning components in prospective remembering: Evidence from a neuropsychological study.* Paper presented at the Workshop on Memory and Mental Representation, Rome, Italy.

Shallice, T., & Burgess, P. (1991). Deficits in strategy application following frontal lobe damage in man. *Brain, 114,* 727–741.

Sheeran, P., & Orbell, S. (1999). Augmenting the theory of planned behavior: Roles for anticipated regret and descriptive norms. *Journal of Applied Social Psychology, 29,* 2107–2142.

Simons, J. S., Scholvinck, M. L., Gilbert, S. J., Frith, C. D., & Burgess, P. W. (2006). Differential components of prospective memory? Evidence from fMRI. *Neuropsychologia, 44,* 1388–1397.

Small, B. J., Rosnick, C. B., Fratiglioni, L., & Bäckman, L. (2004). Apolipoprotein E and cognitive performance: A meta-analysis. *Psychology and Aging, 19,* 592–600.

Smith, R. E. (2003). The cost of remembering to remember in event-based prospective memory: Investigating the capacity demands of delayed intention performance. *Journal of Experimental Psychology: Learning, Memory, and Cognition, 29,* 347–361.

Smith, R. E., & Bayen, U. J. (2004). A multinomial model of event-based prospective memory. *Journal of Experimental Psychology: Learning, Memory, and Cognition, 30,* 756–777.

Smith, R. E., & Bayen, U. J. (2006). The source of adult age differences in event-based prospective memory: A multinomial modeling approach. *Journal of Experimental Psychology: Learning, Memory, and Cognition, 32*, 623–635.

Somerville, S. C., Wellman, H. M., & Cultice, J. C. (1983). Young children's deliberate reminding. *Journal of Genetic Psychology, 143*, 87–96.

Son, L. K., & Metcalfe, J. (2000). Metacognitive and control strategies in study-time allocation. *Journal of Experimental Psychology: Learning, Memory, and Cognition, 26*, 204–221.

Steller, B. (1992). *Vorsätze und die wahrnehmung günstiger gelegenheiten* [Implementation intentions and the detection of good opportunities to act]. Munich, Germany: tuduv Verlagsgesellschaft.

Ste-Marie, D. N., & Jacoby, L. L. (1993). Spontaneous versus directed recognition: The relativity of automaticity. *Journal of Experimental Psychology: Learning, Memory, and Cognition, 19*, 777–788.

Stilley, C. S., Sereika, S., Muldoon, M. F., Ryan, C. M., & Dunbar-Jacob, J. (2004). Psychological and cognitive function: Predictors of adherence with cholesterol lowering treatment. *Annals of Behavioral Medicine, 27*, 117–124.

Stokes, S., Pierroutsakos, S., & Einstein, G. (2005, April). *Prospective memory in children: A multiprocess explanation for the inconsistent effect of age.* Paper presented at the National Conference on Undergraduate Research, Lexington,VA.

Thöne-Otto, A. I. T., Schulze, H., Irmscher, K., & von Cramon, D. Y. (2001). MEMOS—Interaktive elektronische gedachtnishilfe fur hirngeschadigte patienten [Interactive electronic memory support for brain-damaged patients]. *Deutsches Arzteblatt, Ausgabe, 11*, 598–600.

Thöne-Otto, A. I. T., & Walther, K. (2003). How to design an electronic memory aid for brain-injured patients: Considerations on the basis of a model of prospective memory. *International Journal of Psychology, 38*, 1–9.

Thöne-Otto, A. I. T., & Walther, K. (in press). Assessment and treatment of prospective memory disorders in clinical practice. In M. Kliegel, M. A. McDaniel, & G. O. Einstein (Eds.), *Prospective memory: Cognitive, neuroscience, developmental, and applied perspectives.* Mahwah, NJ: Erlbaum.

Tiller, S. J. (2005). *Noticing plus search in event-based prospective memory.* Unpublished doctoral thesis, University of Queensland, Brisbane, Australia.

Tombaugh, T. N., Grandmaison, L. J., & Schmidt, J. P. (1995). Prospective memory: Relationship to age and retrospective memory in Learning and Memory Battery (LAMB). *The Clinical Neuropsychologist, 9*, 135–142.

Tulving, E. (1983). *Elements of episodic memory.* New York: Oxford University Press.

Uttl, B. (2005). Measurement of individual differences: Lessons from memory assessment in research and clinical practice. *Psychological Science, 16*, 460–467.

Vedhara, K., Wadsworth, E., Norman, P., Searle, A., Mitchell, J., MacRae, N., et al. (2004). Habitual prospective memory in elderly patients with type 2 diabetes: Implications for medication adherence. *Psychology, Health, and Medicine, 9*, 17–27.

Vogels, W. W. A., Dekker, M. R., Brouwer, W. H., & de Jong, R. (2002). Age-related changes in event-related prospective memory performance: A comparison of four prospective memory tasks. *Brain and Cognition, 49,* 341–362.

Vortac, O. U., Edwards, M. B., & Manning, C. A. (1995). Functions of external cues in prospective memory. *Memory, 3,* 201–219.

Wechsler, D. (1997). *Wechsler Memory Scale* (3rd ed.). London: The Psychological Corporation Limited.

West, R. (in press). Foundations of the cognitive neuroscience of prospective memory. In M. Kliegel, M. A. McDaniel, & G. O. Einstein (Eds.), *Prospective memory: Cognitive, neuroscience, developmental, and applied perspectives.* Mahwah, NJ: Erlbaum.

West, R., Bowry, R., & Krompinger, J. (2006). The effects of working memory demands on the neural correlates of prospective memory. *Neuropsychologia, 44,* 197–207.

West, R., & Craik, F. I. M. (1999). Age-related decline in prospective memory: The roles of cue accessibility and cue sensitivity. *Psychology and Aging, 14,* 264–272.

West, R., & Craik, F. I. M. (2001). Influences on the efficiency of prospective memory in younger and older adults. *Psychology and Aging, 16,* 682–696.

West, R., Herndon, R. W., & Crewdson, S. J. (2001). Neural activity associated with the realization of a delayed intention. *Cognitive Brain Research, 12,* 1–9.

West, R., Herndon, R.W., & Ross-Munroe, K. (2000). Event-related neural activity associated with prospective remembering. *Applied Cognitive Psychology, 14,* 115–126.

West, R., & Krompinger, J. (2005). Neural correlates of prospective and retrospective memory. *Neuropsychologia, 43,* 418–433.

West, R., Krompinger, J., & Bowry, R. (2005). Disruptions of preparatory attention contribute to failures of prospective memory. *Psychonomic Bulletin & Review, 12,* 502–507.

West, R., Wymbs, N., Jakubek, K., & Herndon, R. W. (2003). Effects of intention load and background context on prospective remembering: An event-related brain potential study. *Psychophysiology, 40,* 260–276.

Whittlesea, B. W. A., & Williams, L. D. (2001a). The discrepancy-attribution hypothesis: I. The heuristic basis of feelings of familiarity. *Journal of Experimental Psychology: Learning, Memory, and Cognition, 27,* 3–13.

Whittlesea, B. W. A., & Williams, L. D. (2001b). The discrepancy-attribution hypothesis: II. Expectation, uncertainty, surprise, and feelings of familiarity. *Journal of Experimental Psychology: Learning, Memory, and Cognition, 27,* 14–33.

Wilkins, A. J. (1979). *Remembering to remember.* Paper presented at a colloquium of the Department of Experimental Psychology, Cambridge University, Cambridge, UK.

Wilkins, A. J., & Baddeley, A. (1978). Remembering to recall in everyday life: An approach to absentmindedness. In M. M. Gruneberg, P. E. Morris, & R. N. Sykes (Eds.), *Practical aspects of memory* (Vol. 1, pp. 27–34). San Diego, CA: Academic Press.

Wilson, B. A., Cockburn, J., & Baddeley, A. (1985). *Rivermead Behavioral Memory Test (RBMT)*. Bury St. Edmunds, UK: Thames Valley Test Company.

Wilson, B. A., Emslie, H., Foley, J., Shiel, A., Watson, P., Hawkins, K., et al. (2005). *Cambridge Prospective Memory Test (CAMPROMPT)*. San Antonio, TX: Harcourt Assessment.

Wilson, B. A., Evans, J. J., Emslie, H., & Malinek, V. (1997). Evaluation of NeuroPage: A new memory aid. *Journal of Neurology, Neurosurgery, and Psychiatry, 70,* 477–482.

Winograd, E. (1988). Some observations on prospective remembering. In M. M. Gruneberg, P. E. Morris, & R. N. Sykes (Eds.), *Practical aspects of memory: Current research and issues* (Vol. 1, pp. 348–353). Chichester, UK: Wiley.

Yaniv, I., & Meyer, D. E. (1987). Activation and metacognition of inaccessible stored information: Potential bases for incubation effects in problem solving. *Journal of Experimental Psychology: Learning, Memory, and Cognition, 13,* 187–205.

Yonelinas, A. P. (1999). The contribution of recollection and familiarity to recognition and source-memory judgments: A formal dual-process model and an analysis of receiver operating characteristics. *Journal of Experimental Psychology: Learning, Memory, and Cognition, 25,* 1415–1434.

Yoon, C., May, C. P., & Hasher, L. (2000). Aging, circadian arousal patterns, and cognition. In D. Park & N. Schwarz (Eds.), *Cognitive aging: A primer* (pp. 151–171). New York: Psychology Press.

Zacks, R. G., & Hasher, L. (1994). Directed ignoring: Inhibitory regulation of working memory. In D. Dagenbach & T. Carr (Eds.), *Inhibitory processes in attention memory and language* (pp. 241–264). San Diego, CA: Academic Press.

Zimmer, H. D. (1986). The memory trace of semantic or motor processing. In F. Klix & H. Hagendorf (Eds.), *Human memory and cognitive capabilities: Mechanisms and performances* (pp. 215–223). Amsterdam: Elsevier.

Zimmer, H. D., & Engelkamp, J. (1985). An attempt to distinguish between kinematic and motor memory components. *Acta Psychologica, 58,* 81–106.

Author Index

Subject Index

ACT (adaptive control of thought) model, of intention superiority effect, 89–90

Age factors. *See* Cognitive neuroscience of prospective memory; Life span development and prospective memory tasks: in adults; Life span development and prospective memory tasks: in adults, event-based tasks

Airline pilot prospective memory examples, 191, 193, 194, 196, 200–202, 207–208, 209, 211, 212

Airline traffic controller prospective memory examples, 106, 196, 199, 200, 201, 208

Alzheimer disease patient research early warning signs, 167–168, 212 external memory aids, 217 spaced-retrieval technique, 104*fig.*, 204–205, 205*fig.* storage and retention of intended actions, 102–103, 105

Anticipated enactment concept, of intended action storage and retention, 91

Brodmann area 10, 174, 180, 190

Cambridge Test of Prospective Memory, 212, 213

Children. *See* Life span development and prospective memory tasks: in children

Classical conditioning, 8–9

Clinical assessment, nonlaboratory investigative technique, 212–213

Closed head injury case study, 173

Cognitive neuroscience of prospective memory: neuroimaging methods event-related brain potentials (ERPs), 182–189, 190 functional magnetic resonance imaging (fMRI), 182–183, 190 positron emissions tomography (PET) technology, 179–182, 190 magnetoencephalography (MEG), 190 *See also* Cognitive neuroscience of prospective memory: neuropsychology of; *specific neuroimaging method*

Cognitive neuroscience of prospective memory: neuropsychology of Brodmann area 10 and, 174, 180, 190 case studies, 171–175 closed head injury, 173 frontal, prefrontal function, 172–174, 175–176, 176*fig.* hippocampal area and, 174, 175, 176*table*, 177–178, 177*fig.*, 190 neuropsychological assessment of normal aging, 175–176 provisional neuropsychological theory, 177–178 schizophrenic patient case study, 173 summary and future directions, 189–190

255

About the Authors

Mark McDaniel received his Ph.D. in experimental psychology from the University of Colorado in 1980. Prior to joining the faculty at Washington University in 2004, he served on the faculties at the University of Notre Dame, Purdue University, and the University of New Mexico. At the University of New Mexico, he chaired the Department of Psychology from 2002 to 2004.

He is past president of the Rocky Mountain Psychological Association and was the associate editor of the *Journal of Experimental Psychology: Learning, Memory, and Cognition* (1995–2000). He currently serves on the editorial boards of *Cognitive Psychology; Journal of Experimental Psychology: Learning, Memory, and Cognition;* and *Psychology and Aging.* He has also served on editorial boards of other prominent journals, including the *Journal of Educational Psychology* and *Memory & Cognition.* He is a fellow of Divisions 3 and 20 of the American Psychological Association, and a member of both the Association of Psychological Science and the Psychonomic Society.

McDaniel has published over 160 articles, chapters, and edited books. His research has been sponsored by various federal funding agencies, such as the Institute of Education Sciences, the National Institutes of Health (NIA, NICHD, NIMH), and NASA, for two decades.

His work is in the general area of human learning and memory, with an emphasis on:

(1) Prospective memory and the influences of aging. This research includes development of theoretical frameworks and experimental investigation of the different processes (retrieval dynamics, encoding, influence of reminders) underlying this important yet relatively neglected memory activity.

(2) Encoding and retrieval processes. His recent work in this area includes a focus on prose memory, specifically on extending basic work to educationally relevant materials and tasks. Other educationally relevant memory work

includes a series of studies on elaborative study techniques, such as the key word method and elaborative interrogation.

(3)   Functional and causal concept learning. This work involves investigation of the learning processes by which humans abstract relations between continuous inputs and outputs, and the use of analogy in learning scientific concepts.

To communicate to the general public the wealth of research findings on aging and memory and their implications for stemming age-related decline in memory, McDaniel recently co-authored with Gil Einstein the book *Memory Fitness: A Guide for Successful Aging*.

Gil Einstein received his Ph.D. in experimental psychology from the University of Colorado in 1977 and has been teaching at Furman University since then. He chaired the department from 1994 to 2006, won Furman University's Meritorious Teaching Award in 1985, and was the first recipient of Furman University's Excellence in Teaching Award in 2006.

He is past president of the Southeastern Workers in Memory, and he has served on the editorial boards of the *Journal of Experimental Psychology: Learning, Memory, and Cognition* and *Memory & Cognition*. He is a fellow of Divisions 2, 3, and 20 of the American Psychological Association and a member of both the Association of Psychological Science and the Psychonomic Society.

He is committed to both teaching and research and believes that research is an excellent learning experience for undergraduates. This commitment is reflected in his service on the Board of Governors of the National Conference on Undergraduate Research and as a counselor in the Council on Undergraduate Research, and in his direction of more than 100 student presentations at conferences. He also chaired the Furman Advantage Program (a program that annually supports about 150 undergraduate summer research fellowships, teaching fellowships, and summer internships) for 14 years.

His research is in the area of human learning and memory and currently focuses on the processes involved in prospective remembering, how these processes break down in important real-world situations, and how they are affected by aging. He has published over 75 articles, chapters, and books, and his research has been supported by the National Institutes of Health (NIA, NICHD) and NASA. In an attempt to capture the explosion of research on aging and memory over the last 10 years, he recently co-authored with Mark McDaniel a book titled *Memory Fitness: A Guide for Successful Aging*.